Y0-EFV-650

Law Enforcement Intelligence:

A Guide for State, Local, and Tribal Law Enforcement Agencies

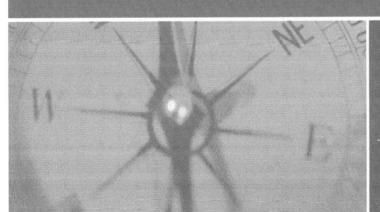

November 2004
David L. Carter, Ph.D.

This project was supported by Cooperative Agreement #2003-CK-WX-0455 by the U.S. Department of Justice Office of Community Oriented Policing Services. Points of view or opinions contained in this document are those of the author and do not necessarily represent the official position or policies of the U.S. Department of Justice or Michigan State University.

Preface

The world of law enforcement intelligence has changed dramatically since September 11, 2001. State, local, and tribal law enforcement agencies have been tasked with a variety of new responsibilities; intelligence is just one. In addition, the intelligence discipline has evolved significantly in recent years. As these various trends have merged, increasing numbers of American law enforcement agencies have begun to explore, and sometimes embrace, the intelligence function. This guide is intended to help them in this process.

The guide is directed primarily toward state, local, and tribal law enforcement agencies of all sizes that need to develop or reinvigorate their intelligence function. Rather than being a manual to teach a person how to be an intelligence analyst, it is directed toward that manager, supervisor, or officer who is assigned to create an intelligence function. It is intended to provide ideas, definitions, concepts, policies, and resources. It is a primer- a place to start on a new managerial journey.

Every effort was made to incorporate the state of the art in law enforcement intelligence: Intelligence-Led Policing, the National Criminal Intelligence Sharing Plan, the FBI Intelligence Program, the array of new intelligence activities occurring in the Department of Homeland Security, community policing, and various other significant developments in the reengineered arena of intelligence.

A number of groups have provided important leadership in this field and afforded me opportunities to learn from their initiatives and experiences. These include the Global Intelligence Working Group (GIWG), Major City

Chiefs' Intelligence Commanders, High-Intensity Drug Trafficking Areas (HIDTA), Counterdrug Intelligence Executive Secretariat (CDX), the Counterterrorism Training Working Group, and the International Association of Intelligence Analysts (IALEIA). In particular, I also would like to thank the COPS Office, FBI, and Bureau of Justice Assistance.

Many people assisted me in this project. First and foremost are the members of my Advisory Board (listed in Appendix A). I appreciate your time, contributions, and expertise. You have added significant value to this work. I particularly thank Doug Bodrero, Eileen Garry, Carl Peed, Maureen Baginski, Tim Healy, Louis Quijas, and Bob Casey for their efforts.

My sincere appreciation also goes to Dr. Andra Katz-Bannister of the Wichita State University Regional Community Policing Institute (RCPI) who gave me constant feedback and support, Dr. Barry Zulauf at the Drug Enforcement Administration (DEA), who always manages to pull off the impossible, Merle Manzi, most recently of the Federal Law Enforcement Training Center (FLETC), who did a yeoman's job of reviewing and editing the manuscript in the waning hours of the deadline, and my Michigan State doctoral assistant, Jason Ingram, who assisted in many of the details and research needed for this project. My thanks also go to my COPS Project Monitor Michael Seelman who provided support and facilitation to get the project completed. Finally, I thank my wife Karen, and children Hilary, Jeremy, and Lauren who put up with the time I worked on this and other projects – you are always in my thoughts.

David L. Carter, Ph.D.
Michigan State University

Executive Summary

New expectations and responsibilities are being placed on law enforcement agencies of all sizes to develop an intelligence capacity as part of a cohesive national strategy to protect the United States from terrorism and the deleterious effects of transjurisdictional organized crime. As part of this trend, particularly after the events of September 11, 2001, unprecedented initiatives have been undertaken to reengineer the law enforcement intelligence function.

Adhering to National Standards

This guide is intended to provide fundamental information about the contemporary law enforcement intelligence function in its application to state, local, and tribal law enforcement (SLTLE) agencies. The guide embodies the Intelligence-Led Policing philosophy, demonstrating how it complements community policing already in use by American law enforcement. It also embodies the principles, ideology, and standards of both the National Criminal Intelligence Sharing Plan and the Global Justice Information Sharing Initiative. It reflects current issues of law, particularly with regard to intelligence records systems (as per 28 CFR, Part 23) and liability issues. .

Definitions and Perspective

At the outset, this guide defines and illustrates law enforcement intelligence with respect to its current application to SLTLE. Because of different jurisdictional responsibilities, federal law enforcement agencies use slightly different definitions. These differences are explained and illustrated to enhance information sharing and ensure clear communications between federal and nonfederal law enforcement. Because of global terrorism, the presence of SLTLE officers on Joint Terrorism Task Forces (JTTF) and a more integrated role between the FBI and SLTLE, discussion is provided on the meaning and implications of national security intelligence as it relates to nonfederal law enforcement.

This guide is intended to provide fundamental information about the contemporary law enforcement intelligence function in its application to state, local, and tribal law enforcement (SLTLE) agencies.

To add perspective, the guide provides a brief history of law enforcement intelligence. There are significant legal and policy implications that have evolved through this comparatively short history, including perspectives from the 9/11 Commission. These are summarized at the end of Chapter 3 as "lessons learned." The "lessons" have been framed essentially as a checklist for policies and procedures that affect many aspects of the intelligence function.

Intelligence-Led Policing

The concept of Intelligence-Led Policing is explained from an operational perspective, illustrating its interrelationship with community policing and CompStat. Moreover, critical issues are addressed ranging from ethics to responsibilities of line officers to the community's role in the intelligence function. This discussion builds on the previous chapters to provide a perspective of intelligence that is "organic" to the law enforcement agency; that is, intelligence is part of the fabric of decision making that can have department-wide implications.

Intelligence Processes and Products

Based on the foundation that has been built, the guide explains current accepted practice of turning "information" into "intelligence." The intelligence cycle and analytic process are explained in summary form to provide the reader with an understanding of the processes. It is important for executives and managers to understand the language and protocols to effectively communicate with analysts and manage the intelligence function.

A discussion of information technology provides some insights into software requirements, networking issues, resources, security issues, and the dynamics associated with open-source information and intelligence. This is followed by a discussion of intelligence products, the different types of intelligence analysis, and how these products are used for both operations and management. Finally, dissemination or information sharing- is discussed, particularly in light of the National Criminal Intelligence Sharing Plan.

> Moreover, critical issues are addressed ranging from ethics to responsibilities of line officers to the community's role in the intelligence function.

Management and Human Resources

Readers of this guide will be experienced in management issues; hence, these sections focus on facets of management unique to law enforcement intelligence. Defining the mission, policy issues, and methods for staying current on trends and practices are addressed, paying particular attention to intelligence file guidelines and ensuring accountability of the intelligence function. As illustrated in the brief history of law enforcement intelligence, these two issues have been paramount, particularly as related to civil lawsuits. The importance of 28 CFR, Part 23, *Guidelines for Criminal Intelligence Records Systems,* is stressed and model intelligence file guidelines prepared by the Law Enforcement Intelligence Unit (LEIU) are included in the appendices. Also included as an appendix is a comprehensive management audit checklist that touches on virtually all aspects of the intelligence function.

With respect to human resources, staffing is discussed, with particular emphasis on the need for professional intelligence analysts. In addition, intelligence training is examined and concludes with a summary of sources and contact information. These facets of management are consistent with the recommendations of the National Criminal Intelligence Sharing Plan.

Networks and Systems

In today's digital world, the heart of effective information sharing is an understanding of the various communications networks available to law enforcement – some are evolving as this is written. The guide presents information about critical secure networks and how law enforcement officers can gain access to the networks. An important recommendation is that all law enforcement agencies should have access to a secure communications system that is based on Internet protocols (IP). Intelligence products and advisories from federal agencies- the FBI and Department of Homeland Security (DHS) in particular – essentially rely on a secure IP system. The issues and processes are discussed in detail.

Defining the mission, policy issues, and methods for staying current on trends and practices are addressed, paying particular attention to intelligence file guidelines and ensuring accountability of the intelligence function.

Intelligence Requirements and Threat Assessment

Another significant change in law enforcement intelligence has been "intelligence requirements" produced by the FBI Intelligence Program. Defining intelligence requirements adds dimensions of specificity and consistency to intelligence processes that previously had not existed. The guide describes the concept and processes in detail. Inherently related to defining intelligence requirements is understanding the threats posed in a jurisdiction. Indeed, the intelligence process is threat-driven with the intent of preventing a terrorist act or stopping a criminal enterprise and, therefore, the guide provides a threat assessment model.

Federal Law Enforcement Intelligence

The penultimate chapter describes federal law enforcement programs and products that SLTLE agencies should be aware of. Because of some confusion on the issue, the chapter begins with a discussion of classified information to clarify some confusion on the issue and provides information on how SLTLE officers can apply for security clearances. Based on the need for information security, the chapter also discusses declassified information for law enforcement, specifically related to the Sensitive But Unclassified (SBU) designation, the FBI Law Enforcement Sensitive (LES) designation, and the DHS For Official Use Only (FOUO) designation.

Building on the classification and information security issues, the guide discusses and illustrates the FBI Office of Intelligence products, FBI counterterrorism programs, and multi-agency initiatives—specifically the Terrorism Threat Integration Center (TTIC) and the Terrorist Screening Center (TSC). Equally prominent in the discussion are the intelligence products and advisories produced by the DHS. The FBI and DHS have established a productive working relationship on intelligence matters, embracing the need to be inclusive with state, local, and tribal law enforcement agencies for two-way information sharing.
Intelligence products and services as well as contact information also are provided for the Drug Enforcement Administration (DEA), El Paso

> Another significant change in law enforcement intelligence has been "intelligence requirements" produced by the FBI Intelligence Program.

Intelligence Center (EPIC), National Drug Pointer Index (NDPIX), National Drug Intelligence Center (NDIC), High-Intensity Drug Trafficking Areas (HIDTA), Bureau of Alcohol, Tobacco, Firearms and Explosives (ATF), the Financial Crimes Enforcement Network (FinCEN), and the High Risk Money Laundering and Related Financial Crimes Areas (HIFCA).

Summary

The intent of this guide is to aid state, local, and tribal law enforcement agencies to develop an intelligence capacity or enhance their current one. To maximize effectiveness, the standards used in the preparation of this guide were to ensure that it is contemporary, informative, prescriptive, and resource rich.

Summary of New Initiatives

- Development of the FBI Intelligence Program with its new emphasis on intelligence requirements, new intelligence products, and creation of the Field Intelligence Group (FIG) in every FBI Field Office as the primary intelligence contact point among state, local, and tribal law enforcement and the FBI.
- Development of new FBI counterterrorism initiatives and programs.
- New intelligence products from the Department of Homeland Security (DHS) as well as a substantive input role of raw information into the DHS intelligence cycle by state, local, and tribal law enforcement agencies.
- Expansion and articulation of the Intelligence-Led Policing concept.
- Implementation of the National Criminal Intelligence Sharing Plan.
- Creation of a wide variety of initiatives and standards as a result of the Global Intelligence Working Group (GIWG) of the Global Justice Information Sharing Initiative.
- Renewed vigor toward the adoption of 28 CFR Part 23, *Guidelines for Criminal Intelligence Records Systems*, by law enforcement agencies that are not required to adhere to the regulation.
- Secure connections for email exchange, access to advisories, reports, and information exchange, as well as integration and streamlining the use of Law Enforcement Online (LEO), Regional Information Sharing Systems' RISS.net, and creation of the Anti-Terrorism Information Exchange (ATIX).
- New operational expectations and training opportunities for intelligence analysts, law enforcement executives, managers, and line officers.

Challenges to be Faced by Law Enforcement Executives

- Recognize that every law enforcement agency – regardless of size or location – has a stake in this global law enforcement intelligence initiative and, as such, must develop some form of an intelligence capacity in order to be an effective consumer of intelligence products.
- Develop a culture of collection among officers to most effectively gather information for use in the intelligence cycle.
- Operationally integrate Intelligence-Led Policing into the police organization.
- Recognize that increased information sharing at and between law enforcement at all levels of government requires new commitments by law enforcement executives and managers.
- Increase information sharing, as appropriate, with the broader public safety and private security sectors.
- Protect data and records along with rigid accountability of the intelligence function.
- Keep law enforcement intelligence and national security intelligence separate, particularly with respect to state and local officers on Joint Terrorism Task Forces.
- Broader scrutiny of intelligence records and practices by civil rights groups.
- Routinely use intelligence to make better tactical and strategic decisions.
- Increase regionalization in all aspects of the intelligence function as an ongoing initiative of law enforcement agencies at all levels of government.
- Ensure that non-law enforcement government officials and the community understand what law enforcement intelligence is and the importance of their role in the intelligence function.

Table of Contents

List of Figures

Introduction

CHAPTER ONE

Introduction

Every law enforcement agency in the United States, regardless of agency size, must have the capacity to understand the implications of information collection, analysis, and intelligence sharing. Each agency must have an organized mechanism to receive and manage intelligence as well as a mechanism to report and share critical information with other law enforcement agencies. In addition, it is essential that law enforcement agencies develop lines of communication and information-sharing protocols with the private sector, particularly those related to the critical infrastructure, as well as with those private entities that are potential targets of terrorists and criminal enterprises.

Not every agency has the staff or resources to create a formal intelligence unit, nor is it necessary in smaller agencies. Even without an intelligence unit, a law enforcement organization must have the ability to effectively consume the information and intelligence products being shared by a wide range of organizations at all levels of government. State, local, and tribal law enforcement (SLTLE) will be its most effective when a single source in every agency is the conduit of critical information, whether it is the Terrorist Intelligence Unit of the Los Angeles Police Department, the sole intelligence analyst of the Lansing, Michigan Police Department, or the patrol sergeant who understands the language of intelligence and is the information sharing contact point in the Mercedes, Texas Police Department. Hence, each law enforcement agency must have an understanding of its intelligence management capabilities regardless of its size or organizational structure.

This document will provide common language and processes to develop and employ an intelligence capacity in SLTLE agencies across the United States as well as articulate a uniform understanding of concepts, issues, and terminology for law enforcement intelligence (LEI). While terrorism issues are currently most pervasive in the current discussion of LEI, the principles of intelligence discussed in this document apply beyond terrorism and include organized crime and entrepreneurial crime of all forms. Drug trafficking and the associated crime of money laundering, for example, continue to be a significant challenge for law enforcement. Transnational computer crime, particularly Internet fraud, identity theft cartels, and global black marketeering of stolen and counterfeit goods, are entrepreneurial crime problems that are increasingly being relegated to SLTLE agencies to investigate simply because of the volume of criminal incidents. Similarly, local law enforcement is being increasingly drawn into human trafficking and illegal immigration enterprises and the often-associated crimes related to counterfeiting of official documents, such as passports, visas, driver's licenses, Social Security cards, and credit cards. Even the trafficking of arts and antiquities has increased, often bringing a new profile of criminal into the realm of entrepreneurial crime. All require an intelligence capacity for SLTLE, as does the continuation of historical organized crime activities such as auto theft, cargo theft, and virtually any other scheme that can produce profit for an organized criminal entity.

To be effective, the law enforcement community must interpret intelligence-related language in a consistent manner. In addition, common standards, policies, and practices will help expedite intelligence sharing while at the same time protecting the privacy of citizens and preserving hard-won community policing relationships.

Perspective

At the outset, law enforcement officers must understand the concept of LEI, its distinction from National Security Intelligence (NSI) and the potential problems an SLTLE agency can face when the two types of intelligence overlap. A law enforcement executive must understand what is meant by an "intelligence function" and how that function can be fulfilled

> In addition, common STANDARDS, POLICIES, and PRACTICES will help EXPEDITE intelligence sharing while at the same time PROTECTING THE PRIVACY of citizens and preserving hard-won community policing RELATIONSHIPS.

through the use of different organizational models. Related executive decisions focus on staffing, particularly when there are fiscal limitations. What kinds of information does the law enforcement agency need (e.g., intelligence requirements) from the federal government to most effectively counter terrorism? How are those needs determined? How is the information requested? When and in what form will the information be received? Will a security clearance be needed to review the information that an executive requests? These are critical questions of a police executive.

From a policy and process perspective, what is meant by intelligence sharing? What information can be collected? What information can be kept in files? How long may it be kept in files? When does a person transcend the threshold of exercising his or her rights to posing a threat to community safety? What resources exist to aid an SLTLE agency in accomplishing its intelligence goals? How can the entire law enforcement agency be integrated into the intelligence function? If a law enforcement organization is to be effective, the answers to these questions must be a product of written policy.

The intent of this document is to provide answers — or at least alternatives — to these questions. To begin the process, every law enforcement administrator must recognize that intelligence and information sharing can be effective in preventing terrorism and organized crime. To realize these ends, however, the intelligence process for law enforcement at all levels of government requires the following:

- Reengineering some of the organization's structure and processes
- Developing a shared vision of the terrorist or criminal threat
- Establishing a commitment to participate and follow through with threat information
- Overcoming the conceptual difficulty of intelligence processes that some personnel find difficult to grasp
- Committing resources, time, and energy from an agency to the intelligence function
- Embracing and using contemporary technology, including electronic access to information and an electronic communications capability through a secure connection
- Having proactive people using creative thought to identify "what we don't know" about terrorism and international organized crime
- Requiring a law enforcement agency to think globally and act locally
- Patience.

Understanding Contemporary Law Enforcement Intelligence: Concept and Definition

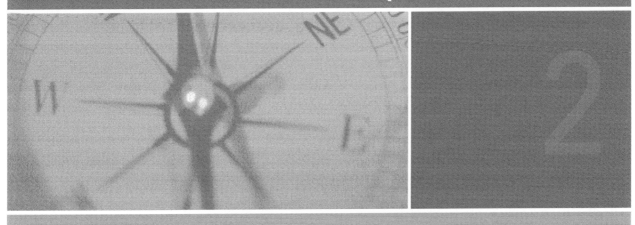

CHAPTER TWO

Understanding Contemporary Law Enforcement Intelligence: Concept and Definition

In the purest sense, intelligence is the product of an analytic process that evaluates information collected from diverse sources, integrates the relevant information into a cohesive package, and produces a conclusion or estimate about a criminal phenomenon by using the scientific approach to problem solving (i.e., analysis). Intelligence, therefore, is a synergistic product intended to provide meaningful and trustworthy direction to law enforcement decision makers about complex criminality, criminal enterprises, criminal extremists, and terrorists.

There are essentially two broad purposes for an intelligence function within a law enforcement agency:

AKA: Tactical Intel.

Prevention. Includes gaining or developing information related to threats of terrorism or crime and using this information to apprehend offenders, harden targets, and use strategies that will eliminate or mitigate the threat. This is known as tactical intelligence.

Planning and Resource Allocation. The intelligence function provides information to decision makers about the changing nature of threats, the characteristics and methodologies of threats, and emerging threat idiosyncrasies for the purpose of developing response strategies and reallocating resources, as necessary, to accomplish effective prevention. This is known as strategic intelligence.

Strategic Intel.

While investigation[1] is clearly part of the information collection[2] process, the intelligence function is often more exploratory and more broadly focused than a criminal investigation, per se. For example, a law enforcement agency may have a reasonable suspicion to believe that a person or group of people have the intent, capacity, and resolve to commit a crime or terrorist act. Evidence, however, may fall short of the probable cause standard, even for an arrest of criminal attempt or conspiracy. Moreover, there may be a compelling community safety reason to keep an enquiry open to identify other criminal offenders – notably leaders – and weapons that may be used.

Because of this broader role, the need to keep information secure and the necessity of keeping records on individuals for whom evidence of criminal involvement is uncertain or tangential,[3] rigid guidelines must be followed. These guidelines are designed to protect the constitutional rights of citizens while at the same time permitting law enforcement agencies to proceed with an inquiry for purposes of community safety. The guidelines are also designed to facilitate accurate and secure information sharing between law enforcement agencies because the nature of terrorism and criminal enterprise threats are inherently multijurisdictional. Further, if law enforcement agencies at all strata of government subscribe to the same guidelines, information sharing can be more widespread because there is surety that regardless of with whom the information is shared, the security and integrity of the records will remain intact.

[1] "Investigation" is defined as the pursuit of information based on leads and evidence associated with a particularly defined criminal act to identify and apprehend criminal offenders for prosecution in a criminal trial.

[2] "Information collection" in the context of law enforcement intelligence is the capture of information based on a reasonable suspicion of criminal involvement for use in developing criminal cases, identifying crime trends, and protecting the community by means of intervention, apprehension, and/or target hardening.

[3] This includes information that would be in the intelligence "Temporary File" as well as "Non-Criminal Identifying Information" as defined in 28 CFR Part 23.

Defining Intelligence

Definitions become problematic because of context, tradition, and the different use of language by specialists, generalists, and lay persons. This guide uses definitions based on generally accepted practice and standards by the law enforcement intelligence community at the local, state, and tribal levels. This does not mean that other definitions of terms are wrong, but provides a common understanding of words and concepts as most applicable to the targeted audience of this guide.

Before defining intelligence, it is essential to understand the meaning of "information" in the context of this process. Information may defined as "pieces of raw, unanalyzed data that identifies persons, evidence, events, or illustrates processes that indicate the incidence of a criminal event or witnesses or evidence of a criminal event."[4] As will be seen, information is collected as the currency that produces intelligence.

4   Global Intelligence Working Group. (2004). *Criminal Intelligence for the Chief Executive*. A Training Program for the Chief Executive. Glossary.

The phrase "law enforcement intelligence," used synonymously with "criminal intelligence," is frequently found in conjunction with discussions of the police role in homeland security. In most cases, the term is used improperly. Too often, intelligence is erroneously viewed as pieces of information about people, places, or events that can be used to provide insight about criminality or crime threats. It is further complicated by the failure to distinguish between law enforcement intelligence and national security intelligence.

> Law enforcement intelligence, therefore, is the PRODUCT of an analytic process that provides an INTEGRATED PERSPECTIVE to disparate information about crime, crime trends, crime and security threats, and conditions associated with criminality."[5]

Pieces of information gathered from diverse sources, for example, wiretaps, informants, banking records, or surveillance (see Figure 1-1), are simply raw data which frequently have limited inherent meaning. Intelligence is when a wide array of raw information is assessed for validity and reliability, reviewed for materiality to the issues at question, and given meaning through the application of inductive or deductive logic. Law enforcement intelligence, therefore, is the product of an analytic process that provides an integrated perspective to disparate information about crime, crime trends, crime and security threats, and conditions associated with criminality."[5] The need for carefully analyzed, reliable information is essential because both policy and operational decisions are made using intelligence; therefore, a vigilant process must be in place to ensure that decisions are made on objective, informed criteria, rather than on presumed criteria.

Figure 1-1: Diverse Information Collected for Intelligence Analysis

Often "information sharing" and "intelligence sharing" are used interchangeably by persons who do not understand the subtleties, yet importance, of the distinction. In the strictest sense, care should be taken to use terms appropriately because, as will be seen in later discussions, there are different regulatory and legal implications for "intelligence" than for "information" (see Figure 1-2). As such, the subtleties of language can become an important factor should the management of a law enforcement agency's intelligence records come under scrutiny.

5   Carter, David L. (2002). *Law Enforcement Intelligence Operations*. 8th ed. Tallahassee, FL: SMC Sciences, Inc.

Figure 1-2: Comparative Illustrations of Information and Intelligence	
Information	**Intelligence**
• Criminal history and driving records • Offense reporting records • Statements by informants, witnesses, and suspects • Registration information for motor vehicles, watercraft, and aircraft • Licensing details about vehicle operators and professional licenses of all forms • Observations of behaviors and incidents by investigators, surveillance teams, or citizens • Details about banking, investments, credit reports, and other financial matters • Descriptions of travel including the traveler(s) names, itinerary, methods of travel, date, time, locations, etc.	• A report by an analyst that draws conclusions about a person's criminal liability based on an integrated analysis of diverse information collected by investigators and/or researchers • An analysis of crime or terrorism trends with conclusions drawn about characteristics of offenders, probable future crime, and optional methods for preventing future crime/terrorism • A forecast drawn about potential victimization of crime or terrorism based on an assessment of limited information when an analysts uses past experience as context for the conclusion • An estimate of a person's income from a criminal enterprise based on a market and trafficking analysis of illegal commodities

Definitions and Context

State and local law enforcement have consistently defined law enforcement intelligence as containing the critical element of "analysis" before any information can be characterized as "intelligence." For example, the Intelligence-Led Policing report funded by the Office of Community Oriented Policing Services observes that:

> ...intelligence is the combination of credible information with quality analysis–information that has been evaluated and from which conclusions have been drawn.[6]

Similarly, the Global Intelligence Working Group, a project funded by the Office of Justice Programs and is part of the Global Information Sharing Initiative, discusses law enforcement intelligence by observing:

> ...the collection and analysis of information to produce an intelligence end product designed to inform law enforcement decision making at both the tactical and strategic levels.[7]

6 International Association of Chiefs of Police. (2002). *Criminal Intelligence Sharing: A National Plan for Intelligence-Led Policing at the Federal, State, and Local Levels*. A summit report. Alexandria, VA: IACP., p. v.

7 Global Intelligence Working Group. (2003). *National Criminal Intelligence Sharing Plan*. Washington, DC: Office of Justice Programs. p. 6.

Following a consistent vision, the International Association of Law Enforcement Intelligence Analysts (IALEIA) states that intelligence is an analytic process:

> ...deriving meaning from fact. It is taking information collected in the course of an investigation, or from internal or external files, and arriving at something more than was evident before. This could be leads in a case, a more accurate view of a crime problem, a forecast of future crime levels, a hypothesis of who may have committed a crime or a strategy to prevent crime.[8]

Beyond these descriptions, the Office of Domestic Preparedness[9] of the Department of Homeland Security simply defines law enforcement intelligence as:

> ...the product of adding value to information and data through analysis.[10]

In creating standards for state, local, and tribal law enforcement, the Commission on Accreditation of Law Enforcement Agencies (CALEA) seeks to provide specific guidance on policies and practices that ensures efficacy and protection from liability on all aspects of law enforcement duties. With respect to intelligence, CALEA's standards note:

> Certain essential activities should be accomplished by an intelligence function, to include a procedure that permits the continuous flow of raw data into a central point from all sources; a secure records system in which evaluated data are properly cross-referenced to reflect relationships and to ensure complete and rapid retrieval; a system of analysis capable of developing intelligence from both the records system and other data sources; and a system for dissemination of information to appropriate components.[11]

It is clear not only from these discussions, but also from the legacy of law enforcement intelligence of various national commissions examining intelligence activities at the state and local level, that a common thread is that information must be analyzed before it is classified as intelligence.

8   International Association of Law Enforcement Intelligence Analysts. (undated). *Successful Law Enforcement Using Analytic Methods.* Internet-published document. p. 2.

9   The Office of Domestic Preparedness is not the Office of State and Local Government Coordination and Preparedness.

10   Office of Domestic Preparedness. (2003). *The Office of Domestic Preparedness Guidelines for Homeland Security.* Washington, DC: U.S. Department of Homeland Security. p.27.

11   Commission on Accreditation of Law Enforcement Agencies. (2002). *Standards for Law Enforcement Accreditation.* "Standard 51.1.1 - Criminal Intelligence." Washington, DC: CALEA.

Chapter 3 will show that there is a fundamental reason for this: regulations applying to state, local, and tribal intelligence records[12] must meet standards of assessment that do not apply to federal agencies.[13] As a consequence, the analytic component is essential for the definition.

It is often stated that for every rule there is an exception. The definition of law enforcement intelligence fits this axiom. As a matter of functional practicality, the FBI Office of Intelligence (OI) categorizes intelligence somewhat differently. As observed by FBI Deputy Assistant Director of the Office of Intelligence Robert Casey:

Exception to def. or intel.

> In the law enforcement/national security business, [intelligence] is information about those who would do us harm in the form of terrorist acts or other crimes, be they property crimes or violent crimes. VS [The FBI OI] produces both "raw" (or un-evaluated *intel*, intelligence) and "finished" intelligence products (those that report intelligence that has had some degree of analysis).[14]

Due to

Given the nature of the FBI OI's responsibilities and the need to get the critical threat information into the hands of the law enforcement community quickly, this definition is more appropriate for its role. Law enforcement executives need to be aware of the different roles and the different context when interpreting information. These differences are not in conflict, rather they exist to support the different missions and responsibilities of agencies at all levels of government. Similarly, the need for a different approach to the "intelligence cycle" exists more for the FBI than for state, local, and tribal law enforcement (SLTLE) because of different intelligence demands (described in Chapter 5).

12   Most notably, 28 CFR Part 23 as well as various court decisions.

13   These issues are described in detail, both in Chapter 3 and Chapter 7.

14   Robert Casey, Deputy Assistant Director, FBI Office of Intelligence. Personal correspondence July 17, 2004.

...a COMMON THREAD is that analysis must be performed on information before it is CLASSIFIED AS "INTELLIGENCE."

The remedy is simple: Those responsible for the intelligence function need to understand the differences and apply policies and practices (described later) that are most appropriate for the types of intelligence being produced and consumed.

National Security Intelligence

In understanding the broad arena of intelligence, some perspective of national security intelligence (NSI) is useful for SLTLE agencies. This primer is meant to familiarize the law enforcement reader with basic terms, concepts, and issues, and is not an exhaustive description.

NSI may be defined as "the collection and analysis of information concerned with the relationship and homeostasis of the United States with foreign powers, organizations, and persons with regard to political and economic factors as well as the maintenance of the United States' sovereign principles."[15] NSI seeks to maintain the United States as a free, capitalist republic with its laws and constitutional foundation intact and identify and neutralize threats or actions which undermine the American way of life.

NSI embodies both policy intelligence and military intelligence. Policy intelligence is concerned with threatening actions and activities of entities hostile to the U.S., while military intelligence focuses on hostile entities, weapons systems, warfare capabilities, and order of battle. Since the fall of the Soviet Union and the rise of threats from terrorist groups, both policy and military intelligence have evolved to grapple with the character of new threats. The organizations responsible for NSI are collectively known as the Intelligence Community (IC) (see Figure 1-3).[16]

As seen in the definition and descriptions of NSI, there is no jurisdictional concern for crime. As a result, constitutional restrictions that attach to criminal cases that law enforcement faces on information collection, records retention, and use of information in a raw capacity do not apply to IC responsibilities where there is no criminal investigation.

15   Carter, David L. (2002). *Law Enforcement Intelligence Operations*. 8th ed. Tallahassee, FL: SMC Sciences, Inc.

16   See also www.odci.gov.

Figure 1-3: Intelligence Community [17]

An Intelligence Community (IC) member is a federal government agency, service, bureau, or other organization within the executive branch that plays a role in the business of national intelligence

- Air Force Intelligence
- Army Intelligence
- Central Intelligence Agency
- Coast Guard Intelligence
- Defense Intelligence Agency
- Department of Energy
- Department of Homeland Security
- Department of State
- Department of Treasury
- Federal Bureau of Investigation
- Marine Corps Intelligence

- National Geospatial-Intelligence Agency
- National Reconnaissance Office
- National Security Agency
- Navy Intelligence

SLTLE agencies have no direct jurisdiction as related to NSI; however, this does not mean that they will not encounter NSI nor receive collection tasks to support NSI. Indeed, given that the FBI is a member of the IC, there is a strong likelihood that SLTLE officers serving on a Joint Terrorism Task Force will encounter or be exposed to NSI. Similarly, officers working on an Organized Crime Drug Enforcement Task Force (OCDETF) may also encounter this intelligence. In both instances the officers typically will have Top Secret or Secret security classifications that provide additional details and background information. Nonetheless, it is a "slippery slope" for SLTLE officers to rely on this information for a criminal investigation because there is a strong likelihood that the methods of collecting the NSI would not meet constitutional muster in a criminal trial. Even if it appeared that constitutional standards may be met, there are other potential problems of using the information in a criminal enquiry. Since the accused in a criminal proceeding has the right to be confronted by his or her accusers, the exercise of this right could compromise sensitive sources and methods. While the Classified Information Procedures Act (CIPA) provides a mechanism to deal with the process, some find that it is cumbersome and may result in greater complications than would otherwise be necessary.[18]

The next issue deals with constitutional law. If the information was collected via NSI sources in a manner inconsistent with the Constitution, it is likely, based on the "Fruits of the Poisonous Tree Doctrine," that any subsequent evidence developed during the course of that investigation

17 On August 28, 2004 President Bush announced: "I have ordered the Director of Central Intelligence to perform the functions of the National Intelligence Director within the constraints of existing law, until Congress establishes that position. I agree with the 9/11 Commission that America needs a single official to coordinate the foreign and domestic activities of the intelligence community with authority over personnel budgeting and policy. I am working with members of Congress to create this position. And while we act, the Director of Central Intelligence will play an expanded role." www.whitehouse.gov/news/releases/2004/08/20040828.html.

18 The author has elected not to discuss CIPA in any detail because it deals with federal investigations rather than state, local, and tribal criminal investigations. For the person interested in further exploring CIPA, see www.usdoj.gov/usao/eousa/foia_reading_room/usam/title9/crm02054.htm.

would be subject to the Exclusionary Rule. Consequently, the evidence would be inadmissible.

A final issue with respect to state, local, and tribal officers' access to NSI is liability. Specifically, if in a criminal investigation SLTLE officers used NSI that was collected in a manner inconsistent with constitutional standards or if that information (including personal records) was kept as intelligence records that were under the custodianship of a state, local, or tribal law enforcement officer, it is possible that the officer(s) and the chain of command (through vicarious liability) of that officer's agency could be liable under 42 USC 1983, *Civil Action for Deprivation of Civil Rights*. As most officers are well aware, under this provision if a state or local officer, acting under the color of state law, violates the civil rights of a person, the officer and his or her chain of command may be sued in federal court. Even though that officer may be working on a federal task force under the supervision of a federal officer such as an FBI agent, the applicable test is whether the officer is paid by and bound by the employment rules of his or her state or local employing jurisdiction.[19]

In sum, based on authorities from the National Security Act of 1947, Executive Order 12333, various Directives from the Director of Central Intelligence, and the U.S. Attorney General Guidelines, the FBI is the lead agency in domestic intelligence collection. It is important that SLTLE understand the distinction between the FBI's authority to both collect and produce intelligence within the territory of the United States and the authority of the Central Intelligence Agency (CIA), National Security Agency (NSA), and other intelligence community members to collect in foreign territories.[20] The Department of Homeland Security can produce intelligence as a result of analysis for dissemination to SLTLE. U.S. foreign intelligence agencies, however, are prohibited from working with state and local law enforcement in a manner that could be interpreted as "tasking intelligence collection." As a result, SLTLE should rely on their relationship with the FBI in matters of intelligence collection in the territory of the U.S., including where those matters involve international terrorism activity.

19 The FBI may keep such records in its custody on the basis of its national security responsibilities. While it is possible to hold a federal officer liable based on what is known as a *"Bivens Suit"* - derived from the case of *Bivens v. Six Unknown Agents* 403 US 388 (1971) – it would be difficult, particularly under the conditions of counterterrorism.

20 The Coast Guard of the Department of Homeland Security is the only other IC member authorized to collect intelligence in U.S. territory.

The lessons learned from this brief review of national security intelligence are threefold:

1. State, local, and tribal law enforcement officers have no jurisdiction to collect or manage national security intelligence.
2. Use of NSI in a criminal investigation by a state, local, or tribal law enforcement officer could derail the prosecution of a case because of Fourth Amendment protections afforded by the Fruits of the Poisonous Tree Doctrine and the Exclusionary Rule.
3. Use of NSI in a criminal investigation by an SLTLE officer and/or retention of NSI in a records system or in the personal records of an SLTLE officer could open the possibility of civil liability from a Section 1983 lawsuit.

CONCLUSION

The intent of this chapter was to give the reader insight into what intelligence is, its role, and some of the complications that emerge from using the term. Law enforcement intelligence, for example, is defined somewhat differently by the FBI than it is by SLTLE. The reason for the difference is based on the sources of information used by the FBI and the responsibility it holds for disseminating unique critical information in a timely fashion. The important point is that the consumer simply needs to know the different definitions and the different context. With this knowledge, information can be interpreted and used most effectively.

Chapter 2 also addressed the meaning of NSI and the complications it conceivably can pose for SLTLE agencies. Once again, it is important to understand the issues and parameters of each type of intelligence. The proverbial bottom line is that understanding the definitions and their application is an essential foundation for the remaining topics discussed throughout the guide.

∨

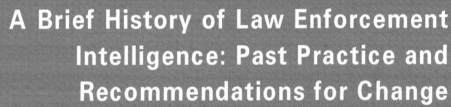

A Brief History of Law Enforcement Intelligence: Past Practice and Recommendations for Change

CHAPTER THREE

A Brief History of Law Enforcement Intelligence: Past Practice and Recommendations for Change

Controversies have surrounded law enforcement intelligence because of past instances where the police maintained records of citizens' activities that were viewed as suspicious or anti-American, even though no crimes were being committed. This, of course, violates fundamental constitutional guarantees and offends the American sense of fairness with respect to government intrusiveness. Unfortunately, the boundary is not precise regarding the types of information the police can collect and keep. Some legal guidelines appear contradictory and the application of law to factual situations is often difficult. Beyond the legal ramifications, early intelligence initiatives by the police typically lacked focus, purpose, and process. Important lessons can be learned from these historical experiences that provide context and guidance for law enforcement intelligence today.

21

Aggravating these factors has been the tenuous relationship between law enforcement intelligence and national security intelligence that has changed continuously since the mid-20th century. These changes have been both politically and legally controversial, responding to changing socio-political events in American history and most recently through post-9/11 counterterrorism efforts. As a result, there is value in understanding selected portions of history from both types of intelligence to gain context and understand the lessons learned.

Law Enforcement Intelligence: The Years of Evolution

Early law enforcement intelligence units, notably going back to the 1920s, borrowed an old method from the military known as the "dossier system." Essentially, intelligence files were nothing more than dossiers—files with a collection of diverse raw information about people who were thought to be criminals, thought to be involved with criminals, or persons who were thought to be a threat to the safety and order within a community. Bootleggers during prohibition and many of the high-profile criminals of the early twentieth century – for example, Bonnie and Clyde, the Barker Gang, Machine Gun Kelly, Al Capone – were the typical kinds of persons about whom police agencies kept dossiers.

During the depression of the 1930s, little was done in the law enforcement intelligence arena. Other priorities were simply higher; the pervasive threat to the country was the economy, not criminality. Circumstances began to change in the latter part of the decade as Communism – or the "Red Scare" – became predominant. The police relied on the only system they had used: the dossier.

In 1937, U.S. Representative Martin Dies (D-Texas) became the first chairman of the House Committee on Un-American Activities. Dies, a supporter of the Ku Klux Klan, fueled the fire of concern about Communism in the United States, including labeling people as Communists that often resulted in their loss of jobs and functional displacement from society. Concern about Communism was pervasive, but was of secondary interest in the 1940s because of World War II. After the war, when the Soviet Union was formed and built its nuclear arsenal, the Red Scare re-emerged with even greater vigor.

> ... local law enforcement agencies began creating **INTELLIGENCE DOSSIERS** on persons who were suspected Communists and Communist sympathizers, these often became known as "RED FILES."

The fires were fanned significantly in 1950 by Senator Joseph McCarthy (R-Wisconsin) who was using this national concern as the foundation for his floundering re-election bid to the Senate. McCarthy railed against the American Communist Party and called for expulsion from government, education, and the entertainment industry anyone who was an avowed Communist or Communist sympathizer. Because of fear from the Soviet Union among the American public, this war on Communism resonated well.

Responding to expressions of public and governmental concern, local law enforcement agencies began creating intelligence dossiers on persons who were suspected Communists and Communist sympathizers, these often became known as "Red Files." Thus, police agencies were keeping records about people who were expressing political beliefs and people who were known to sympathize with these individuals. The fact that these people were exercising their constitutional rights and had not committed crimes was not considered an issue because it was felt that the presence of and support for Communism within the nation was a threat to the national security of the United States.[21]

The dossier system had become an accepted tool for law enforcement intelligence; hence, when new over-arching challenges emerged, it was natural for law enforcement to rely on this well-established mechanism for keeping information. In the 1960s law enforcement met two challenges where intelligence dossiers appeared to be an important tool: the Civil

21   It was rationalized that such activities were warranted on the grounds of a "compelling state interest." This argument, however, did not meet political or constitutional scrutiny.

Rights movement and the anti-Vietnam War movement. In both cases, participants appeared to be on the fringe of mainstream society. They were vocal in their views and both their exhortations and actions appeared to many as being un-American. This was aggravated by other social trends: World War II baby boomers were in their teens and twenties, exploring their own newly defined world of "sex, drugs, and rock n' roll" contributing to the stereotype of the "dope-smoking, commie-hippie spies" – a sure target for a police traffic stop.

An overlap among these social movements was viewed by many as conspiratorial. Moreover, rapidly changing values, stratified in large part along generational and racial lines, created a sense of instability that appeared threatening to the mainstream. Rather than being culturally unstable, as we have learned on hindsight, it was simply social evolution. Because of the dissonance in the 1960s and the largely unsupported assumption that many of the activists and protesters "might" commit crimes or "might" be threats to our national security, police agencies began developing dossiers on these individuals "just in case." The dossier information typically was not related to specific crimes, rather, it was kept as a contingency should the information be needed in an investigation or prosecution. There is little doubt that law enforcement was creating and keeping these dossiers with good faith to protect the community from activities then viewed as threats; however, that faith does not mitigate unconstitutional practices.

There was additional concern during this time because of the activist nature of the U.S. Supreme Court during the era of Chief Justice Earl Warren (1953 – 1969). Many of the liberal decisions of the Warren Court were met with disfavor and the often-expressed belief that the Court's decisions[22] were "handcuffing the police." With regard to the current discussion, perhaps most important was that the Warren Court led a generation of judicial activism and expanded interpretations of the Constitution. Moreover, it symbolically motivated activist attorneys from the 1960s to try new strategies for the protection of constitutional rights. Among the most successful was reliance on a little-used provision of the Civil Rights Act of 1871, codified as Title 42 of the U.S. Code, Section 1983, *Civil Action for Deprivation of Civil Rights.*

22 Among the most often cited are *Miranda v. Arizona* - police must advise arrestees of their Fifth and Six Amendment rights prior to a custodial interrogation; *Mapp v. Ohio* - applying the Exclusionary Rule to the states; *Gideon v. Wainwright* - right to appointed counsel; and *Escobedo v. Illinois* - right to counsel when the process shifts from investigatory to accusatory.

Commonly referred to as 1983 suits, this provision essentially provides that anyone who, under color of state or local law, causes a person to be deprived of rights guaranteed by the U.S. Constitution or federal law may be civilly liable. The initial lawsuits focused on whether a city, police department, and officers could be sued for depriving a person of his or her constitutional rights. The Supreme Court held that they could. A significant

> It was increasingly discovered that POLICE AGENCIES were keeping INTELLIGENCE FILES on people for whom there was NO EVIDENCE of criminality.

aspect of the case was that the police could be sued if there was "misuse of power possessed by virtue of state law and made possible only because the wrongdoer is clothed with the authority of state law."[23] This opened the proverbial floodgates for lawsuits against the police (and correctional institutions).

Initial lawsuits focused on various patterns of police misconduct; for example, excessive force and due process violations. The reach of lawsuits against law enforcement grew more broadly with decisions holding that the police chain of command could be held vicariously liable for the actions of those under their command. Moving into the late 1960s and early 1970s, this movement of lawsuits reached toward law enforcement intelligence units. It was increasingly discovered that police agencies were keeping intelligence files on people for whom there was no evidence of criminality. The practice of keeping intelligence dossiers on a contingency basis was found to be improper, serving no compelling state interest and depriving those citizens of their constitutional rights. As a result, the courts repeatedly ordered intelligence files to be purged from police records and in many cases police agencies had to pay damage awards to plaintiffs. The decisions also permitted citizens to gain access to their own records. Many activists publicized their intelligence files as a badge of honor, often to the embarrassment of the police.[24] Law enforcement intelligence operations were cut back significantly or

23 *Monroe v. Pape* 365 U.S. 167 (1961).

24 For example, it was not uncommon to find notations and even photographs of an "intelligence target" having dinner or attending a public event such as a movie or the theater. The citizen would then pose a rhetorical question, "Is this how you want your tax dollars spent?"

eliminated as a result of the embarrassment and costs associated with these lost lawsuits. The lessons learned from this era suggest caution in the development of intelligence files; information must be collected, maintained, and disseminated in a manner that is consistent with legal and ethical standards.

This lesson is reinforced by the findings of the United States Senate Select Committee to Study Government Operations:[25] the Church Committee, named after its chairman, Frank Church (D - Idaho),[26] which held extensive hearings on domestic intelligence, most notably the FBI's Counter Intelligence Program (COINTELPRO) which spanned the years of 1959 to 1971. The committee concluded that:

> Domestic intelligence activity has threatened and undermined the Constitutional rights of Americans to free speech, association and privacy. It has done so primarily because the Constitutional system for checking abuse of power has not been applied.

Early Intelligence Recommendations

After World War II, the major focus of the Intelligence Community[27] (IC) was to direct intelligence activities at the Soviet Union to prevent the perceived threat of Soviet world domination.[28] Accordingly, the congressional commissions in charge of investigating the IC's operations at this time were largely concerned with the IC's efficiency in conducting such activities. The main focus of these investigations was to recommend ways to improve the IC's structure, organization, and coordination. Indeed, most of the recommendations made by the committees addressed deficiencies in coordination and organization.[29] Three specific commission investigations made recommendations that were particularly relevant to law enforcement intelligence.

In 1948, the Hoover Commission recommended developing better working relationships between the Central Intelligence Agency (CIA) and the rest of the IC. The commission had found a lack of coordination within the IC and of a lack of information sharing which led to redundant intelligence activities. In 1949, the Dulles Report recommended that the CIA provide

25   United States Senate Select Committee to Study Government Operations. (1976). *Intelligence Activities: Final Report.* Washington, DC: Library of Congress.

26   Also alternately known as the Church Commission.

27   For an explanation of the Intelligence Community and those departments and agencies that are current members see www.intelligence.gov.

28   R. Best. & H.A. Boerstling. (1996). The intelligence community in the 21st century. House of Representatives 104 Congress: Permanent Select Committee on Intelligence. www.access.gpo.gov/congres s/house/intel/ic21/ic21018 .html.

29   *Ibid.*

greater coordination for the rest of the community, particularly between the Director of Central Intelligence (DCI) and the FBI. The report also recommended that the director of the FBI become a member of the Intelligence Advisory Committee to help coordinate intelligence functions with the rest of the IC. Finally, results from the Schlesinger Report in 1971 recommended a reorganization of the IC. The report noted that failures in coordinating the IC and the lack of centralized leadership could be corrected by creating a Director of National Intelligence, increasing the authority of the DCI, and creating a White House position to oversee the entire IC.

Not all intelligence recommendations, however, have looked solely at improving the efficiency and effectiveness of intelligence operations. In the mid-1970s, a number of intelligence abuses surfaced indicating that both the CIA and the FBI had conducted intelligence operations that violated American citizens' civil rights. The CIA was charged with conducting questionable domestic intelligence activities, and the FBI was charged with abusing its intelligence powers, mainly within COINTELPRO.[30] These abuses, coupled with the public's frustration over the Vietnam War and the Watergate scandal, led to a shift in focus of the congressional committees' inquiries toward what is now referred to as the era of public investigations.

Intelligence Recommendations in the Era of Public Investigations

During this era, investigations of the IC moved away from assessing the efficiency of intelligence operations and toward assessing the legality and the appropriateness of the actual operations conducted. As will be seen, the recommendations made by three congressional committees would result in major changes in both the jurisdiction and roles of IC members with respect to law enforcement and national security intelligence. This would lead to the separation of the two types of intelligence activities, the so-called "wall between domestic and international intelligence."

30   For an illustration of the types of information collected during COINTELPRO, see the FBI's Freedom of Information website, foia.fbi.gov.

In 1975, the Rockefeller Commission recommended limiting the CIA's authority to conduct domestic intelligence operations. Furthermore, the commission also recommended that the DCI and the director of the FBI set jurisdictional guidelines for their respective agencies. In 1976, the House Select Committee on Intelligence (the Pike Committee, chaired by Representative Otis Pike, D - New York) also made recommendations to further limit the jurisdictional overlap between agencies responsible for national security intelligence and agencies primarily responsible for law enforcement intelligence. It was the recommendations of the Church Committee, however, that were the most important in developing the wall of separation.

> The RECOMMENDATIONS of the Church Committee have been widely recognized as a PRIMARY REASON for the SEPARATION of law enforcement intelligence from national security intelligence. The call for this separation, however, DID NOT MEAN that the AGENCIES SHOULD STOP WORKING with each other.

31 L. Johnson. (1985). *A season of inquiry: The Senate intelligence investigation.* Lexington, KY: The University Press of Kentucky.

32 For a more complete review of the formation of the Church committee see note 14.

The Church Committee, an inquiry formed by the Senate in 1976, examined the conduct of the IC in a broader fashion than did the Rockefeller Commission.[31] The recommendations made by this inquiry led to jurisdictional reformations of the IC. Most of the recommendations were directed at developing new operational boundaries for the FBI and CIA. Out of the committee's 183 recommendations, the following illustrate how law enforcement intelligence was separated from national security intelligence:[32]

- The committee recommended that agencies such as the NSA, CIA, and military branches not have the power to conduct domestic intelligence operations (i.e., law enforcement intelligence functions). Specific attention was given to the role of the CIA, noting that "the CIA should be prohibited from conducting domestic security activities within the United States."[33]

- The committee recommended that the FBI have "sole responsibility" in conducting domestic intelligence investigations of Americans.
- The FBI should "look to the CIA as the overseas operational arm of the intelligence community."[34]
- All agencies should ensure against improper intelligence activities.

The recommendations of the Church Committee have been widely recognized as a primary reason for the separation of law enforcement intelligence from national security intelligence. The call for this separation, however, did not mean that the agencies should stop working with each other. In fact, the Church Committee also recommended that the FBI and CIA continue sharing information and make a better effort to coordinate their initiatives. This was operationally complicated: How do the two agencies work together and coordinate initiatives when there are substantial limitations on the kinds of information that can be collected and shared? The result was increased compartmentalization between the agencies and within each agency.[35] Recommendations to improve law enforcement intelligence, however, have not been limited to the federal level. Such recommendations have also been made for state and local law enforcement agencies.

Law Enforcement Intelligence at the State, Local, and Tribal Levels

One of the first recommendations to address local law enforcement intelligence came from the Warren Commission's 1964 report on the assassination of President John F. Kennedy. While the majority of the commission's recommendations were directed at federal agencies, notably the Secret Service and FBI, it also recommended that these agencies work more closely with local law enforcement. Specifically, the commission called for increased information sharing and stronger liaison between local and federal agencies.[36]

33 United States Senate Select Committee to Study Governmental Operations with Respect to Intelligence Activities. (26 April 1976). *Intelligence activities and the rights of Americans: Final report.* Book II.

34 *Ibid.*

35 For example, because of the regulations - or at least the interpretation of the regulations - FBI agents working within the Foreign Counter Intelligence Division (FCI) were often barred from sharing information with agents working on criminal investigations.

36 The Warren Commission Report. (2003). *Report of the president's commission on the assassination of President John F. Kennedy.* New York: Barnes and Noble, Inc. [Originally published in 1964].

With the increased problems associated with organized crime and domestic terrorist threats, more recommendations to improve state and local law enforcement intelligence were made throughout the 1960s and 1970s. In 1967, the President's Commission on Law Enforcement and Administration of Justice recommended that every major city police department have an intelligence unit that would focus solely on gathering and processing information on organized criminal cartels. Furthermore, it recommended staffing these units adequately and evaluating them to ensure their effectiveness.[37]

In 1971, the National Advisory Commission on Criminal Justice Standards and Goals (NAC) was created to make recommendations for increased efficacy of the entire criminal justice system. "For the first time national criminal justice standards and goals for crime reduction and prevention at the state and local levels" were to be prepared.[38] Included in the commission's report were recommendations directed at establishing and operating intelligence functions for state and local law enforcement agencies. These recommendations included the following:

Establishing Intelligence Functions

- Each state should develop a centralized law enforcement intelligence function with the participation of each police agency within the state.[39]
- States should consider establishing regional intelligence networks across contiguous states to enhance criminal information-sharing processes.[40]
- Every local law enforcement agency should establish its own intelligence function in accordance with its respective state's intelligence function.[41]

Intelligence Function Operations

- Each state and local intelligence function should provide support to federal agencies.
- Operational policies and procedures should be developed for each local, state, and regional intelligence function to ensure efficiency and effectiveness.[42]
- Each agency should have a designated official who reports directly to the chief and oversees all intelligence operations.

37 The President's Commission on Law Enforcement and Administration of Justice. (1967). Task force report: Organized crime. Washington, DC: U.S. Government Printing Office.

38 National Advisory Commission on Criminal Justice Standards and Goals. (1973). Police. Washington D.C.: U.S. Department of Justice, Law Enforcement Assistance Administration.

39 Ibid.

40 National Advisory Commission on Criminal Justice Standards and Goals. (1976). Report of the task force on organized crime. Washington DC: U.S. Department of Justice, Law Enforcement Assistance Administration.

41 Ibid.

42 Ibid.

- Each agency should develop procedures to ensure the proper screening, securing, and disseminating of intelligence-related information.[43]

Although the recommendations provided by the NAC were made to strengthen law enforcement's capabilities to fight organized crime, by the mid-1980s, criminal enterprises had grown dramatically and encompassed a diverse array of illegal activities, from drug trafficking to counterfeiting consumer commodities. Investigators and intelligence units had neither the expertise nor the personnel to contain the problem effectively. This was aggravated by a failure of law enforcement to generally understand the nature of the problem and by poor information sharing between law enforcement agencies at all strata of government.[44] Organized crime was characterized as a "rapidly changing subculture" that was outpacing the capability of law enforcement to control it. Increasingly, state and local law enforcement viewed it as a federal responsibility. As a result, law enforcement intelligence units were often relegated to being little more than an information clearinghouse or, in some cases, viewed as a failed initiative.[45]

Despite the lack of success, many within the law enforcement community still viewed the intelligence function as important to police agencies. As a result, new critical assessments of the intelligence function resulted in more recommendations to improve its operations. A primary limitation of state and local intelligence units was their inability to move beyond the collection of information to a systematic method of analyzing the collected data. The solution, then, was to have "the analytical function…guide the data collection [procedure]" rather than vice versa.[46]
Another limitation of law enforcement intelligence was that many police executives either did not recognize the value of intelligence and/or did not have the skills necessary to use intelligence products effectively. Furthermore, intelligence personnel did not possess the analytic (and often reporting) skills needed to produce meaningful intelligence products. The need for training was considered an important solution to this problem.

Another issue was that intelligence units tended to be reactive in nature, often viewed as a repository of sensitive information rather than a

43   National Advisory Commission on Criminal Justice Standards and Goals. (1976). *Report of the task force on disorder and terrorism.* Washington DC: U.S. Department of Justice, Law Enforcement Assistance Administration.

44   President's Commission on Organized Crime. (1987). Washington, DC: U.S. Government Printing Office.

45   F. Martens. (1987). "The intelligence function." In Herbert Edelhertz (ed.), *Major Issues in Organized Crime Control.* Washington, DC: U.S. Government Printing Office.

46   *Ibid.*

proactive resource that could produce information critical for preventing crime and apprehending offenders. Similarly, intelligence units tended not to produce consistent, specifically defined products. Instead, intelligence reports tended to be written on an ad hoc basis to address critical matters.

A final limitation was that intelligence products were not disseminated in a timely or comprehensive manner. This, perhaps, was the greatest setback because the character of organized crime was constantly changing: different commodities were being trafficked, methods of operations tended to change, and participants in the operation of the enterprise changed. The need for timely and relevant information was seen as a necessary component to improving law enforcement intelligence operations.

While the majority of the past recommendations focused on the development and operations of intelligence units, recommendations have also been made regarding the ethical issues associated with state and local intelligence operations. Similar to the concerns that led to the formation of the Church Committee at the federal level, potential abuses of power was also a concern at the state and local levels. Accordingly, recommendations were made to ensure citizens' civil rights remain intact.

47 Commission on Accreditation for Law Enforcement Agencies. (1998). *Standards for law enforcement agencies*. 4th ed. www.calea.org/newweb/newsl etter/no79/criminalintelligence .htm.

…the development of the INTELLIGENCE-LED POLICING concept and the creation of the NATIONAL CRIMINAL INTELLIGENCE SHARING PLAN have been important milestones in the evolution of law enforcement intelligence.

For example, the Commission on the Accreditation of Law Enforcement Agencies (CALEA) has recommended that every agency with an intelligence function establish procedures to ensure that data collection on intelligence information is "limited to criminal conduct that relates to activities that present a threat to the community" and to develop methods "for purging out-of-date or incorrect information."[47] In other words, the CALEA standard identified the need for law enforcement agencies to be held accountable for abuses of power associated with their intelligence activities.

As will be seen later, the development of the Intelligence-Led Policing concept and the creation of the National Criminal Intelligence Sharing Plan have been important milestones in the evolution of law enforcement intelligence. By creating both an overarching intelligence philosophy and a standard for operations, state, local, and tribal law enforcement intelligence is becoming more professional. It is embracing more sophisticated tools, developing greater collaboration for one voice from the law enforcement intelligence community, and moving with a greater sense of urgency because of 9/11.

Recent Developments: Law Enforcement Intelligence and the 9/11 Commission

Most recently, the issue of information sharing was addressed both in public hearings and in a staff report from the National Commission on Terrorist Attacks Upon the United States (the 9/11 Commission). One issue of concern was the effectiveness of information sharing by the FBI with state and local law enforcement. The commission's staff report stated, in part:

> We heard complaints that the FBI still needs to share much more operational, case-related information. The NYPD's Deputy Commissioner for Counterterrorism, Michael Sheehan, speculated that one of the reasons for deficiencies in this information sharing may be that the FBI does not always recognize what information might be important to others. ... Los Angeles Police Department officials complained to us that they receive watered-down reports from the FBI. ... We have been told that the FBI plans to move toward a "write to release" approach that would allow for more immediate and broader dissemination of intelligence on an unclassified basis.[48]

Both of these issues are being addressed through the National Criminal Intelligence Sharing Plan (NCISP) and more specifically through the

48 National Commission on Terrorist Attacks Upon the United States (2004). *Staff Statement No. 12: Reforming Law Enforcement, Counterterrorism, and Intelligence Collection in the United States,* p. 8. http://www.9-11commission.gov/staff_statements/staff_statement_12.pdf.

creation of Intelligence Requirements by the FBI. Moreover, FBI Executive Assistant Director for Intelligence Maureen Baginski specifically stated in remarks at the 2004 annual COPS community policing conference that included in the initiatives of the FBI Office of Intelligence was a revised report-writing style that would facilitate information sharing immediately, including with those intelligence customers who did not have security clearances.[49]

Interestingly, the 9/11 Commission's staff report on reformation of the intelligence function included many of the issues and observations identified in previous commission reports over the previous 40 years. The difference, however, is that substantive change is actually occurring, largely spawned by the tragedy of September 11, 2001.

The final 9/11 Commission report issued a wide range of recommendations related to intelligence. Cooperative relationships, the integration of intelligence functions, and a general reengineering of the intelligence community were at the heart of the recommendations. In commentary, the commission noted the role of state, local, and tribal law enforcement agencies, stating the following:

> There is a growing role for state and local law enforcement agencies. They need more training and work with federal agencies so that they can cooperate more effectively with those authorities in identifying terrorist suspects.[50]

The commission went on to recognize that:

> The FBI is just a small fraction of the national law enforcement community in the United States, a community comprised mainly of state and local agencies. The network designed for sharing information, and the work of the FBI through local Joint Terrorism Task Forces, should build a reciprocal relationship in which state and local agents understand what information they are looking for and, in return, receive some of the information being developed about what is happening, or may happen, in their communities.[51]

49 Maureen Baginski, FBI Executive Assistant Director for Intelligence. Remarks in a keynote address to "Community Policing for America's Future: National Community Policing Conference", Office of Community Oriented Policing Services, Washington, DC (June 22, 2004).

50 National Commission on Terrorist Attacks Upon the United States. (2004). *The 9/11 Commission Report.* Washington, DC: U.S. Government Printing Office, p. 390. Also available in full online at www.9-11 commission.gov/report/911Report.pdf.

51 *Ibid.*, p. 427.

The commission also recommended creation of a new domestic intelligence entity that would need to establish "...relationships with state and local law enforcement...."[52] In proposing a new National Counterterrorism Center (NCTC), the commission stated that the center should "... [reach] out to knowledgeable officials in state and local agencies throughout the United States."[53] Implicit in the commission's recommendations is that terrorism is a local event that requires critical involvement of state and local government in prevention and response.[54]

> Implicit in the [9/11] COMMISSION'S recommendations is that TERRORISM is a local event that requires critical involvement of STATE and LOCAL GOVERNMENT in prevention and response.

LESSONS LEARNED

While we have evolved in our expertise and professionalism, many of the same issues remain. What are the lessons learned from history?

- Building dossiers full of raw, diverse information provides little insight; analysis is needed to give meaning to the information.
- The improper collection of information can have a negative impact on our communities, including a "chilling effect" on the constitutional right of freedom of speech.
- To be effective, intelligence units must be proactive, developing unique products and disseminating the products to appropriate personnel on a consistent and comprehensive basis.
- A clear distinction is needed between law enforcement intelligence and national security intelligence. While there is information that can support the goals of both forms of intelligence, the competing methodologies and types of information that may be maintained in records mandates that the distinction remain clear and that overlap

52   *Ibid.*, p. 424.

53   *Ibid.*, p. 404.

54   *Ibid.*

occurs only for clear purposes of public safety, including the apprehension of offenders and prevention of criminal and/or terrorists' acts.

- Targeting people is unlawful…without some evidence of a criminal predicate:
  - If the reason for the target is the support of an unpopular cause.
  - If they are being targeted because of their political beliefs, religion, race, ethnicity, or other attribute or characteristic that is inherently lawful.
  - Targeting without lawful justification can result in civil rights suits and vicarious liability lawsuits which can be both costly and embarrassing to the police department.
- Monitoring an individual's behavior is proper if reasons can be articulated that reasonably support the notion that:
  - The person may be involved in criminality now or in the future.
  - There is a reasonable threat to public safety.
- Retaining information in intelligence files about an individual is improper if there is no sustainable evidence of his or her criminal involvement, unless that information is used only as noncriminal identifying information and is labeled as such.
- A full-time law enforcement intelligence function should be organized professionally and staffed with personnel who are specifically trained in analysis and intelligence product preparation.
- There must clear lines of communications between the intelligence unit and decision makers.
- Law enforcement intelligence units must be evaluated regularly to ensure functional utility and operational propriety.
- Information sharing remains an important priority with few major improvements since the original recommendations in the 1964 Warren Commission.

Intelligence-Led Policing: The Integration of Community Policing and Law Enforcement Intelligence

CHAPTER FOUR

Intelligence-Led Policing: The Integration of Community Policing and Law Enforcement Intelligence

A common concern expressed by police executives is that the shift toward increased counterterrorism responsibilities may require a shift of resources away from community policing. Instead the question should be how community policing and counterterrorism should be integrated. As will be seen, there are more commonalities between the two than one may intuitively expect. Indeed, new dimensions of law enforcement intelligence and counterterrorism depend on strong community relationships. Crime will continue to be a critical responsibility for the police as will the need for community support. Moreover, with increased social tension as a result of this terrorism environment, the need is even greater to maintain a close, interactive dialogue between law enforcement and the community.

39

Community policing has developed skills in many law enforcement officers that directly support new counterterrorism responsibilities: The scientific approach to problem solving, environmental scanning, effective communications with the public, fear reduction, and community mobilization to deal with problems are among the important attributes community policing brings to this challenge. The National Criminal Intelligence Sharing Plan (NCISP) observed these factors, noting the following:

> Over the past decade, simultaneous to federally led initiatives to improve intelligence gathering, thousands of community-policing officers have been building close and productive relationships with the citizens they serve. The benefits of these relationships are directly related to information and intelligence sharing: COP officers have immediate and unfettered access to local, neighborhood information as it develops. Citizens are aware of, and seek out COP officers to provide them with new information that may be useful to criminal interdiction or long-term problem solving. The positive nature of COP/citizen relationships promotes a continuous and reliable transfer of information from one to the other. It is time to maximize the potential for community-policing efforts to serve as a gateway of locally based information to prevent terrorism, and all other crimes.[55]

55   http://it.ojp.gov/topic.jsp?topic_id=93.

COMMUNITY POLICING has DEVELOPED SKILLS in many LAW ENFORCEMENT OFFICERS that directly support new COUNTERTERRORISM RESPONSIBILITIES.

Furthermore, the Office of Domestic Preparedness (ODP) *Guidelines for Homeland Security* describes the roles community policing has in the intelligence process. These include the following:

- Provide examples and materials that may aid the recognition of terrorism to community policing contacts in order to make members of the community aware of those actions, behaviors and events that constitute "suspicious."
- Organize community meetings to emphasize prevention strategies, vigilance, and public awareness.
- Ensure that members of the community are aware of the means of and processes for relaying observed data to police officers and police organizations, just as they are, or should be, aware of methods to relay information to community policing officers.
- Encourage prevention, proactive policing, and close working relationships between the police and the community.[56]

Intelligence-Led Policing

These factors were precipitated by the development of Intelligence-Led Policing (ILP) as an underlying philosophy of how intelligence fits into the operations of a law enforcement organization. Rather than being simply an information clearinghouse that has been appended to the organization, ILP provides strategic integration of intelligence into the overall mission of the organization. In many ways, ILP is a new dimension of community policing, building on tactics and methodologies developed during years of community policing experimentation. Some comparisons illustrate this point. Both community policing and ILP rely on:

- Information Management
  - Community policing - Information gained from citizens helps define the parameters of community problems.
  - ILP - Information input is the essential ingredient for intelligence analysis.
- Two-way Communications with the Public
  - Community policing - Information is sought from the public about offenders. Communicating critical information to the public aids in crime prevention and fear reduction.
  - ILP - Communications from the public can provide valuable information for the intelligence cycle. When threats are defined with specific

[56] http://www.ojp.usdoj.gov/odp/docs/ODPPrev1.pdf.

information, communicating critical information to citizens may help prevent a terrorist attack and, like community policing, will reduce fear.

- Scientific Data Analysis
  - Community policing - Crime analysis is a critical ingredient in the CompStat[57] process.
  - ILP - Intelligence analysis is the critical ingredient for threat management.
- Problem Solving
  - Community policing - Problem solving is used to reconcile community conditions that are precursors to crime and disorder.
  - ILP - The same process is used for intelligence to reconcile factors related to vulnerable targets and trafficking of illegal commodities.

The importance of these factors is illustrated in the comments of FBI Director Robert Mueller in announcing an increased concern for terrorism at major national events during the summer of 2004. When referring to the photographs of seven terror suspects believed to be in the United States, Director Mueller stated:

> We need the support of the American people ... to cooperate when called upon, as agents will be reaching out to many across the nation to help gather information and intelligence ... to be aware of your surroundings and report anything suspicious ... to "BOLO" [Be On the LookOut] for those pictured above. ... Have you seen them in your communities? Have you heard that someone might be helping them to hide? Do you have any idea where they might be? If so, we need you to come forward.[58]

These words reflect the operational essence of the interrelationship of law enforcement intelligence and community policing. Like community policing, ILP requires an investment of effort by all components of the organization as well as the community. Gone are the days when intelligence units operated in relative anonymity. Based on the precepts of the ILP philosophy and the standards of the NCISP, law enforcement intelligence is an organization-wide responsibility that relies on a symbiotic relationship with residents.

57 For a good contemporary discussion of CompStat, see: Shane, Jon. (2004). "CompStat Process." *FBI Law Enforcement Bulletin*. Vol. 73, No. 2. (April). pp 12-23.

58 http://www.fbi.gov.

Ethical Issues

Another important characteristic similar to both community policing and ILP is the emphasis on ethical decision making. In community policing the need for ethical decision making was based, among other reasons, on the need to develop trust between the police and community. Without this trust, the public would not provide the critical information needed for crime control. The need for ethical decision making in ILP is similar, but goes a step further. Because of concerns about the types of information being collected by law enforcement and how that information is retained in records, concerns have been expressed that law enforcement may violate citizens' rights in the quest for terrorists. As a result of these concerns, the aura of ethical decision making and propriety of actions must be unquestioned in the law enforcement intelligence function.

The Similarity to CompStat

One of the best examples of the community policing/ILP interrelationship can be seen in the latest tool of community policing: CompStat. Drawing its name from "COMPuterized STATistics," CompStat may be defined as the

Figure 4-1: Comparison of CompStat and Intelligence-Led Policing		
CompStat	**Commonalities**	**Intelligence-Led Policing**

• Single jurisdiction
• Incident driven
• Street crime and burglary
• Crime mapping
• Time sensitive (24-hour feedback and response)
• Disrupt crime series (e.g., burglary ring)
• Drives operations:
  – Patrol
  – Tactical Unit
  – Investigators
• Analysis of offender MOs
	• Each have a goal of prevention
	• Each require…
	  – Organizational flexibility
	  – Consistent information input
	  – A significant analytic component
	• "Bottom-up" driven with respect to operational needs
		• Multijurisdiction
		• Threat driven
		• Criminal enterprises and terrorism
		• Commodity flow; trafficking and transiting logistics
		• Strategic
		• Disrupt enterprises
		• Drives Operations
		  – JTTF
		  – Organized Crime Investigations
		  – Task Forces
		• Analysis of enterprise MOs

Correlated goals and methodologies make both concepts complement each other		

timely and effective deployment of people and resources to respond to crime, disorder, and traffic problems and trends which are detected over a relatively short time. The process is much more than performing a sophisticated data analysis and mapping. It requires accountability at all levels of the organization, necessary resource allocation, and both immediate triage and long-term solutions to problems.

> In many ways, [INTELLIGENCE-LED POLICING] is a new dimension of community policing, BUILDING ON TACTICS and METHODOLOGIES DEVELOPED during years of community policing experimentation.

59 Training is discussed in detail – including line officer training – in Chapter 8.

60 On a related note, following the terrorists' attacks of September 11, 2001, the FBI developed a series of interview questions for persons who may have knowledge about terrorism. State and local law enforcement were asked to participate in the questioning of some persons who were in the U.S. on visas. There was a mixed response, largely based on the perspective of local government leaders. Despite this, the questions were also intended to provide insight and information for officers. More information as well as the protocol questions can be found in: General Accounting Office. (2003). *Justice Department's Project to Interview Aliens After September 11, 2001.* Report Number GAO-03-459. Available at: www.gao.gov.

As illustrated in Figure 4-1, both community policing and ILP are prevention oriented and are "driven" by an information flow coming from the line-level upward. Intelligence awareness training for street officers recognizes that officers on patrol have a strong likelihood of observing circumstances and people that may signify a threat or suggest the presence of a criminal enterprise. The patrol officer must be trained[59] to regularly channel that information to the intelligence unit for input into the intelligence cycle for analysis. Like community policing, this requires new responsibilities for patrol officers and organizational flexibility to permit officers to explore new dimensions of crimes and community problems that traditionally have not been part of a patrol officer's responsibilities.

Similarly, to be effective, both community policing and ILP require feedback on information analysis – whether it is crime analysis or intelligence analysis – to be consistently informed of potential problems or threats that may be encountered during the course of their shift.

In this regard, what types of information do street officers need from the intelligence unit? Ideally, intelligence analysis should address four broad questions:[60]

- <u>Who poses threats?</u> This response identifies and describes people in movements or ideologies who pose threats to community safety.
- <u>Who's doing what with whom?</u> This includes the identities, descriptions, and characteristics of conspirators or people who provide logistics in support of terrorism and criminal enterprises.
- <u>What is the modus operandi of the threat?</u> How does the criminal enterprise operate? What does the terrorist or extremist group typically target and what are the common methods of attacking? How do members of the extremist group typically integrate with the community to minimize the chance of being discovered?
- <u>What is needed to catch offenders and prevent crime incidents or trends?</u> What specific types of information are being sought by the intelligence unit to aid in the broader threat analysis?

The Flow of Illicit Commodities

Beyond these questions, it is useful to provide street officers with information on *commodity flows*. Criminal enterprises exist to earn illegal profits through the trafficking of illegal commodities: drugs, stolen property, counterfeit goods, and other contraband where there is a consumer demand. Terrorists also rely on trafficking in illegal commodities: explosives, weapons, false identity credentials, and money to support terrorists' networks and cells. Historical evidence demonstrates that once regular commodity flow networks are established, they typically will be consistent and change infrequently. While conventional wisdom may suggest that changing transaction processes will minimize the probability of detection, in practice it is often difficult to change transaction methodologies. Moreover, it is a fundamental characteristic of human behavior to perform tasks in a consistent manner. As a result, commodity flow patterns provide an avenue of consistent behavior that may be recognized as evidence of unlawful activity.

In many cases, there is evidence of illegal commodity transactions "on the streets" where direct observations of suspicious behaviors may be made by officers. In other cases, law enforcement may need to educate the public on what to look for and seek community input on such observations. Once again, this relies on a trusting relationship between law enforcement officers and members of the community. In both instances, effective observations rely on information provided by intelligence analysis.

It is important to recognize that clear social, personal, and organizational interrelationships exist between terrorists and organized crime groups as well as among different criminal enterprises. An important reason for these relationships centers on the commodities they need to either further their enterprise or to sustain a terrorist organization. As such, understanding and monitoring illicit commodity flows can be an important avenue for penetrating a wide range of complex criminality.

One of the important factors to note in this process is the need for public education. Advisories warning the community to be aware of suspicious activity often leads to the question of "what is suspicious?" The police must provide context to community members. Using intelligence analysis, the law enforcement organization will be able to identify threats within the community and be more specific about defining suspicious behavior. When the patrol officer receives specific information from the intelligence unit, he or she can pass a more detailed educational process on to citizens. Armed with more detailed information concerning what actions may constitute "suspicious" behavior, the public can be more aware. With this greater awareness, citizens will not only know what to look for, but also what to report to the law enforcement agency.

The success of this process relies on three elements:

- effective intelligence analysis
- effective information dissemination to street officers
- trusting relationships and effective communications between law enforcement and community members.

This is the essence of the integration of community policing and intelligence analysis.

Public Education

As noted previously, public education is critical for effective ILP. The lessons learned from community policing provides important insights. The public encompasses many different groups and different public education initiatives need to be provided to each of those constituent groups. For example, what does the agency want to accomplish with a public education program: Fear reduction? Resolve community tensions? Develop volunteers for the police department? Is the goal simply to give citizens information about terrorism indicators to aid in prevention? The important point to note is that a specific goal should be related to the public education initiative.

Such a program may also stratify the community in order to give specific types of information to different targeted audiences. Who in the community should be targeted for an education program: The business community? Civic and church groups? Graduates of the Citizens' Police Academy (CPA)? Non-law enforcement government employees? Teachers and students? The general community? Demographically defined segments of the community?

> Different segments of the COMMUNITY may have different needs. For example, since 85 percent of America's critical INFRASTRUCTURE is owned by the private sector, a special public education program may focus on THREAT-RELATED ISSUES for this narrowly defined community.

Different segments of the community may have different needs. For example, since 85 percent of America's critical infrastructure is owned by the private sector, a special public education program may focus on threat-related issues for this narrowly defined community. Conversely, a completely different kind of public education may be directed toward graduates of the CPA who may be trained to work as volunteers during crises or a heightened alert status. Yet a different public education agenda would be directed toward a particular ethnic or religious community within a city. Each segment of the community has a different goal. In this case, the business sector to harden potential targets, the CPA graduates to aid the police in response to increased service demands, and the ethnic community to gain information about suspicious persons and their actions.

These segments may be further divided, particularly if there are unique targets within the community. For example, the business community may be broken down into different segments: There are different threats may target a nuclear plant or telecommunications switching station (both are critical infrastructure) or a meat processing plant or university genetic research laboratory (both of which may be a target of domestic environmental extremists).[61] The law enforcement agency will have to conduct a threat assessment to fully understand the character of the threat within the community as well as to understand the agency's intelligence requirements.[62] Collectively, these elements have a symbiotic relationship to aid in the development of a public education program.

Community education programs should also have a specific outcome intended. Whether it is to reduce fear or to enlist support for volunteer efforts, all public education initiatives should incorporate four factors related to the intelligence function:

- Know how to observe.
- Know what is suspicious.
- Know how to report.
- Know what to report.
- Know what happens next.

To maximize the quality and quantity of information provided by the community, law enforcement must provide a framework of knowledge. The more that law enforcement can educate the community, the more robust the feedback from the community.[63] In this regard, Figures 4-2 and 4-3 illustrate a range of items that may be incorporated into a public education program from both a topical and an outcome perspective.

Civil Rights Issues

A reality that law enforcement must face on matters related to law enforcement intelligence is discussion of citizens' civil rights. Different

61 Oftentimes, targets may not be readily apparent in a community. Does East Lansing, Michigan appear to be a terrorist target? In 1992, the Animal Liberation Front (ALF) started a fire in the Michigan State University mink research facility and caused more than $2 million in damages. On December 31, 1999, a fire in MSU's Agricultural Hall caused $700,000 in damages and destroyed years of research. Earth Liberation Front (ELF) claimed responsibility, targeting genetic research.

62 The threat assessment and intelligence requirements will be discussed in a later chapter.

63 Ideally, the law enforcement agency would be able to provide feedback to the citizen about information that was reported. Many times this is not feasible in the "intelligence environment"; however, it serves as positive reinforcement to the citizen when feedback is provided.

Figure 4-2: Examples of Topics in Public Education Program

- Understanding Terrorism
- What is terrorism (defined/explained)
- Why people commit terrorist acts
- Perspectives of terrorism
- Asymmetric warfare
- An act of terror is defined by the victim
- How terrorism can touch your community
  - As a target
  - Logistics and support provided to terrorists
  - Activities that fund terrorist organizations
- New preparedness resources for local emergency services

- What is being done at the national level
  - National level
  - National strategies developed
  - National threat assessment by FBI
  - FBI reprioritized and re-organized to aid state and local law enforcement
- What is being done state and local level
  - Participation in Joint Terrorism Task Forces (JTTF)
  - Officers receiving antiterrorism training (SLATT)
  - New communications and information sharing (ATIX, RISS, LEO) give local law enforcement more access

Figure 4-3: Examples of Actions the Public Can Take

- Keep informed to know what to look for and report to the police
  - Law enforcement must be prepared for information sharing with public
- Be aware, yet be fair
- Be cognizant of threats, but avoid stereotyping and hyperbole
- Information on how to talk/deal with children regarding terrorism
  - http://www.ed.gov/admins/ lead/safety/ emergencyplan/index.html
  - http://www.fema.gov/kids/
  - http://www.atf.gov/kids/index.htm

- Information on how to protect family http://www.ready.gov
- Safety checklist
- Communications information
- What "awareness" means
- Explain the Alert System
- How to help children cope with fear
- Safety issues
- Equipment and resource checklist
- Understand the Homeland Security Advisory System and its effect

groups of citizens – some more vocal than others – have expressed concerns at the national level concerning the USA PATRIOT Act and at the local level concerning the types of personal information that is being collected and retained in files at the local law enforcement agency. As part of a public education effort, law enforcement officers should be informed about civil rights issues and the agency's policies and responses to those issues. Among the more common concerns expressed are the types of records a law enforcement agency can keep on citizens; whether a citizen may see what information, if any, is being kept about him or her; the types of electronic surveillance that may be used; whether the FBI can view library records and monitor both email and Internet sites visited; and USA PATRIOT Act in general.[64] While a law enforcement officer may not be able to answer all citizens' questions, providing some information is more useful than not responding at all.

Community Members as Law Enforcement Volunteers

Oftentimes community members ask what they may do to aid in counterterrorism. One important element is serving as a volunteer for the law enforcement agency. Experience has shown that community volunteers can save the agency money as well as often provide unique expertise. Money can be saved when citizens are able to perform tasks that would otherwise have to be performed by a law enforcement employee. For example, the Austin, Texas Police Department uses volunteers as part of its Civil Defense Battalion to accomplish these goals. (Figure 4-4 describes the mission, philosophy, organization, and duties for the citizen volunteers.)

Obviously, an agency needs to develop some means to screen volunteers as well as provide structure for their work agreement and for administrative controls when they are performing activities on behalf of the law enforcement agency. In this regard, an important resource is Volunteers in Police Service (VIPS).[65] The VIPS website provides a wide

> EXPERIENCE has shown that community volunteers can save the agency money as well as often provide UNIQUE EXPERTISE.

array of resources, documents, policies, and tips that can make a law enforcement volunteer program functional and easy to manage. Volunteers with unique occupational experience may be particularly valuable to the intelligence function. An attorney, accountant, people with

64 The official Justice Department website on the USA PATRIOT Act, including frequently asked questions, is http://www.lifeandliberty.gov.

65 http://www.policevolunteers.org.

experience in researching land titles, and academic researchers and scholars are illustrations of professional volunteers who could provide important assistance to the intelligence function. (Of course, background checks and nondisclosure agreements must be required of all such volunteers.)

CONCLUSION

As noted in a recent publication by the staff of the Office of Community Oriented Police Services:

> For the past 20 years, community policing has encouraged law enforcement to partner with the community to proactively identify potential threats and create a climate of safety. Its emphasis on problem-solving has led to more effective means of addressing crime and social disorder problems. In the 21st Century the community policing philosophy is well positioned to take a central role in preventing and responding to terrorism and in efforts to reduce citizen fear.[66]

The prudent executive will explore these avenues as part of a comprehensive, community-wide homeland security strategy. Because of the concern for terrorism and Islamic extremism, the need to embrace all elements of the community becomes an even higher priority. As noted by the Muslim Public Affairs Council:

> "Ultimately, U.S. counterterrorism efforts will require a partnership between policymakers and the American Muslim community…"[67]

66   Scheider, Matthew, Robert Chapman, and Michael Seelman. (2004). *Connecting the Dots for a Proactive Approach.* Border and Transportation Security. Washington, DC: Office of Community Oriented Policing Services. http://www.cops.usdoj.gov/mime/open.pdf?Item=1046.

67   Muslim Public Affairs Council. (2003). *A Review of U.S. Counterterrorism Policy: American Muslim Critique and Recommendations.* Washington, DC: Muslim Public Affairs Council, p. 8.

Figure 4-4: Austin, Texas Police Department Civil Defense Battalion[68]

Mission Statement

To be in readiness as well trained civil defense volunteers to support the work of the Austin Police Department.

Executive Summary:

The Austin Police Department (APD) is well-positioned and well-trained to respond to critical incidents as defined by events prior to September 11, 2001. The terrorist attacks on the United States on September 11 necessitated a fresh look at our ability to respond to a catastrophic event of heretofore unimagined proportions. An assessment of strengths and needs underscored our confidence in many areas of training and staffing. However, the identified areas needing additional resources led to the creation of a Major Event Team (MET) equipped and trained to handle terrorist attacks and/or civil unrest or panic resulting from such attacks. A natural part and extension of the MET is the creation of a Police Civil Defense Battalion, consisting of a well-trained corps of volunteers prepared to respond quickly to supplement the work of APD officers. These volunteers would begin working within APD immediately to become familiar with departmental procedures and to work in areas needing assistance at this time. The Police Civil Defense Battalion would consist of four companies, each trained to handle specially identified tasks with the goal of freeing officers to handle assignments requiring highly-trained police officers. The Office of Community Liaison (OCL) has responsibility for recruitment, coordination and scheduling for training, and placement of volunteers

Training in all areas will be offered and some immediate assignments will be given. Ongoing training will be offered to maintain readiness. Volunteers working outside of the police facilities will work in pairs only.

Structure:

The four companies would be designed to work in clearly defined areas.
- **Company "A" (Aviation Detail)** - Assigned to the Aviation Police, assignments would include:
    1. Information dissemination to airport visitors through the Airport Ambassadors program
    2. Assist in getting housing and/or transportation for stranded passengers in the event of a crisis or if closure of the airport
- **Company "B" (Homeland Security Supplemental Services)** - Assigned to the MET for immediate assignments in various areas within the department to ensure continued services and provide for newly identified needs:
    1. Daylight perimeter patrol of city facilities
    2. Parking control and building access control for police and other city facilities
    3. Work special events (i.e., New Year's Eve - work the barricades with officers providing information to citizens and reporting disturbances)

68 *Source:*
http://www.ci.austin.tx.us/polic
e/civildb.htm.

4. Daylight patrol in areas where multiple offenses of similar types have been reported

- **Company "C" (Headquarters Detail)** - Immediate assignments to assist officers in critical areas:
  1. Work in the control booth at the main police station greeting visitors, providing information and escorting visitors through the building
  2. Abandoned Vehicle Volunteer Program - increase the number of volunteers tagging abandoned/junked vehicles on public property (opening up neighborhood streets for easier access by emergency vehicles)
  3. Assist in answering phones and providing information in all police facilities
  4. Make copies and distribute information as needed

- **Company "D" (Homeland Security)** - Activated should a critical incident occur, assigned to the MET to provide centralized services:
  1. Former police officers may receive special assignments
  2. Activate phone tree to call in volunteers and provide information to the community
  3. Supplement 3-1-1 call takers to handle callers seeking information only
  4. Daylight incident perimeter control - maintaining police lines
  5. Traffic control - freeing officers to work inside incident perimeters
  6. Supplement Red Cross efforts by providing food and water for officers and victims - recruit restaurants to provide these provisions in the event of need; arrange for portable toilets and dumpsters at incident sites
  7. Maintain list of volunteers who speak various languages
  8. Maintain a "message board" for missing persons
  9. Call the families of officers and other emergency workers at an incident scene with reassurance and information
  10. Call neighborhood groups to enlist assistance as needed and contact congregational groups who have agreed to open facilities as shelters in each area command
  11. Chaplains would respond to the scene and provide services as outlined in their volunteer protocol
  12. Should dispatch fail, volunteers to go to each fire station to take calls and relay messages to officers

How do you apply?

You must be at least 18 years old and live or work in the Austin area. The Civil Defense Battalion requires its personnel to meet some physical demands. They are:

1. Vision and hearing corrected to normal range.
2. Ability to stand for 2 or more hours at a time.
3. Ability to lift at least 20 pounds.

Figure 4-4: Austin, Texas Police Department Civil Defense Battalion *(Cont.)*

Each applicant must complete the <u>Civil Defense Battalion Application</u> and the <u>Personal History Form</u>. Once these forms are completed please deliver them in person as your thumbprint will be taken for a Criminal Background Check. The address is 1009 E. 11th St., Austin, TX 78701. The Office of Community Liaison is located at the corner of San Marcos and E. 11th St., 2nd Floor.

- The <u>Civil Defense Battalion Application</u> and the <u>Personal History Form</u> requires the <u>Adobe Acrobat Reader</u> plug-in.

After downloading and printing the application and personal history form, complete them and hand deliver them to:

The Office of Community Liaison
1009 E. 11th Street

For information contact: Contact (512) 974-4738

The Intelligence Process

CHAPTER FIVE

The Intelligence Process

In defining intelligence, it was previously noted that the key factor that transforms information to intelligence is analysis. The British National Crime Squad, when referring to intelligence, observed the following:

> The processing of reliable intelligence is the cornerstone of successful law enforcement. Analysis organizes and interprets the intelligence in a way that significantly enhances its value and the possibility of its success in combating organized crime. Analysis identifies and predicts trends, patterns or problem areas requiring action.[89]

Many larger law enforcement agencies have an intelligence unit, but in too many cases the unit is limited in its utility because of failures in structure or direction.[70] Perhaps the most common limitation is that the unit collects, but does not analyze information. Instead, the information is stored in a database simply awaiting access. For example, in some agencies field interview reports are managed by the intelligence function. While this descriptive report on an intelligence subject typically is forwarded to the intelligence unit, too often it is only entered into a database. When information sits passively in an information system, its use will be limited. If, however, the intelligence unit closely examines, analyzes, and compares the field interview forms with other information, the information can be used more effectively. Having a group of people whose primary job is simply responding to information requests about possible wanted subjects but not providing proactive analysis is not a contemporary intelligence unit.

All too frequently when an intelligence unit performs some type of analysis, no distinction is made within the unit about the different types of intelligence outputs and how they can contribute to the agency's goals. As a result, the unit provides far less support and awareness on crime issues and crime threats than could be done. Moreover, intelligence units too often are treated as a support unit, when they can proactively guide many investigative functions. In reality, a police intelligence unit may be placed best organizationally within an operations unit or division. The direct line of communication and the high degree of interaction required between intelligence analysts and investigators provide a richer interchange of information and ideas, thereby enhancing the quality of analysis.

INTELLIGENCE ANALYSIS starts at the most basic level – COLLECTING INFORMATION ABOUT THE "CRIME TRIANGLE" – just as in the case of PROBLEM ORIENTED POLICING.

Intelligence analysis starts at the most basic level – collecting information about the crime triangle: the offender, victim/commodity, and location – just

69   See
      http://www.nationalcrimesqua
      d.police.uk

70   In a survey conducted by the
      Police Executive Research
      Forum (PERF) after the
      September 11 attacks, 60%
      stated that they needed better
      intelligence. For further
      information on this survey,
      *Local Law Enforcement Role
      in Preventing and
      Responding to Terrorism*, see
      the PERF report at
      http://www.policeforum.org/libr
      ary.asp.

as in the case of problem oriented policing (see Figure 5-1). In a terrorist attack, for example, collecting and analyzing information about the victim and location can lead to information about the offender. Since terrorist groups typically have distinct methods, motives, and targets, these can be derived from the victim and location. With a criminal enterprise, the variable victim would be replaced by the commodity. In each instant, the type of information being sought should be driven by intelligence requirements. Defining the requirements (discussed in detail in Chapter 10) will provide greater efficacy to intelligence processes.

Each piece of information needs to be assessed for its validity and reliability to determine how much weight, if any, it contributes to understanding the crime, identifying suspects, and developing a case that can be prosecuted. Once the dependability of the information is assessed, an assessment of its substantive contribution to the investigation must be made, determining the information's relevance and materiality. This process is done for all evidence and information gathered during the course of an investigation.

Figure 5-1: Crime Triangle

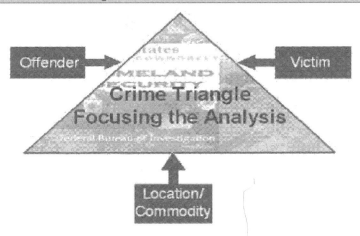

As the body of assessed information accumulates, the intelligence analyst asks two questions:

1. What does this information mean?
2. Can I prove it?

In an example, an analyst receives the following information about a person that represents each activity over a 6-month period:

- A pen register indicating calls made from a targeted suspect's telephone.
- A printout of travel destinations from the suspect's travel agent.
- An accounting of ATM withdrawals from the bank.
- A credit card record of purchases.

In looking at the content of each of these items, the analyst uses both deductive reasoning to develop a hypothesis of what the information means within each type of record, and inductive reasoning to hypothesize what the collective information suggests about the suspect and his or her behavior related to criminality. Examples of questions are as follows:

71   N.B. = "nota bene" means "of particular note".

- Is there a pattern to the telephone calls based on the person called, locations called, and times called?
- Is there a pattern to the travel locations traveled to, days of the week, times of the day, and hotels stayed at?
- Is there a correlation between the telephone calls and the travel on any set of variables?
- Is there any pattern or evidence in the ATM withdrawals or any credit card purchases to show additional travel (such as driving to a location), specific or unique purchases, consistency in cash or credit transactions (either consistent amounts or amounts always ending even, full dollars, no change)?

After determining answers to these questions, the analyst may start drawing conclusions for which additional information is needed: Can the hypotheses be corroborated with other evidence? To corroborate the hypotheses, the analyst may request surveillance of the target(s), conduct an interview, or obtain information from a confidential informant. The analyst must also be looking for evidence of motive (N.B.,[71] motive helps explain the criminality and provide guidance on where to seek additional evidence), intent (N.B., to establish the mens rea or criminal intent) as well as specific criminal transactions (N.B., to document the actus reus or physical act of the crime).

This simple example demonstrates the general process of analysis. As diverse pieces of evidence are added to the investigation, the analyst often prepares an illustration which shows the linkages, as established by evidence among people, places, and organizations. This is referred to as link diagram (Figure 5-2). When transactions are involved, such as drug trafficking, illicit weapons sales, or money laundering, the analyst often prepares a diagram called a commodity flow (Figure 5-3). These two analytic tools are useful in visualizing the relationships and process in complex criminal investigations.[72] They not only help guide the investigation but are also useful in presenting the case in court.

As the analysis progresses, the analyst writes reports to describe to administrators, supervisors, investigators, and/prosecutors, the progress that is being made on the case, the direction that the investigation should follow, new information or concerns, and resources or assistance needed to develop the case further. Certain types of information derived from the reports also need to be disseminated to a broader group, for example, giving information to patrol officers and neighboring jurisdictions in the form of BOLOs.[73] If the intelligence is not disseminated, then much of its value is lost.

[72] Various commercial software programs are available to aid in preparing these diagrams. Most software permits the user to embed photographs, images of evidence, and even video to further illustrate the relationships within a criminal enterprise or the commodity flow.

[73] BOLO = Be On the Look Out.

Figure 5-2: Link Diagram Illustration

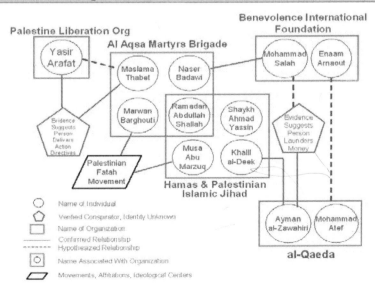

Figure 5-3: Commodity Flow Chart Illustration

Intent: Purchase weapons for terrorists w/laundered money through "fronts"

"Invested" Money to Buy Weapons

Money Laundering Process

} Weapons Transactions

"CHARITABLE" FOUNDATION

WEAPONS BROKER → Weapons → WEAPONS SMUGGLER

Financial Investment

Weapons

WEAPONS SOURCE COUNTRY

Weapons

Cash

Financial Investment

Cash

Cash

WEAPONS BOUGHT BY TERRORISTS

Cash

Cash

Cash

MONEY LAUNDERING

MONEY LAUNDERING

WEAPONS PAID FOR

Payment in Swiss Francs

Dollars

BANK OF SWITZERLAND

One of the greatest weaknesses in the organizational culture of intelligence
units is the unwillingness to share information. Police leadership must
ensure that intelligence is proactively shared with the people who need the
information, both inside the organization and with external agencies. Too
many times, intelligence units act as a sponge, absorbing information from
diverse sources, but are reluctant to share what they have gathered and
learned. This gate-keeping practice is dysfunctional, wastes resources,
and contributes to the reluctance of field personnel to submit information.
Having stated that the information must be shared, there are some caveats
about disseminating law enforcement intelligence. First, care must be
taken to ensure security of the information so that an investigation will not
be compromised. While this is a real concern, some intelligence units
become overly cautious. Like most things in life, there must be a
reasonable balance. A second concern is that tactical and operational
intelligence is often accusatory, but not conclusive. The amount of
information in a developing case may strongly suggest a person's criminal
activity but not meet the standard of probable cause. As such, the
intelligence may be used for further inquiry, gathering more information to
either expand or conclude the investigation. However, if the intelligence

and related information should become public and cannot be linked effectively to an evidence-based criminal investigation, the agency may risk liability for a civil rights lawsuit.

With complex criminal behavior like terrorism, an effective law enforcement intelligence unit can be critical to both the prevention of a terrorist attack and the apprehension of offenders. Law enforcement agencies need to review their intelligence function carefully, ensuring that it is structured, directed, and staffed in a manner that can provide the critical information, through analysis, that is needed. They should give consideration to developing a regional intelligence capacity to develop more comprehensive, multijurisdictional information on community problems and threats. The value of state and regional approaches is multifaceted. First, it is more cost-efficient because there would be just one intelligence structure for multiple agencies sharing resources to operate the intelligence unit. Second, it is more effective because there is a broader array of information input covering a wider geographical area. Third, since criminals regularly cross jurisdictional boundaries, a regional approach gives law enforcement more flexibility in criminal investigations. When all variables are factored in, a regional intelligence capacity is organizationally and operationally the most efficacious approach.

The Intelligence Cycle

This brief summary of analysis followed a process known as the intelligence cycle (Figure 5-4). It is an ongoing process that seeks continuous input so that every new piece of information which meets the standards of rigor can be added to the evidentiary picture. As is evident, this can be a labor-intensive process which requires eclectic knowledge and strong analytic ability to be successful.

The fundamental point to draw from this discussion is that pieces of information gathered through the collection process are not intelligence. Rather, intelligence is the knowledge derived from the logical integration and assessment of that information and is sufficiently robust to enable law enforcement to draw conclusions related to a particular crime.

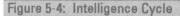

Figure 5-4: Intelligence Cycle

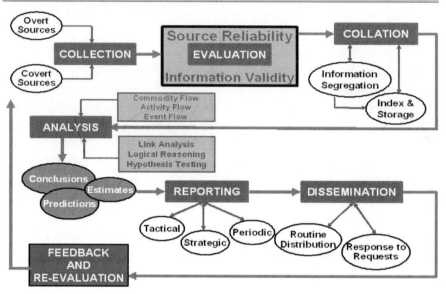

As noted previously, the FBI has broad responsibility (and authority) in the intelligence process that integrates both law enforcement and national security intelligence. As a result, the FBI Intelligence Program approaches the cycle somewhat differently. Figure 5-5 provides definitions of the FBI Intelligence Cycle – information that is important for state, local, and tribal law enforcement (SLTLE) personnel to understand to be effective consumers of the FBI intelligence products and communicate effectively on matters related to FBI intelligence operations.

INFORMATION MANAGEMENT AND INTELLIGENCE PROCESSES[74]

Information is the currency of intelligence. In the era of digital communications and networking, it is virtually impossible to deal with the management and sharing of information without considering technological implications. Technology and information transcend a number of boundaries which are often blurred. Internet protocols (IP), for example, are often critical for collecting, analyzing, and sharing information. The sections that follow serve as a primer for information technology and intelligence. Concepts, trends, resources, and issues are discussed to provide familiarization to the manager.

Figure 5-5: FBI Intelligence Cycle Definitions and Processes

FBI INTELLIGENCE PROGRAM
DEFINITION AND PROCESS OF THE FBI INTELLIGENCE CYCLE

1. REQUIREMENTS: Requirements are identified information needs – what we must know to safeguard the nation. ... Requirements are developed based on critical information required to protect the United States from National Security and criminal threats.

2. PLANNING AND DIRECTION: Planning and direction is management of the entire effort from identifying the need for information to delivering the intelligence product to the consumer. It involves implementation plans to satisfy requirements levied on the FBI as well as identifying specific collection requirements based on FBI needs. Planning and direction is also responsive to the end of the cycle because current and finished intelligence, which supports decision making, generates new requirements.

3. COLLECTION: Collection is the gathering of raw information based on the requirements. Activities such as interviews, technical and physical surveillances, human source operations, searches, and liaison relationships results in the collection of intelligence.

4. PROCESSING AND EXPLOITATION: Processing and exploitation involves converting the vast amount of information collected to a form usable by analysts. This is done through a variety of methods including decryption, language translation, and data reduction. Processing includes the entering of raw data into databases where it can be exploited for use in the analysis process.

5. ANALYSIS AND PRODUCTION: Analysis and production is the converting of raw information into intelligence. It includes integrating, evaluating, and analyzing available data, and preparing intelligence products. The information's reliability, validity, and relevance is evaluated and weighed. The information is logically integrated, put in context, and used to produce intelligence. This includes both "raw" and "finished" intelligence. Raw intelligence is often referred to as "the dots". ... "Finished" intelligence reports "connect the dots" by putting information in context and drawing conclusions about its implications.

6. DISSEMINATION: Dissemination...is the distribution of raw or finished intelligence to the consumers whose needs initiated the intelligence requirements. The FBI disseminates information in three standard products – FBI Intelligence Information Reports, FBI *Intelligence Bulletins*, and FBI *Intelligence Assessments*) described and illustrated in Chapter 11). FBI intelligence customers make decisions – operational, strategic, and policy – based on the information. These decisions may lead to the levying of more requirements, thus continuing the FBI intelligence cycle.

From: FBI Office of Intelligence. The FBI Intelligence Cycle: *Answering the Questions....* A desk reference guide for FBI employees. (Pamphlet form). (July 2004).

Software to Aid the Intelligence Process[75]

Just like any other aspect of police management, there are a number of vendors who will develop proprietary software for intelligence records, analysis, and secure electronic dissemination.[76] Such systems can be expensive to purchase and maintain and may not be a viable option for many medium and small agencies because of fiscal constraints. For most agencies, a wide array of off-the-shelf software can aid the intelligence function. Most obvious are word processing and presentation software programs for preparing reports and briefings. Beyond these, a number of software programs that can be useful to the intelligence function include the following:

- **Databases:** A law enforcement agency can use commercially available databases to create an intelligence records system that is searchable on a number of variables. Most current databases permit the user to custom design the variable fields and include images as well as text.[77]
- **Spreadsheets:** The analytic capacity of most current versions of spreadsheet software is reasonably robust. For example, data from a pen register can be entered and compared, complete with different graphing options, to identify associations and trends. Virtually any kind of data can be analyzed and converted to bar graphs, scatter plots, line charts, area charts, radar graphs, surface charts, and other graphing options to aid in data interpretation and presentation.
- **Mapping Programs:** Inexpensive mapping software, such as Microsoft Streets and Maps, can be useful for both analysis and presentation of intelligence data. The maps can be used for strategic intelligence illustrations of any geographic-based variable of interest (e.g., people, groups, meetings, commodity distribution, trafficking of contraband). In addition, programs such as these have integrated databases which, although typically limited in character, nonetheless provide sufficient capability to include descriptive information about entries on the map. (see Figure 5-6 as an illustration.)
- **Statistical Programs:** For strategic analysis, statistical software with a graphic capability is very useful. Perhaps the best known, and most powerful, is SPSS.[78] To be most effective, the SPSS user must have a sound knowledge of statistics. A number of other statistical analysis programs

75 Of course, software compatibility issues still remain and should be considered in any purchase. One can not assume compatibility. For example, even though a system is operating on Windows XP, if there is some type of proprietary software on the system, it could cause incompatibility issues with off-the-shelf software that would otherwise operate normally with Windows XP. For more information, see *The Law Enforcement Tech Guide: How to Plan, Purchase and Manage Technology (successfully)!* at: www.cops.usdoj.gov/default.asp?Item=512. See also, SEARCH technical assistance: www.search.org/programs/technology.

76 See the summary of Information Technology Initiatives of the U.S. Office of Justice Programs at http://it.ojp.gov/topic.jsp?topic_id=85 as well as the International Association of Chiefs of Police Technology Clearinghouse at http://www.iacptechnology.org.

77 For examples of databases, see dir.yahoo.com/Computers and internet/software/databases.

78 www.spss.com.

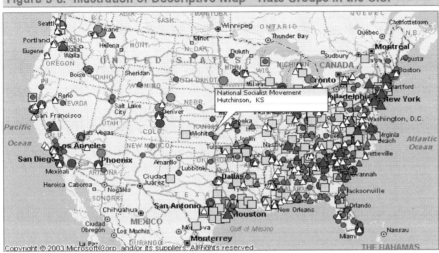

Figure 5-6: Illustration of Descriptive Map - Hate Groups in the U.S.

cost less and are somewhat easier to use; however, such programs have fewer analytic features and options.

- **Intelligence Analysis Software:** Software to assist in organizing, collating, integrating, and presenting data for analysis is an invaluable tool. Perhaps the most widely used analytic software is offered by I2 Investigative Analysis Software.[79] As illustrated in Figure 5-7, the software integrates a number of features that aid in the analysis of data. For a law enforcement agency that is able to have an intelligence analyst on staff, analytic software is an essential investment.

Information Technology Management

There are additional technology concerns beyond those of software described above. The increasingly lower costs of networking technology, the commonality of Internet Protocols for information sharing, the ability to share not only text but also images, audio, and video, and the ease of access to information contribute to the growth of law enforcement intranets and extranets for secure information sharing. As agencies develop these networks, two important elements must be kept in mind: Security and compatibility.

With the pervasive presence of computer crime and unauthorized network intrusions,[80] it is essential to build exceptional security into any network. The significant growth of wireless networks and Bluetooth[R] peripheral

79 www.i2.co.uk/Products.

80 See http://www.cybercrime.gov and http://www.crime-research.org.

connections only serve to aggravate the security problem. Among the security issues to be considered are these:

1. *Manual Assurance of Data Handling:* Virtually all data is handled manually at some point. There must be security standards and quality control of data that is entered into the system.
2. *Physical Security:* There must be effective measures in place to ensure the security of the facility housing computer(s), servers, and any other related hardware (e.g., PDAs) and peripherals (e.g., printers) that have access to the system.
3. *Operations Security:* Processes for quality control of personnel who are system operators/managers as well as security monitoring of people who have access to the secure area where computers and servers are housed. This includes maintenance and custodial personal, clerical personnel, and others who may have access to the secure area.
4. *Management-Initiated Controls:* This includes…
   - Management oversight of system operations.
   - Administrative policy for computer access and use.
   - Fair use policies if a public website is provided.
   - Establishment of data security management policies.
   - Establishing data classification protocols for control and access.

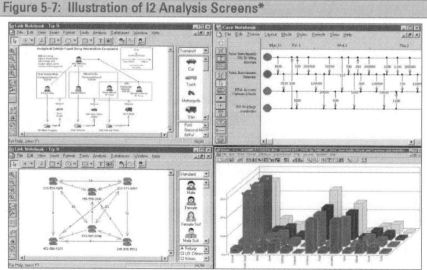

Figure 5-7: Illustration of I2 Analysis Screens*

*Copyright © 2004 i2 Ltd. All Rights Reserved. The Visual Space, Capital Park, Fulbourn, Cambridge, CB1 5XH, UK

5. *Computer System Control:* Strict access to the system should be controlled by:
   - <u>Authorization of personnel</u>. Defining policies and standards as to who may have access to the system, for what purposes access is granted, and defined standards of acceptable use of the system.
   - <u>Software access controls</u>.[81] Beyond standard user name and password controls, and all the well-known security precautions associated with these, the system should be protected by a Virtual Private Network (VPN) for access control by authorized users.
   - <u>System protection and inoculation</u>. All networked systems should have a multistage firewall and constantly updated virus definitions.
6. *Encryption for wireless devices:* Network encryption should be enabled if wireless devices are used with an intelligence records system or intelligence-related communications.
7. *Access audit controls:* A real-time auditing system should monitor all accesses to the system, user identification, activity during the user period, length of time, and IP number of the computer accessing the system.
8. *Control of remote storage media:* Policies need to be established and technological controls instituted to monitor the use and control of restricted data related to remote storage media (e.g., disks, CDs, thumb drives, etc.).

Following these procedures will not only protect intelligence records, they will meet the data security standards of 28 CFR Part 23.

On the issue of compatibility, a report from the Global Justice Information Sharing Initiative observed the following:

> During the past 30 years, the lack of standards for linking justice information systems has been responsible for a substantial part of the high costs involved with information exchange and has contributed significantly to the associated difficulties of exchanging information between justice agencies. Now that a variety of organizations have acknowledged the importance of data exchange standards, it is critical that the adoption of justice

81 At this writing, the Bureau of Justice Assistance is developing a "Trusted Credentials Project" that would identify a process (which may include both software and hardware) that would allow different systems to recognize and accept any credential previously identified as trustworthy. For example a LEO user could pass seamlessly between networks with a single sign-on once that user was validated to the network. This would enable network users to integrate between networks without the need to sign on and off each of them separately.

information exchange standards take into account emerging technologies which will serve as the basis for information exchange in a broad spectrum of industry sectors.[92]

As a result, the initiative has done a significant amount of work in developing consistent definitions, protocols, and data standards — including the XML standard for IPs — to ensure system compatibility. The results will increase connectivity, interoperability, and, consequently, better information sharing.[83]

Information Technology Resources

Other resources are available that will aid in training and program development for the intelligence function. While these resources address issues broader than intelligence, per se, they are nonetheless valuable for the intelligence manager. The websites contain training resources, documents, and links that are useful.

- National White Collar Crime Center[84]
- SEARCH - The National Consortium for Justice Information and Statistics[85]
- Crime Mapping Analysis Program[86]
- Crime Mapping and Problem Analysis Laboratory of the Police Foundation[87]
- Office of Justice Program Information Technology Website.[88]

Open-Source Information and Intelligence

Volumes of information have been written on open-source intelligence.[89] The intent of the current discussion is to simply familiarize the law enforcement manager with the open-source concept and its application to a law enforcement agency.

Open-source *information* is any type of lawfully and ethically obtainable information that describes persons, locations, groups, events, or trends. When raw open source information is evaluated, integrated, and analyzed it provides new insight about intelligence targets and trends — this is open-

82   *Technology Considerations in the Development of Integrated Justice Data Exchange Standards.* A report of the Global Justice Information Sharing Initiative, p. 1. http://www.it.ojp.gov/technology/files/IJIS-Standards.pdf.

83   For more information, see the OJP Information Technology Initiatives website at http://www.it.ojp.gov/topic.jsp?topic_id=85, the Global Justice XML website at http://www.it.ojp.gov/topic.jsp?topic_id=43 and the report: National Law Enforcement and Corrections Technology Center. (2001). *A Guide for Applying Information Technology to Law Enforcement.* Washington, DC: Office of Science and Technology, National Institute of Justice (http://www.nlectc.org/pdffiles/infotechguide.pdf).

84   http://www.nw3c.org.

85   http://www.search.org.

86   http://www.nlectc.org/cmap/justnet.html.

87   http://www.policefoundation.org/docs/crime_mapping.html.

88   http://it.ojp.gov/index.jsp.

89   As one example, see http://www.oss.net.

source intelligence. Open-source information is wide-ranging and includes the following:

- All types of media[90]
- Publicly available data bases[91]
- Directories[92]
- Databases of people, places, and events[93]
- Open discussions, whether in forums, classes, presentations, online discussions on bulletin boards, chat rooms, or general conversations
- Government reports and documents[94]
- Scientific research and reports[95]
- Statistical databases[96]
- Commercial vendors of information[97]
- Websites that are open to the general public even if there is an access fee or a registration requirement
- Search engines of Internet site contents.[98]

> Importantly, OPEN-SOURCE INFORMATION about individuals must still meet the CRIMINAL PREDICATE REQUIREMENT to be retained in an agency's INTELLIGENCE FILES.

The main qualifier that classifies information as open source is that no legal process or clandestine collection techniques are required to obtain the data. While open-source data has existed for some time, networking has increased its accessibility significantly. For example, if an analyst was preparing a strategic intelligence report on trends in international terrorism, the analyst may go to the websites of the U.S. Department of State Counterterrorism Office,[99] the FBI terrorism reports,[100] and the Israeli Defense Force terrorism statistics center[101] to download the various reports and data. If the analyst was preparing a report on right-wing extremists, he or she may visit the Southern Poverty Law Center[102] to download reports or

90 See http://www.newslink.org.

91 See as an example http://www.searchsystems.net and http://www.factfind.com/database.htm.

92 One of the most extensive directories is in http://www.yahoo.com. However, other sources of directories exist, such as http://www.search-it-all.com/all.aspx.

93 See as an example http://www.namebase.org, http://www.searchsystems.net and http://www.crimetime.com/online.htm.

94 See http://www.clearinghouse.net/cgi-bin/chadmin/viewcat/Government___Law/government?kywd, http://www.theore.com/links/fedgov-links.html, http://www.firstgov.gov/Topics/Reference_Shelf.shtml and http://www.firstgov.gov/Citizen/Topics/PublicSafety.shtml.

95 See http://www.fas.org.

96 See http://www.lib.umich.edu/govdocs-stats-pilot and http://www.ojp.usdoj.gov/bjs.

97 See as an example http://www.accudatalists.com/index1.cfm.

go to a white supremacy website, such as Stormfront[103] to read the information, conduct further research by reading materials, and following hyperlinks to gain more raw data to prepare an independent report.

Raw information obtained from open sources tends to fall into two categories that have important significance for an SLTLE agency: (1) Information about *individuals* and (2) *aggregate* information. As a general rule, civil rights attach to open source information about individuals, such as a credit report or a legal notice in a newspaper about a lawsuit, *when it is in the intelligence records system* of an SLTLE agency. As a general rule, no civil rights attach to aggregate information, such as the advocacy of terrorism against the U.S. on an Islamic radical website or the threat by a radical environmental group to burn down a university research facility. If, however, individuals are named in an aggregate information source, such as a news story about radical anarchists, some civil rights protections may attach. These instances must be assessed on case-by-case before being retained by the law enforcement agency.

Importantly, open-source information about individuals must still meet the criminal predicate requirement to be retained in an agency's intelligence files. The key is not the source of the information, but *what is being retained* by a law enforcement agency about a person. Illustrations of issues to consider include the following:

- What types of open-source information about a person should be kept on file by the police concerning a "person of interest" who is not actually a suspect?
- How aggressive should a police agency be in gaining open-source information on people who expressly sympathize and/or support a terrorist group as determined by statements on a web page, but do not appear to be part of a terrorism act nor active in the group?
- How does a police agency justify keeping information on a person when a suggestive link between the suspicious person and a terrorist group has been found through open-source research, but not a confirmed link through validated and corroborated evidence?

See pg. 71

98   Beyond the commonly used Internet search engines such as Google, Lycos, Yahoo, Ask Jeeves, and others, a unique web search site is http://www.itools.com.

99   http://www.state.gov/s/ct.

100   http://www.fbi.gov/publications/terror/terroris.htm.

101   http://www1.idf.il/DOVER/site/homepage.asp?clr=1&sl=EN&id=-8888&force=1.

102   http://www.splcenter.org.

103   http://www.stormfront.org.

Creating intelligence dossiers is both tempting and easy using open-source data. The question to consider, however, is whether it is proper. The reader is asked to reflect on the earlier discussion of history and the lessons learned. Among those lessons was the fact that the police cannot retain intelligence dossiers on persons for whom a criminal predicate is not articulated in the facts. Essentially, by applying the Terry[104] test, if the police do not have an articulable reason to link a suspect to a crime, they cannot keep these records in a dossier. As noted previously, the issue is not whether the information was from an open source, but whether the police could properly keep the information. Law enforcement agencies must consider the reason for which information is being retained, not the *source*.

Data can also be gathered on individuals through open-source information on the Internet (often for a fee). Companies such as AutoTrack,[105] Accurint,[106] and Lexis-Nexis[107] have merged a wide array of public databases coupled with data migration techniques to permit merging of extraordinarily detailed information about people into a summary report. Marketing data available through subscription from many companies and even news searches — notably through the comprehensive databases of Lexis-Nexis[108] — can provide a surprising amount of detail about people which, when analyzed, presents a detailed profile that may be useful in varying aspects of an investigation. In addition, university libraries offer a wide array of research and resource tools that are often available at no cost.[109]

The fact that information is open source should not dissuade a law enforcement officer or analyst from using it. Indeed, there is often very high-quality, insightful evidence available from open sources. So much so, that the 9/11 Commission, in its Final Report, recommended that a new Open Source Agency be added to the U.S. intelligence structure.[110] For example, news services have global networks of sophisticated communications and informants with trained staff to conduct research and investigate virtually all issues that would be of interest to a consuming public. As a general rule, responsible news organizations also have editorial policies to ensure that the information is valid, reliable, and

104 This refers to the U.S. Supreme Court "stop and frisk" case of *Terry v. Ohio* 392 US 1 (1968) wherein the Court held that police officers could stop, detain, and frisk a person whose actions, based on the experience of a police officer, suggested that the person was committing, had committed, or was about to commit a crime.

105 http://www.autotrack.com.

106 http://www.accurint.com.

107 http://www.lexis-nexis.com/ risksolutions/lawenforcement.

108 http://www.lexis-nexis.com.

109 As examples, see http://www.lib.msu.edu/harris2 3/crimjust/index.htm and http://er.lib.msu.edu.

110 National Commission on Terrorist Attacks Upon the United States. (2004). The 9/11 Commission Report. Washington, DC: U.S. Government Printing Office, p. 413. Also available in full online at http://www.9-11commission.gov/report/911 Report.pdf.

corroborated. As such, the news media is a tremendous source of information that should be part of a law enforcement agency's "intelligence toolkit."

As an illustration, the Anti-Terrorism Information Exchange (ATIX), a website operating on the Regional Information Sharing Systems secure network, RISS.net, is designed to provide groups of defined users with secure interagency communication, information sharing, and dissemination of terrorist threat information. Part of the ATIX site includes news stories on all aspects of terrorism (Figure 5-8). Not only does this help users stay up-to-date on focused terrorism-related news stories, but the ongoing consumption of this news develops an "intellectual database" wherein the user becomes aware of issues, trends, locations, and methodologies related to terrorism.

Open-source information can be a tremendous resource for a law enforcement agency and should be incorporated as part of an agency's intelligence plan. The important caveat, however, is to ensure that all file requirements are applied to open-source data.

CONCLUSION

This chapter familiarized the reader with terminology and concepts that transform information to intelligence. Most law enforcement officers will not be involved in the analytic process; however, understanding that process provides important insights into understanding the kinds of information an intelligence analyst needs and what kind of output can be expected.

Police LEADERSHIP must ensure that intelligence is proactively SHARED with the people who need the information—both inside the ORGANIZATION and with EXTERNAL AGENCIES.

Figure 5-8: Illustration of Open-Source News Stories on RISS ATIX

ATIX News
Archive

National Organizations Partner to Launch National Preparedness Month

The U.S. Department of Homeland Security (DHS), The America Prepared Campaign, the American Red Cross, the National Association of Broadcasters and the U.S. Department of Education have joined a coalition of more 50 national organizations to engage Americans in emergency preparedness by launching National Preparedness Month on September 9. *Posted 09/11/04*

New Terror Threat Info Warns of Plans With Helicopters, Limos

The FBI is warning that al-Qaeda could attempt to commandeer helicopters, limousines and other rental vehicles to launch attacks inside the United States. *Posted 08/09/04*

Vaccine Protects Mice Against Ricin

U.S. military researchers say they have produced a vaccine that protects mice from the deadly effects of inhaled ricin -- one of the most toxic substances known. *Posted 08/04/04*

Major Exercises Set For NORAD and USNORTHCOM

Two major exercises, Amalgam Virgo 04 (AV04) & Determined Promise 04 (DP04), kick off this week for the North American Aerospace Defense Command and the U.S. Northern Command to test the commands? response to terrorist events on a national, state, and local level. *Posted 08/04/04*

Intelligence Agencies Next in Line for Reorganization

With the president's endorsement yesterday of a national intelligence czar, the government appears on track for another major restructuring. *Posted 08/04/04*

This led into a discussion of software and technology issues that may be used in support of the SLTLE intelligence function. Needs will vary by agency; hence, the discussion was a broad buffet of software and technology tools from which a manager may begin making resource decisions. Finally, transcending the line between analysis and technology, open-source information and intelligence was discussed with respect to its use, value, resources, and limitations.

The reader should take away from this chapter a thorough understanding of information management and analysis issues as they relate to the development of an intelligence function.

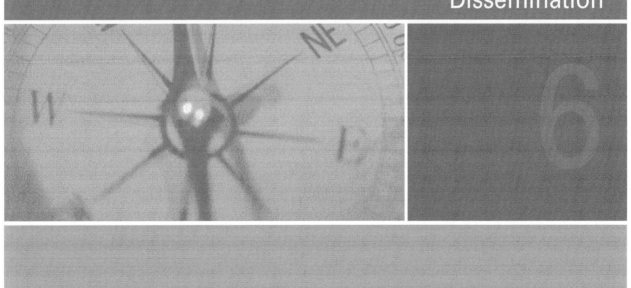

Law Enforcement Intelligence
Classifications, Products, and
Dissemination

CHAPTER SIX

Law Enforcement Intelligence Classifications, Products, and Dissemination

A range of terms describe different types of law enforcement intelligence. A brief discussion of these as they relate to state, local, and tribal law enforcement (SLTLE) will provide some context for the reader when these terms are encountered.

79

Intelligence Based on the Nature of Analysis

Two terms are often used in this category: "raw intelligence" and "finished intelligence." Typically, raw intelligence is information that has been obtained from generally reliable sources; however, it is not necessarily corroborated. It is deemed valid not only because of the sources but also because it coincides with other known information. Moreover, raw intelligence usually is time sensitive and its value is perishable in a relatively short period. Because of its time sensitivity and critical relationship to the community or individual safety, an advisory is disseminated as a preventive mechanism.

Finished intelligence is when raw information is fully analyzed and corroborated. It should be produced in a consistent format to enhance utility and regularly disseminated to a defined audience. Different types of finished intelligence reports meet the needs of diverse consumers and are referred to as the "products" of an intelligence unit.

Intelligence Products

To accomplish its goals, intelligence and critical information need to be placed in a report format that maximizes the consumption and use of the information. The report should do the following:

1. Identify the targeted consumer of the information (patrol officers, administrators, task force members, others).
2. Convey the critical information clearly.
3. Identify time parameters wherein the intelligence is actionable.
4. Provide recommendations for follow-up.[111]

Such products are a series of regularly produced intelligence reports that have a specific format and type of message to convey. They are most useful when each product has a specific purpose; is in a consistent, clear, and aesthetic format; and contains all critical information the consumer needs and no superfluous information. The types of products will vary by the character of the agency (e.g., state/local, urban/rural, large/small) as

111 For example, follow-up instructions may direct a patrol officer to complete a field interview card, notify a special unit, conduct surveillance of the target, or take safety precautions.

well as the collection and analytic capacity of unit personnel. As a general rule, only about three products may be needed:

- Reports that aid in the investigation and apprehension of offenders.
- Reports that provide threat advisories in order to harden targets.
- Strategic analysis reports to aid in planning and resource allocation.

Without fixed, identifiable intelligence products, efforts will be wasted and information will be shared ineffectively.

> "PRODUCTS" are a series of regularly produced intelligence reports that have a SPECIFIC FORMAT and type of message INTENDED TO CONVEY.

Operational ("non-product") Intelligence

SLTLE often find a need to maintain information, in either raw or finished form that can place them in a controversial position. For purposes of community safety, law enforcement needs to maintain information on some people and organizations for two reasons: (1) The have the potential to commit crimes and (2) They pose a bona fide threat, although the parameters of that threat are often difficult to specify. Their actions are monitored and affiliations recorded to help prevent future crimes and/or build a future criminal case. Inherently problematic is the idea of a future crime: what is the rationale for keeping information on a person who has not committed a crime, but might do so? Essentially, if there is a compelling interest for community safety, an effective argument can be made to maintain records on individuals who threaten that safety as long as reasonable justification can be presented to show a relationship to criminality.

In this type of intelligence there is no product, per se, but regularly prepared and disseminated operational records on people and groups who are associated with terrorists or criminal enterprises. The important, yet difficult, balance is to ensure that there is no violation of constitutional rights during the course of the process, but at the same time maintaining a resource of credible information for legitimate law enforcement purposes.

An example is anarchists who advocate the "Black Bloc" tactic of property destruction, confrontation with the police, and disruption of the public's right to movement. Typically, the simple advocacy of such forms of protest would be expressions of free speech and therefore inappropriate to maintain in an intelligence records system. However, a legacy of anarchists using the Black Bloc tactic that includes causing property damage – some of it significant – and public disruption is a circumstance where operational intelligence becomes important because of the potential for criminal law violations.

If anarchists who advocate the use of the Black Bloc held a public meeting, it would be proper for an undercover agent to attend, take notes, describe participants, and take literature for inclusion in the intelligence records system.

Beginning in the fall of 2001, the police faced new challenges for operational intelligence. In the wake of the terrorists attacks in New York, Washington, and Pennsylvania, the U.S. Department of Justice began identifying people who entered the United States under the grant of entry afforded by various types of visas. Some were detained for several weeks on civil immigration violations. Others were detained on grounds that they had conspired with the terrorist, had materially assisted the terrorists, or had knowledge of the terrorist's plans. In an effort to expand the investigation, for both resolution of the September 11 attacks and to prevent future attacks, the FBI began a systematic identification of specific people who had entered the U.S. on a visa with the intent of interviewing the visa holders.[112] Evidence of knowledge about any aspect of the terrorists' attacks was not a precursor for a person to be interviewed.

Because of the potential for civil litigation and ethical concerns about the propriety of these interviews, some police departments – beginning with Portland and Corvallis, Oregon – declined to comply with the FBI's request to assist in the interviews. It is probable that future conflicting interests will emerge in the war on terror and the prudent police manager must carefully consider the legal and ethical concerns of such practices and balance them with the need to protect the community.

112 The questions asked of people in the U.S. on non-immigrant visas: If they.......noticed anybody who reacted in a surprising way to the news of the September 11 attacks. ...know anyone who has helped plan or commit terrorism or anybody capable of or willing to commit terrorism. ...have sympathy for the September 11 hijackers or other terrorists and the causes they support. ...have heard of anybody recruiting people to carry out terrorism against the United States, or if anyone has tried to recruit them. ...know anyone who has received financing or training for terror activities. ...are willing to provide information in the future. ...know anyone capable or developing any biological or chemical weapon such as anthrax.

Intelligence Based on the Orientation of the Analysis

Traditionally, intelligence for SLTLE agencies has also been described according to whether the output of the analysis is either *tactical or strategic*.

Tactical intelligence is used in the development of a criminal case that usually is a continuing criminal enterprise, a major multijurisdictional crime, or other form of complex criminal investigation, such as terrorism. Tactical intelligence seeks to gather and manage diverse information to facilitate a successful prosecution of the intelligence target. Tactical intelligence is also used for specific decision making or problem solving to deal with an immediate situation or crisis. For example, if there is a terrorist threat to a target, tactical intelligence should provide insight into the nature of both the threat and the target. As a result, decisions can be made on how to best secure the target and capture the offenders in a way that increases the probability of some form of action, such as prosecution or expulsion from the country if the person(s) involved is(are) not United States citizen(s).

Strategic intelligence examines crime patterns and crime trends for management use in decision making, resource development, resource allocation, and policy planning. While similar to crime analysis, strategic intelligence typically focuses on specific crime types, such as criminal enterprises, drug traffickers, terrorists, or other forms of complex criminality. Strategic intelligence also provides detailed information on a specified type of crime or criminality.[113] For example, terrorists cells[114] related to Al-Qaeda within the United States might be described to the extent possible on their characteristics, structure, philosophy, numbers of members, locations, and other distinguishing characteristics. Similarly, a strategic intelligence report may document attributes of "eco-extremists"[115] by describing typical targets and methods used in their attacks. This information helps police understand the motivations of the intelligence targets and can help in deploying investigative resources, developing training programs for police personnel to better understand the threat, and provide insights which may help in target hardening. Such ongoing

113 For examples of strategic intelligence reports related to drug trafficking, see the Drug Enforcement Administration's intelligence publications at http://www.dea.gov.

114 A terrorist cell refers to a loosely structured working group with a specific terrorism-related mission that has multiple targets depending on how leaders decide to operationalize the mission. Typically, there is a loose hierarchy within the cell based largely on the idea of having one person who is the "first among equals"—this is the individual who communicates with decision makers and is generally responsible for handling expenses and logistics of the cell members. The relationship is not actually a "supervisory" one. Cell members typically live in close geographic proximity and may share a habitat. The activities of the cell may change, but that is determined by hierarchical leaders external to the cell, not a cell member.

115 The eco-extremist movement represents environmental activism that is aimed at political and social reform with the explicit attempt to develop environmental-friendly policy, law, and behavior. As stated by one group, "The work of Green social transformation is only partially a matter of electoral and legislative victories. A far more important aspect of this work involves a fundamental retooling of the basic cultural values and assumptions that have led us to our current ecological and social problems."

strategic intelligence keeps officials alert to threats and potential crimes. Each type of intelligence has a different role to fulfill. When performed properly, the different forms of intelligence can guide investigations; provide insights for resource allocation; suggest when priorities should be expanded or changed; suggest when new training and procedures may be needed to address changing threats; and permit insight when there is a change in the threat level within a specific community or region.

> … the different forms of intelligence can GUIDE INVESTIGATIONS; PROVIDE INSIGHTS for resource allocation; suggest when PRIORITIES should be expanded or changed; suggest when new training and procedures may be needed to address CHANGING THREATS; and permit insight when there is a change in the threat level…

115 (Cont.)

http://www.well.com/user/smendler/green/gmculture.htm As is the case with virtually any political or religious group, the eco-extremists also have members who commit acts of terrorism in the name of ecological conservation, such as the Environmental Liberation Front's (ELF) arsons of condominiums in the Rocky Mountains.

116 As an example, for the first time the HSAS was raised for a specific target (financial institutions) in specific areas (Washington, DC; northern New Jersey, and New York City) in the summer of 2004.

On this last point, the federal government created the color-coded Homeland Security Advisory System (HSAS) to provide information to communities when indications and warnings (I&W) arise resulting from the analysis of collective intelligence. A formal and deliberate review process occurs within the interagency process of the federal government before a decision is made to elevate the threat level. The HSAS continues to be refined[116] and adjustments are made in line with security enhancements across the major critical infrastructure sectors. Additionally, as intelligence is assessed and specific areas are identified, the HSAS is sufficiently flexible to elevate the threat within the specific sector, city, or region of the nation. This was not something that could have been done in the infancy of the Department of Homeland Security or at the creation of the HSAS. As the intelligence capacity of the DHS continues to mature, along with the FBI's increased domestic intelligence capability supported by state and local law enforcement intelligence, threats can be targeted on geographic and temporal variables with greater specificity. As a result, the system becomes more useful to law enforcement and citizens alike.

Assuming these developmental factors converge, there may well be greater interplay between the HSAS alert level and the emphasis given to the different forms of intelligence. For example, when the alert level increases, there will be a greater need for raw and operational intelligence to increase the probability of identifying and apprehending those involved in planning and executing a terrorist attack as well as to harden potential targets. As the alert level decreases, there will be a greater need to focus on strategic intelligence as a tool to assess trends, identify changes in targets and methods, or develop a pulse on the mood of the various terrorist groups to sense changes in their strategies. Tactical intelligence, involving criminal case development, should continue at a pace dictated by the evidence to identify and prosecute perpetrators. Law enforcement should seek all lawful tools available to secure the homeland through prevention, intervention, and apprehension of offenders.

DISSEMINATION[117]

The heart of information sharing is dissemination of the information. Policies need to be established for the types of information that will be disseminated and to whom. Critical to appropriate dissemination of information is understanding which persons have the "right to know" and the "need to know" the information, both within the agency and externally. In some cases, there may need to be multiple versions of one product. For example, an unclassified public version of a report may be created to advise citizens of possible threats. A second version may be "Law Enforcement Sensitive" and provide more detailed information about potential suspects that would be inappropriate to publicize.[118]

When considering disseminating sensitive material, a law enforcement organization should impose the "Third Agency Rule." This means that any recipient of intelligence is prohibited from sharing the information with another (i.e., third) agency. This affords some degree of control and accountability, yet may be waived by the originating agency when appropriate.

Clearly, the most efficient way to share information is by electronic networking. With the availability of secure connections, i.e., RISS.net, Law

117 On August 28, 2004, President Bush announced, "I have ordered the Director of Central Intelligence to ensure that we have common standards and clear accountability measures for intelligence sharing across the agencies of our government. I have established a new Information Systems Council to identify and break down any remaining barriers to the rapid sharing of threat information by America's intelligence agencies, law enforcement agencies, and state and local governments. To continue to protect the freedoms and privacy of our citizens, I've established a civil liberties board to monitor information-sharing practices." No additional details were available at this writing. http://www.whitehouse.gov/news/releases/2004/08/20040828.html.

118 This is conceptually similar to what federal agencies use as a "tear line". In a classified report there may be a summary of critical information, without a description of sources and methods that is below a designated line on the report. This portion may be "torn off" of the report, making it Sensitive But Unclassified (SBU) and may be disseminated to law enforcement personnel who do not have a security clearance as "Law Enforcement Sensitive".

Enforcement Online (LEO), and the Joint Regional Information Exchange System (JRIES),[119] — as well as intranets in growing numbers of agencies, dissemination is faster and easier. The caveat is to make sure the information in the intelligence products is essential and reaching the right consumer. If law enforcement officers are deluged with intelligence reports, the information overload will have the same outcome as not sharing information at all. If officers are deleting intelligence products without reading them, then the effect is the same as if it had never been disseminated.

National Criminal Intelligence Sharing Plan

Formally announced at a national signing event in the Great Hall of the U.S. Department of Justice on May 14, 2004, the National Criminal Intelligence Sharing Plan (NCISP) (see Figure 6-1) signifies an element of intelligence dissemination that is important for all law enforcement officials. With endorsements from Attorney General John Ashcroft,[120] FBI Director Robert Mueller, Homeland Security Secretary Tom Ridge, and the Global Information Sharing Initiative,[121] the plan provides an important foundation on which SLTLE agencies may create their intelligence initiatives. The intent of the plan is to provide local police agencies (particularly those that do not have established intelligence functions) with the necessary tools and resources to develop, gather, access, receive, and share intelligence information.

Following a national summit on information-sharing problems funded by the Office of Community Oriented Policing Services of the Department of Justice, the International Association of Chiefs of Police (IACP) proposed the development of a plan to overcome five barriers that inhibit intelligence sharing:

1. Lack of communication among agencies.
2. Lack of equipment (technology) to develop a national data system.
3. Lack of standards and policies regarding intelligence issues.
4. Lack of intelligence analysis.
5. Poor working relationships/unwillingness to share information.

119 The newly developed Homeland Security Information Network (HSIN) is intended to become the overarching information-sharing backbone.

120 http://www.usdoj.gov/opa/pr/2004/May/04_ag_328.htm.

121 http://it.ojp.gov/topic.jsp?topic_id=8.

As a result, the Global Intelligence Working Group (GIWG) was formed to create the plan to address these issues:

- Blueprint for law enforcement administrators to follow
- Mechanism to promote Intelligence-Led Policing
- Outreach plan to promote intelligence sharing
- Plan that respects individual's civil rights.

The NCISP has 28 recommendations that address four broad areas. Among the key points are these:

1. The establishment of a Criminal Intelligence Coordinating Council
   - Consist of local, state, tribal, and federal agency representatives who will provide long-term oversight and assistance with implementing the plan (Recommendation #2)
   - Develop the means to aide and advance the production of "tear line" reports (Recommendation #17)
   - Develop working relationships with other professional law enforcement organizations to obtain assistance with the implementation of intelligence training standards in every state (Recommendation #19)
   - Identify an "architectural" approach to ensure interoperability among the different agencies' intelligence information systems (Recommendation #23)
   - Develop centralized site that allows agencies to access shared data (Recommendation #28)
2. Individual Agency Requirements
   - Adopt the minimum standards for Intelligence-Led Policing and develop an intelligence function (Recommendation #1)
   - Provide criminal intelligence training to all levels of personnel
3. Partnerships
   - Form partnerships with both public and private sectors to detect and prevent attacks on infrastructures (Recommendation #7)
   - Expand collaboration and sharing opportunities by allowing other types of organizations with intelligence information to work with law enforcement agencies (Recommendation #24)

Figure 6-1: Fact Sheet – National Criminal Intelligence Sharing Plan

"This plan represents law enforcement's commitment to take it upon itself to ensure that the dots are connected, be it in crime or terrorism. The plan is the outcome of an unprecedented effort by law enforcement agencies, with the strong support of the Department of Justice, to strengthen the nation's security through better intelligence analysis and sharing."

Attorney General John Ashcroft, May 14, 2004

The Department of Justice is effectively pursuing the goals of the National Criminal Intelligence Sharing Plan by ensuring that all of its components are effectively sharing information with each other and the rest of the nation's law enforcement community.

Activities by DOJ and Related Agencies:

- Through the Global Justice Information Sharing Initiative, the Attorney General captures the views of more than 30 groups representing 1.2 million justice professionals from all levels of government. Global members wrote the National Criminal Intelligence Sharing Plan and published guides, best practices, and standards for information sharing.
- The Department's Chief Information Officer, under the authority of the Deputy Attorney General, has formed a Law Enforcement Information Sharing Initiative to establish a strategy for the Department of Justice to routinely share information to all levels of the law enforcement community and to guide the investment of resources in information systems that will further this goal. The strategy identifies how the Department of Justice will support the implementation of the Plan.
- The newly established Criminal Intelligence Coordinating Council (CICC) under Global will serve to set national-level policies to implement the Plan and monitor its progress on the state and local level. The CICC will work with the Department's Law Enforcement Information Strategy Initiative and with the Justice Intelligence Coordinating Council, created by a directive of the Attorney General, to improve the flow of intelligence information among federal, state, and local law enforcement agencies.
- The Federal Bureau of Investigation (FBI) has built an enterprise-wide intelligence program to fulfill its responsibility to get vital information about those who would do us harm to those who can act to prevent that harm. To that end, the FBI has built robust intelligence production and sharing processes enabled by technologies developed and operated by the Criminal Justice Information Systems (CJIS) Division. The FBI has established an intelligence requirements process to both drive its investigative work against common threats and to satisfy the information needs of the larger U.S. national security community, including other partners in law enforcement. This process ensures that the FBI produces not only the information it can produce, but also the information it must produce to safeguard the nation.

In addition, the FBI has implemented a policy of "writing to release" to ensure the maximum amount of information is pushed to key customers and partners at the lowest possible classification level. The FBI Intelligence Webpage on Law Enforcement Online was created to make this information available at the unclassified level for FBI partners in state, local, and tribal law enforcement. Finally, the FBI has established Field Intelligence Groups (FIG) in each FBI field office to ensure the execution of the intelligence program in FBI field divisions. The FIGs are the bridge that joins national intelligence with regional and local intelligence information through entities like the Joint Terrorism Task Forces.

- The Drug Enforcement Administration (DEA), in partnership with the High Intensity Drug Trafficking Area Program and the Regional Information Sharing Systems (RISS), is developing the National Virtual Pointer System (NVPS) that will allow federal, state, local, and tribal law enforcement agencies access to pointer databases through a single point of entry. Through NVPS, participating agencies will be able to determine if any other law enforcement entity is focused on the same investigative target–regardless of the crime. They will be linked to the agent or law enforcement officer who has information on the related case. Information will be transmitted over the National Law Enforcement Telecommunications System and RISSnet, the secure web-based communication system operated by a collaborative organization of state and local justice officials.
- All components of the Department of Justice have adopted a common language for sharing information among differing computer systems, the Justice XML Data Dictionary. All federal grant programs to criminal justice agencies will also include a special condition calling for the use of this standard.
- The Department of Justice, through the FBI, Office of Justice Programs (OJP) and the Office of Community Oriented Policing Services (COPS), is providing training and technical assistance to criminal justice policy leaders, law enforcement professionals, and information technology professionals in standards and policies to enable information sharing, improve the use of intelligence by law enforcement, and build systems that tie into the nation's existing information-sharing networks.
- The Department of Justice is investing in research and development of new tools and methods to improve the use of intelligence in law enforcement. This work includes the continued development of XML standards, new analytical tools, security standards, and policing methods to improve the safety and effectiveness of police officers. In addition, through OJP and COPS, the Department is sponsoring pilot projects across the nation to improve the interoperability of information systems and show the impact of improved information sharing on fighting crime and terrorism.

Source: http://www.fbi.gov/dojpressrel/pressrel04/factsheet051404.htm

4. Intelligence Information and the Public
- Ensure the protection of individual's civil rights (Recommendation #6)
- Develop trust with communities by promoting a policy of openness to public (Recommendation #14)
- Promote accountability measures as outlined in 28 CFR Part 23 (Recommendation #15)[122]

CONCLUSION

The message of this chapter is twofold: First, when developing an intelligence capacity, there must be clearly thought out and articulated intelligence products. With this clearly defined output, the intelligence function will operate with greater efficacy.

Second, intelligence reports, bulletins, and advisories must be broadly disseminated to all persons who can use the information effectively. This refers not only to intelligence products developed by the agency, but also those products that are distributed from federal sources, regional intelligence centers, and other entities. Without effective dissemination, much of the value of intelligence is lost. All too often, patrol officers, private security, and citizens are excluded from dissemination. Certainly, there must be careful evaluation of the types of information that is disseminated, but nonetheless, a broad array of recipients should be included in the dissemination process.

122 At this writing, changes to 28 CFR Part 23 are being considered, but have not yet been implemented. A key element of the proposed changes is that provisions of 28 CFR Part 23 must be covered by policy. It is important that law enforcement executives and intelligence managers monitor legislative and regulatory activity related to this provision. If revisions to the regulation are implemented, it is highly recommended that appropriate personnel from SLTLE agencies attend new training programs that will be available. Training will be available at no charge, funded by the Bureau of Justice Assistance. See http://www.iir.com.

Managing the Intelligence Function

CHAPTER SEVEN

Managing the Intelligence Function

Most American law enforcement agencies will not have a formal intelligence unit, but will still have an intelligence function to manage. With the growing symbiosis among federal and state, local, and tribal law enforcement (SLTLE), adoption of the National Criminal Intelligence Sharing Plan and the growth of networked intelligence information systems, along with the responsibility to keep the homeland secure, virtually every law enforcement agency in the country needs to develop some type of intelligence capacity. That capacity may be a full-scale unit or one person who serves part time as an agency's point of contact to receive and disseminate critical information. In some form, an intelligence capacity has become a de facto requirement for U.S. law enforcement agencies. As a result, new intelligence processes for SLTLE provides challenges such as the following to the executive:

- Reengineering some of the organization's structure and processes
- Developing a shared vision of the terrorist or criminal threat among all law enforcement agencies in the region and at the federal level.
- Participating in intelligence processes and following through with threat information
- Committing resources, time, and energy to the intelligence function
- Developing a proactive spirit and creative thought to identify "what we don't know" about terrorism and international organized crime
- Developing a culture within the law enforcement agency that is able to think globally and act locally
- Providing vigilance, patience, and entrepreneurial leadership.

To operationalize these components into a functional intelligence mechanism, SLTLE agencies of all sizes need, at a minimum, fundamental operational components. These include the following:

123 For information on the Global Justice Information Standard, see http://it.ojp.gov/topic.jsp?topic_id=43.

- A person designated as the intelligence point of contact to whom external agencies may direct inquiries, warnings, and advisories and from whom information and questions may be sent. This person must have sufficient training to understand the language, processes, and regulations incumbent on the law enforcement intelligence community.
- A secure electronic communications system for sending and receiving information that is Law Enforcement Sensitive (LES) and For Official Use Only (FOUO). Several systems are available, including Law Enforcement Online (LEO), RISS.net, Anti-Terrorism Information Exchange (ATIX), National Law Enforcement Telecommunications System (NLETS), and Joint Regional Information Exchange System (JRIES) – some of which are available at no charge to the user. With the growth of the XML standard,[123] access to these systems will be essential for the most accurate information sharing.
- Established policies for information collection, reporting, and dissemination. If an agency of any size is going to maintain intelligence records, the agency must have policies in place to control that data or risk exposure to liability. In many cases, adoption of the Law Enforcement Intelligence Unit (LEIU) File Guidelines (see Appendix B) will serve the purpose.

- Establishing the ability to determine the kinds of information/intelligence that is needed to effectively prevent terrorism and disrupt criminal enterprises. This is a more difficult challenge and requires a greater labor investment. Understanding the threats and targets within a community and developing responses to neutralize those threats is essential. As observed by FBI Executive Assistant Director of Intelligence Maureen Baginski, "The absence of evidence is not the absence of a threat."[124] It is essential that American law enforcement discover the evidence that may be in its backyard.

Beyond these factors, a number of management factors may be considered when developing an intelligence capacity. This chapter provides a perspective on issues from which the reader may choose those applicable elements that apply to one's respective law enforcement organization.

Establishing an Organizational Framework

Just as any other function in a law enforcement agency, organizational attention must be given to the administrative structure of the law enforcement intelligence (LEI) unit. Administrators and managers must examine the following:

- The *need* for the LEI unit
- How it functions every day
- Issues of *resource* acquisition, deployment, and management
- *Future agency needs* for the intelligence function.

Properly organized and staffed, the intelligence function serves as an internal consultant to management for resource deployment. It should be designed as an integrated and organic element of the law enforcement organization, not a distinct function. Intelligence defines the scope and dimensions of complex criminality – including terrorism – facing the jurisdiction and provides alternatives for policy responses to those problems. Importantly, it also serves as a focal point for information sharing and dissemination to maximize community safety. Some law enforcement agencies have been reluctant to fully develop an intelligence unit – including both tactical and strategic activities – for several reasons.

124 Baginski, Maureen, EAD-I, Federal Bureau of Investigation. Remarks in an address to the Major City Chiefs Intelligence Commanders Conference. Washington, DC. May 2004.

Perhaps at the top of the list is the past abuses and subsequent lawsuits from poorly organized and managed intelligence activities. In many cases, law enforcement executives eliminated the intelligence unit to reduce liability and to minimize criticism from persons in the community who did not understand the intelligence role and/or generally opposed law enforcement intelligence for philosophical reasons. Similarly, the need and value of an LEI unit has not been fully recognized by managers who often do not understand that the intelligence function can be an important resource for agency planning and operations. For example, intelligence analysts are frequently assigned clerical tasks instead of proactive analysis, largely because the manager does not recognize the value of intelligence analysis as a management resource.

> Properly ORGANIZED and STAFFED, the intelligence function serves as an internal consultant to management for RESOURCE DEPLOYMENT.

125 For more information on these organizations see their respective web pages at http://www.ialeia.org and http://www.leiu-homepage.org.

As a consequence of several factors, the Zeitgeist – or "spirit of the times" – is now present for American law enforcement to embrace law enforcement intelligence of the 21st century. Many SLTLE agencies have established a legacy of proactive law enforcement through the use of community policing and its activities of problem solving, CompStat, crime analysis, effective internal and external communications, multidisciplinary responses to crime, and a "bottom-up" approach for operational direction. Moreover, since 9/11, there has been a greater development of resources and training to make intelligence activities more easily adapted and functional. Finally, the law enforcement intelligence function has become professionalized through greater involvement of academic institutions, federal initiatives, and long-standing activities by groups such as the International Association of Law Enforcement Intelligence Analysts (IALEIA) and the Law Enforcement Intelligence Unit (LEIU).[125]

"Chartering" an Intelligence Unit

One of the first steps in creating an intelligence unit is to "charter" the function. This includes the following:

- Determining its organizational priority and placement
- Resource allocation
- Defining its mission and goals
- Establishing the unit's authority and responsibility,

A number of publications describe these processes.[126] The current discussion will identify specific points related to the intelligence function. The creation of an intelligence unit should be based on a needs assessment.[127] This includes identifying current intelligence-related competencies of the law enforcement agency and desired competencies. One of the main outcomes of an effective needs assessment is identifying how an intelligence unit can influence the drive toward greater efficiency and responsiveness. Importantly, the needs assessment will also define personnel and resource needs.

Resource allocation is always a difficult process because it typically involves diminishing one function to develop another. In most cases, the creation of a new unit will not come with a new appropriation of funding to fully staff and operationalize it; therefore, part of the resource allocation process is to determine where the intelligence function fits in the organizational priorities of the law enforcement agency.

The mission is the role that the unit fulfills in support of the agency's overall mission. It specifies in general language what the unit is intended to accomplish and establishes the direction and responsibility for the LEI unit for which all other administrative actions and activities are designed to fulfill. Figure 7-1 presents a sample mission statement for a law enforcement agency's intelligence unit.

A goal is the end to which all activity in the unit is directed. It is broad based, yet functionally oriented. Importantly, the goal must be mission-related, that is, accomplishing goals supports the broader mission of the

126   Most police management textbooks describe these processes in detail. Perhaps of particular value are publications available from the International City Management Association http://bookstore.icma.org. See also the on-line performance management database of the Royal Canadian Mounted Police at http://www.rcmp-learning.org.

127   A good illustration of a law enforcement needs assessment and how it can be performed, which includes multiple applications is: Healy, J.J., Superintendent, International Training and Peacekeeping Branch, Royal Canadian Mounted Police. http://www.rcmp-learning.org/docs/ecdd1134.htm.

law enforcement agency. Moreover, the goals will give the unit direction in support of the mission. Since the mission of an LEI unit will be comprehensive and incorporate diverse functions, several goals will be stipulated. The purpose of goals is to not only provide operational direction but to also serve as performance standards.[128] The environment of the community will change over time as will crime patterns and problems; therefore, the law enforcement agency should review goal statements annually and change or revise them to reflect current issues and trends. (Figure 7-1 also includes an illustration of intelligence goals for a law enforcement agency.)

Authority is the right to act or command others to act toward the attainment of organizational goals. Operational authority includes decisions that must be made concerning the degree and type of activities the LEI unit may perform without seeking administrative authorization, financial flexibility of the unit to fulfill its objectives, and the degree of direction or precedence the LEI unit can exercise over other departmental units. Each of these factors has significant organizational implications and must be developed conceptually and stipulated by policy.

128 Performance standards are often characterized as effectiveness and efficiency, wherein effectiveness is "Doing the right job," and efficiency is "Doing the job right."

Figure 7-1: Sample Mission Statement and Goals of an LEI Unit

Sample Intelligence Mission Statement

The mission of the Intelligence Unit of the Hypothetical Police Department is to collect, evaluate, analyze, and disseminate intelligence data regarding criminal activity in this city/county and any criminal activity in other jurisdictions that may adversely effect on this city/county. This includes providing processes for collating and analyzing information collected by operational units of the law enforcement agency. The Intelligence Unit will furnish the Chief of Police with the necessary information so that Operations Units charged with the arrest responsibility can take the necessary enforcement action.

Sample Intelligence Goals

1. The Intelligence Unit shall supply the Chief of Police with accurate and current strategic intelligence data so that the Chief will be kept informed of changing criminal activity in the jurisdiction.

Figure 7-1: Sample Mission Statement and Goals of an LEI Unit (Cont.)

2. The Intelligence Unit shall provide a descriptive analysis of organized crime systems operating within the jurisdiction to provide operational units with the necessary data to identify organized crime groups and individuals working as criminal enterprises.

3. The Intelligence Unit will concentrate its expertise on the following crimes...

    a. Islamic extremists in support of terrorism – activities, participants, funding, and logistical support, all of which are of a criminal nature.

    b. Domestic extremists in support of criminal acts – activities, participants, funding, and logistical support, all of which are of a criminal nature.

    c. Labor/strike activity – monitor and gather strategic intelligence to be supplied to the Operations Bureau with regard to this activity.

    d. Organized crime – identify crimes and participants, including new and emerging criminal enterprises.

    e. Major Narcotics Traffickers – provide tactical intelligence and information analysis to the Operations Bureau on persons identified as being involved in narcotics trafficking enterprises.

The Intelligence Unit recognizes the delicate balance between the individual rights of citizens and the legitimate needs of law enforcement. In light of this recognition, the unit will perform all of its intelligence activities in a manner that is consistent with and upholds those rights.

129 http://it.ojp.gov/process_links. jsp?link_id=3774.

Responsibility reflects how the authority of a unit or individual is used for determining if goals have been accomplished and the mission fulfilled in a manner that is consistent with the defined limits of authority. The unit and its members must be held accountable for its charge and administrative mechanisms must be set in place to assess the degree to which the unit is meeting its responsibilities.

IACP Model Policy on Criminal Intelligence.

The International Association of Chiefs of Police (IACP) has taken a proactive role in all aspects of developing a contemporary intelligence capacity in America's law enforcement agencies. The IACP Model Policy[129] on Criminal Intelligence provides a policy statement and procedures that are of particular benefit to a small agency. As in the case of all models, the language of the IACP policy needs to be adjusted to meet the needs of different jurisdictions. Nonetheless, it provides a sound foundation for starting the process.

Adhering to 28 CFR Part 23

Throughout this guide, reference is made to a federal regulation entitled Criminal Intelligence Systems Operating Policies, cited as 28 CFR Part 23. As is becoming apparent, it is essential that SLTLE intelligence records system adhere to the provisions of this regulation if the system is a multi-jurisdictional and supported with federal funding. The best way to demonstrate and ensure adherence is for the law enforcement agency to develop specific policies and procedures to cover segments of the regulation, including the following:

- Security
- Accessing the system to make inquiries
- Defining standards for identifying and classifying "Non-Criminal Identifying Information"
- Entering data in the criminal intelligence system
- Reviewing data quality and propriety
- Purging
- Disseminating intelligence.

Even if 28 CFR Part 23 guidelines do not apply to a specific law enforcement agency, use of the guideline and these policies is good practice for the agency to follow.

Auditing the Intelligence Function

Perhaps one of the best ways to understand management of the intelligence unit is to examine the variables used in the audit process. Appendix C is an audit questionnaire created by the author that includes 180 variables to assess in an intelligence audit. The necessity for an audit is essential for both operational reasons and risk management. By reviewing the questionnaire, which has been used by the author to assess compliance with a U.S. District Court settlement in one city's intelligence unit, it will become clear that there are myriad factors that are incumbent on ensuring organizational control of the intelligence function.

In addition, the Global Intelligence Working Group and the LEIU are preparing intelligence unit audit guidelines. At the time of this writing, the guidelines were not completed; however, they will likely appear on the Global Intelligence Working Group website when they available and ready for distribution.[130]

Establishing and Managing Partnerships

The nature of the intelligence function requires that a law enforcement agency enter into partnerships. Critical information is shared through collaboration, typically with other law enforcement agencies, but often with other organizations ranging from private security to non-law enforcement government agencies, such as public health or emergency services. These various relationships have different dynamics related to needs, responsibilities, and limitations on access to information. As such, the parameters of each formal partnership should be articulated in a formal partnership agreement.

130 http://it.ojp.gov/topic.jsp?topic_id=56.

> Critical information is **shared** through collaboration, typically with other law enforcement agencies, but often with

Broadly speaking, two types of partnerships are related to the intelligence function. These are the following:

- *Users:* Organizations with which information and/or intelligence products are shared. Users are consumers.
- *Participants:* Organizations that provide resources and actively contribute to the intelligence activity, such as a regional intelligence center. Participants have a shared responsibility for operations.

A formal agreement is simply sound management because it articulates mutually agreed-on operational provisions related to resource management; clear identification of responsibilities and accountability; adherence to legal standards; and conditions associated with liability. Certainly these agreements apply to a wide range of law enforcement activities or services; however, the current discussion is limited to the intelligence function. While the language varies between states, as a general rule there are three forms of written partnerships:

- *Memorandum of Agreement (MOA):* Users/consumers of an intelligence unit or system, including a records system, that use the system on an ongoing basis would typically sign the MOA. Essentially, the MOA acknowledges that the user will abide by the "rules" established for the system or activity, aid in cost recovery, and adhere to legal and accountability standards. Obviously, the character of the activity will dictate more detail. As an example, if one agency's intelligence records system can be accessed by another agency, the user may have to agree to pay a monthly fee, adhere to 28 CFR Part 23, and agree to the Third Agency Rule. Failure to meet these standards would result in ending access to the system.
- *Mutual Aid Pact (MAP):* The MAP is an agreement that is in place to deal with special circumstances, rather than an ongoing service, and establishes the agreed-on conditions when one agency would provide assistance to another. Oftentimes assistance is reciprocal, except for real costs that may be incurred in extended activities. As an intelligence-related example, two law enforcement agencies may agree to aid each other when conducting a surveillance.
- *Memorandum of Understanding (MOU):* The MOU is more detailed and involves a partnership in an activity. Essentially a contract, the MOU would specify all obligations and responsibilities and typically share liabilities in the endeavor. For example, if multiple agencies agree to develop a regional intelligence center, the MOU may be a fairly detailed document outlining all aspects of governance, management, structure, funding, accountability, and operations of the center.

A key element to understand is that, regardless of the nature of the agreement, its content and detail is to ensure that all parties understand their obligations. Figure 7-2 identifies some of the provisions that may be included in a partnership agreement. While not all of these provisions will be required of every agreement, it is important to have a formal document that clearly defines expectations and responsibilities.

Figure 7-2: Sample Provisions for a Partnership Agreement	
• Activities • Civil liability/indemnification • Dispute resolution • Funding • Governance • Information – access and use • Information – adherence to 28 CFR Part 23 • Information – dissemination to "Third Agency" • Information – entry into a system • Information – ownership • Location • Mission, purpose, goals	• Operating procedures • Payments and costs • Personnel assignment • Personnel evaluation • Personnel removal • Physical plant considerations • Property - purchase and maintenance • Reports to be prepared • Security clearances of staff • Security of information • Security of the facility • Time limit/term of the agreement

Sources for Intelligence Management and Resource Trends

Effective management of an intelligence unit requires that the manager be constantly informed of emerging issues, technologies, and trends. This is a difficult process; however, one of the more effective methods is to monitor online newsletters of reliable organizations. Topics can range from actions and activities of extremists groups to new products and new policy and legislation. As an illustration (not an endorsement), some of the more substantive news letters include (in alphabetical order) the following:

- Anti-Defamation League http://www.adl.org/learn/default.htm – there are two newsletters – the *Law Enforcement Newsletter* and the *Breaking News*
- Center for Digital Government (three newsletters; one specifically on homeland security) http://www.centerdigitalgov.com/center/enewsletters.phtml
- *Computer and Information Security* http://www.securitypipeline.com (newsletter subscription in lower left portion of homepage)

- *Federation of American Scientists Secrecy News*: http://www.fas.org/sgp/news/secrecy
- *Foundation for Defense of Democracies Weekly Update*: http://www.defenddemocracy.org (subscription is toward the bottom of the left side of the page – enter your email address.)
- *Government Computer News* http://www.gcn.com/profile
- *Government Computing* http://www.kablenet.com/kd.nsf/EmailListFormNew?OpenForm
- *Government Technology* http://www.govtech.net/magazine/subscriptions/mailings.php?op=getaddy
- *Homeland Security Institute Newsletter*: http://www.homelandsecurity.org/newsletterSignup.asp
- *Homeland Security Update* (DFI International) http://www.dfi-intl.com
- *Homeland Security Week* http://www.govexec.com/email
- Information Warfare and Cyberterrorism http://www.iwar.org.uk/mailman/listinfo/infocon
- Israeli Defense Force Intelligence and Terrorism Research Center http://www.intelligence.org.il
- National White Collar Crime Center http://www.nw3c.org (subscription information for both electronic and print versions of the newsletter on this page.)
- PoliceOne.com (*Law Enforcement News*) http://www.policeone.com
- Saudi-U.S. Relations Information Service (quite a bit of information on terrorism) http://www.saudi-us-relations.org
- Southern Poverty Law Center http://www.splcenter.org/center/subscribe.jsp
- *Terrorism Central Newsletter* http://www.terrorismcentral.com/Newsletters/CurrentNewsletter.html
- Terrorism Research Center http://www.terrorism.org/mailman/listinfo (three newsletters)

- U.S. Department of Justice, Justice Technology Network
  http://www.nlectc.org/justnetnews/nlectc_subscribe.asp
- U.S. Department of State, Overseas Security Advisory Center (OSAC)
  http://www.ds-osac.org

As is the case with any information, a newsletter will reflect the agenda of its sponsor. Keeping this in mind, valuable information can be gained for an intelligence manager to remain current on the issues for which one is responsible.

CONCLUSION

As a rule, the application of management principles may be applied generally regardless of the unit or assignment within a law enforcement agency. It is just as true that some substantive knowledge of the unit or function must also be developed. Criminal investigation commanders need to understand caseload differentials for crimes, patrol commanders must know minimum staffing requirements to handle calls for service, and traffic commanders must understand traffic analysis and its application to selective enforcement. It is no different with the intelligence commander. This chapter identified critical substantive elements of the intelligence function that will aid the law enforcement manager to manage this activity more effectively.

Human Resource Issues

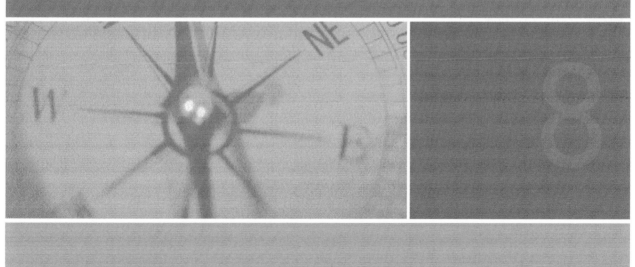

CHAPTER EIGHT

Human Resource Issues

Who should perform the intelligence function in a state, local, and tribal law enforcement (SLTLE) agency and what qualifications should that person have? This question is impossible to answer conclusively because it depends on myriad variables tied to the attributes of a given law enforcement agency. The agency's size, jurisdiction, the priority intelligence is given, resource flexibility, competing crime and calls for service issues, and collective bargaining agreements must be calculated into the formula. Rather than provide for the ideal situation, this chapter will present issues and guidelines that will enable the law enforcement executive to make an informed decision about options available for staffing the intelligence function.

STAFFING

131 For more detail, see: Wells, Ian. (2000). "Staffing the Intelligence Unit". (2000). Intelligence 2000: Revising the Basic Elements. A joint publication of the Law Enforcement Intelligence Unit and the International Association of Law Enforcement Intelligence Analysts, pp. 53-66.

132 The General Counterdrug Intelligence Plan (GCIP), discusses issues related to human resources in Section E: Analytic Personnel Development and Training. While not specifically addressing the issues in this discussion, nonetheless provide some observations and recommendations are germane to the issues presented herein. See http://www.whitehousedrugpolicy.gov/publications/gcip/sectione.html.

Clerical and support staffing decisions can be made for the intelligence function just as for any other assignment in the agency, taking into consideration professional staff workloads, service demands, nonprofessional work activities (e.g., data entry, clerical work), and budget, among others. The key positions are with the professional staff.[131]

The Intelligence Analyst

The intelligence analyst is a professional who collects various facts and documents circumstances, evidence, interviews, and other material related to a crime and places them in a logical, related framework to develop a criminal case, explain a criminal phenomenon, or describe crime and crime trends. The analyst should have at least a baccalaureate degree and receive training in the intelligence process, criminal law and procedure, statistical analysis, and factual and evidentiary analysis. The analyst should be an objective, analytic thinker with good writing and presentation skills. This is a professional position that should be compensated accordingly.

> The intelligence analyst is a professional who takes varied facts, documentation of circumstances, evidence, interviews, and any other material related to a crime and places them into a logical and related framework for the purpose of developing a criminal case, explaining a criminal phenomenon, or describing crime and crime trends.

An ongoing issue is whether the intelligence analyst will be sworn or nonsworn. Different agecies use different models, each with its advantages and disadvantages.[132] Those who advocate that the intelligence analyst position would be best served by a nonsworn employee argue that the nonsworn analyst's characteristics and background may provide a more creative and less restrictive view of data when compared to sworn personnel. Further, a sworn employee is likely to be either transferred or promoted out of the intelligence unit, thereby reducing the unit's overall efficiency. Advocates of having a nonsworn employee argue that the position does not require law enforcement authority; therefore placing a sworn person in an analyst's position may be viewed as an ineffective use of personnel. Finally, the role of an analyst is highly experiential: Over the years the experienced analysts accumulates a mental repository of names, locations, businesses, and so forth, that can be highly useful in an analysis. If this person is a sworn employee who is transferred out of the unit, that accumulated knowledge is lost.

Conversely, opponents argue that nonsworn employees do not have the substantive knowledge and experience for conducting investigations nor do they understand, with the same degree of insight, the life of the street where many intelligence targets live and operate. The analyst builds his or her expertise and knowledge cumulatively throughout his or her work life. Much of this expertise is substantive knowledge and information (persons, crime patterns, locations, and so forth) learned while working on a variety of criminal cases. The analyst needs to view crime problems from the big picture—a picture that is most precisely focused with years of law enforcement "street" experience.

Other factors not related to the conceptual responsibilites will enter the equation such as the compensation package, collective bargaining agreement, civil service regulations, organizational culture, the candidate pool, and so forth. This is a critical position requiring an effective analytic capability and care should be taken to hire the "the right person" to fit the agency's needs. It should not be, as has too often been the case, an appointment of convenience or a "reward appointment" to a good clerical person who has "worked hard for the department." Professional output from the intelligence unit will occur only if the position is filled by a professional analyst.

TRAINING

The Bureau of Justice Assistance-funded Criminal Intelligence Training Coordination Strategy (CITCS) Working Group, conducted a needs assessment of intelligence training in spring of 2004. Among the findings were the following:

- That training is lacking in all of the training classifications. However, respondents rated Intelligence Analyst and Intelligence Manager as the classes most lacking in adequate training. Surprisingly, 62 percent of respondents stated they are receiving adequate training, but over a third (36 percent) indicated they were not receiving adequate training.
- The majority of respondents cited lack of funding as the primary impediment of training, but respondents also rated high on difficulty finding good trainers, travel and lodging costs, and unsure of available training. Only a handful of respondents selected unsure of appropriate training for personnel as an impediment. *One respondent indicated that in order to support the tenets of the NCISP, additional training guidelines and opportunities are needed. Other respondents indicated that training can be sporadic, which dovetails into the need for core minimum standards that can be used consistently nationwide. Other respondents indicated that their agency has not needed intelligence training because they do not have the staff or resources to engage in an intelligence function.*[133] (Emphasis in original).

Clearly, intelligence training currently represents the proverbial mixed bag of content, availability, and structure. The content or subject matter of law enforcement intelligence can be divided in two broad categories.[134] The first category is *protocols and methodology of the intelligence process*. This includes subjects such as information collection methodologies; laws and regulations associated with intelligence records systems; analytic methods and tools; intelligence reporting structures and processes; and intelligence dissemination. Essentially, these elements constitute the discipline of law enforcement intelligence.

The second category is somewhat more amorphous. Broadly speaking, this is *subject matter expertise*. It includes understanding the motives, methods, targets, and/or commodities of criminal intelligence targets. Intelligence researchers and analysts must have subject matter knowledge of the types of enterprises that are being investigated and the context within which these enterprises occur. Whether the target crime is

133   Bureau of Justice Assistance, Criminal Intelligence Training Coordination Strategy Working Group. (2004). *Survey of Law Enforcement on Intelligence Training.* Unpublished staff report.

134   Carter, David L. and Richard N. Holden. (2004). "Chapter 2: Law Enforcement Intelligence." *Homeland Security for State and Local Police.* Englewood Cliffs, NJ: Prentice Hall.

terrorism, drug trafficking, money laundering, or the trafficking of stolen arts and antiquities, the intelligence specialist must be a subject matter expert on the genre of criminality being investigated, both broadly speaking as well as with the unique facts associated with a specific investigation. For example, an intelligence analyst working on cases of terrorism by Islamic extremists needs to substantively understand the distinctions between Shiite and Sunni Muslims, the role of sectarian extremism (notably as related to Palestine), the different Islamic terrorist groups (e.g., al-Qaida, HAMAS, Hezbollah, Islamic Jihad, etc.) and their methods, the culture of Islamic nations, different leaders, methods of funding, and so forth. This type of substantive knowledge is essential for an analyst to be effective. All training programs currently available contain some aspect of the protocols and methodology of the intelligence process, although most programs for nonanalysts provided an overview of these items rather than detailed instruction. Fewer programs contained subject matter information for intelligence as part of the training. For those that did provide this information, it was typically because the agency sponsoring the training had a specific jurisdictional responsibility (e.g., the Regional Counterdrug Training Academy's "Operational Intelligence" course integrates "intelligence concepts" with more specific "drug intelligence indicators"). Training programs continue to emerge on intelligence related topics, particularly since the Office of State and Local Government Coordination and Preparedness of the Department of Homeland Security is preparing to fund a series of new training programs on various aspects of counterterrorism, including intelligence.[135] Perhaps the best single source to monitor training programs of all types is through the Bureau of Justice Assistance Counterterrorism Training website[136] which includes not only training opportunities but funding and related information as well.

135 At this writing not all programs have been announced. One program that has been funded was awarded to the School of Criminal Justice at Michigan State University. Under this program, law enforcement agencies will have access to no-cost training to help create an intelligence capacity within their department, regardless of size. For more information see: http://www.intellprogram.msu.edu.

136 http://www.counterterrorismtraining.gov.

> Perhaps the best single source to monitor training programs of all types is through the BUREAU OF JUSTICE ASSISTANCE COUNTERTERRORISM TRAINING website which includes not only training opportunities but also funding and related information.

Figure 8-1: Intelligence Training Categories and Descriptions

Training Category	Description
Awareness	The broadest, most diverse, types of intelligence training could best be described as "awareness" training. These programs, which vary in length from 2 hours to 4 days, tend to include information about the intelligence discipline (i.e., definitions, methods, processes, etc.) as integrated with a specific subject matter (e.g., drugs, terrorism, auto theft, etc.).
Intelligence Analyst	Intelligence Analysts training programs have a reasonable degree of consistency in the subject matter topics; however, the hours of training on each topic has more variability. In some cases, the curricula include substantive modules on subject matter: For example, the FBI College of Analytic Studies program integrates intelligence methods specifically with crimes within FBI jurisdiction. Similarly, the DEA curricula integrates intelligence methods with material on drug trafficking.
Investigators and Intelligence Unit Researchers	Some intelligence training programs exist which lack the depth of training found in the Analyst curricula, but are more detailed than simply "awareness" training. It appears that the intended audience for these programs is investigators, "investigative analysts", or "intelligence researchers". In each of the cases, the curricula are similar. Notable among these courses are the 2-week DEA FLEAT course and the FLETC intelligence course.
Management Issues for Intelligence	One program, offered at the Regional Counterdrug Training Academy at NAS Meridian, Mississippi is specifically labeled as being an intelligence course for managers.[137] Some other courses could be labeled as such, but were more likely to be "issues" courses. In some cases, intelligence issues for managers have been discussed in broader venues, such as in courses offered by the FBI National Academy.
Specialized Training	This training focuses on a narrow aspect of the entire intelligence process. The best known of these courses is the Criminal Intelligence Analysis course offered by Anacapa Sciences, Inc.,[138] that focuses exclusively on the "analysis" component of the intelligence cycle. Other courses that fall into this category are generally "software courses" such as classes on how to use a particular type of intelligence software (typically either analytic software or databases).

137 See http://www.rcta.org/counter drug/catalog/ipm.htm for a course description and enrollment information.

138 Anacapa is a private company. This reference should not be considered an endorsement of the product by the author, the Department of Justice, or any of its components. It is used only as a descriptive illustration.

Categories of Currently Available Intelligence Training Programs

A wide range of programs has been developed on various aspects of law enforcement intelligence. Virtually all of these were developed before the standards and specifications in the National Criminal Intelligence Sharing Plan. Figure 8-1 describes the five categories of available training programs.

A few law enforcement intelligence training programs serve as the core programs because of their consistency and the expertise they offer. A great deal of experience and thought has served as the basis for their development and, as such, they provide models for good practice. The following summary descriptions of the most notable programs will provide more insight.

Federal Bureau of Investigation College of Analytic Studies[139]

After the terrorists' attacks of 9/11, the attorney general mandated the FBI to focus on terrorism as its top priority. This necessitated a number of changes in the Bureau, including expanding its law enforcement intelligence capability and working closely with state and local law enforcement agencies on terrorism investigations through Joint Terrorism Task Forces (JTTF) and Field Intelligence Groups (FIG). Among the needs precipitated by these changes was a significant broadening of the capacity for intelligence analysis among FBI personnel as well as among state and local JTTF and FIG intelligence staff. The FBI's College of Analytic Studies (CAS), created in 2002 and located at the FBI Academy, is a seven week course that focuses on analysis functioning and tradecraft for terrorism, counterintelligence, and criminal intelligence analysis as well as specific FBI intelligence systems and practices related to terrorism. Twenty-five percent of each session of course capacity is reserved for state and local law enforcement personnel who have federal security clearances and are working with the JTTF in their region.[140]

139 For enrollment information contact the Training Coordinator at your local FBI Field Office - see http://www.fbi.gov/contact/fo/fo.htm - or the FBI Academy http://www.fbi.gov/hq/td/academy/academy.htm.

140 Some variation in the 25% state-local training allocation may occur in the short term as the FBI significantly increases the number of Intelligence Analysts being hired by the Bureau.

The FBI intelligence curriculum is based on a number of successful concepts, processes, and tradecraft found in intelligence practices in the U.S. Intelligence Community; federal, state, and local law enforcement in the U.S.; and in friendly foreign services around the world. In addition to the CAS, the FBI is developing online intelligence training at its Virtual Academy and will be available to SLTLE agencies in the coming months. The Training Coordinator in the local FBI Field Office will be able to provide more details on the availability of the Virtual Academy courses and enrollment processes.

New specialized courses are being developed for intelligence analysts, as well, including a course on reporting raw intellignece. Beyond the CAS, a greater presence of intelligence issues is found in the curricula of the new agent's basic academy, the FBI National Academy (FBINA), the Law Enforcement Executive Development Seminar (LEEDS), and the National Executive Institute (NEI). In addition, training coordinators in each FBI Field Office can help facilitate different types of intelligence-related training programs for SLTLE.

141 For further information on DEA training see http://www.usdoj.gov/dea/programs/training.htm.

Drug Enforcement Administration (DEA)[141]

The DEA has long been recognized for the quality of training provides through the Intelligence Training Unit of the DEA Academy at Quantico, Virginia. DEA intelligence training focuses on information research and intelligence analysis through the 9-10 week (it varies) Basic Intelligence Research Specialist (BIRS) program. DEA also offers an advanced intelligence training program as well as specialized programs related to the use of different data bases and the classified DEA proprietary intelligence computer system, MERLIN.

Because of the DEA's historic role of working with state and local law enforcement agencies, and the inherent need for intelligence in the Organized Crime Drug Enforcement Task Forces (OCDETF) and the High Intensity Drug Trafficking Areas (HIDTA), DEA developed a 4-week Federal Law Enforcement Analyst Training (FLEAT) program specifically directed toward state and local law enforcement agencies. The program is offered in different cities throughout the U.S. to enhance the ability of state and local agencies to send intelligence personnel to this tuition-free program. While the program has historically focused exclusively on drug enforcement and money laundering, it is being revised to include a component related to both domestic and international terrorism.

Federal Law Enforcement Training Center (FLETC)[142]

Serving 72 federal law enforcement agencies, FLETC has a massive training responsibility. For several years the Financial Fraud Institute (FFI) of FLETC has offered a 4-week intelligence course that focused on intelligence concepts, research, and analysis. Given that the Department of Homeland Security (DHS) has a significant intelligence responsibility through its Information Analysis and Infrastructure Protection (IAIP) directorate,[143] the need for revitalizing intelligence training has emerged.

Analyst training has been revised and now consists of a 2-week core Intelligence Analyst Training Program (IATP) that provides the basic substantive skills. Personnel may then opt for a wide variety of follow-up specialized classes to further enhance their skills, ultimately earning an Intelligence Analyst certificate after 4 to 6 weeks of total training.

In addition, FLETC also assessed the need for intelligence training and, in light of the mandate for state and local law enforcement to be involved in counterterrorism efforts, defined the need for intelligence training to focus on different responsibilities: intellligence analysts, managers, and intelligence "awareness" for line-level personnel.[144] As a result, the FFI has worked cooperatively with the FLETC National Center for State and Local Law Enforcement Training to conduct a needs assessment among state and local law enforcement agencies and develop intelligence courses that meet their needs. As of this writing, a 2-day intelligence awareness course, specifically for nonanalyst SLTLE agencies has been developed and will be offered beginning in the fall of 2004 at no cost at geographically decentralized locations throughout the U.S.[145]

142 FLETC is part of the Department of Homeland Security. For more detail and contact information see http://www.fletc.gov.

143 See http://www.intelligence.gov/1-members_dhs.shtml.

144 Manzi, Merle. Intelligence Program Coordinator, Financial Fraud Institute, Federal Law Enforcement Training Center. *Intelligence Training for State and Local Law Enforcement Agencies in Support of Homeland Security.* An internal concept paper. (May 2003).

145 See http://www.fletc.gov/osl/index.htm.

General Counterdrug Intelligence Plan (GCIP)[146]

The General Counterdrug Intelligence Plan (GCIP) of February 2000 was revisited in 2002 and once again called for the creation of an interagency-validated, basic law enforcement analytical course that could be used by law enforcement at all levels of government. The result of this initiative was the creation of an intelligence analyst training curriculum called "The Community Model." Guiding the process was the Counterdrug Intelligence Executive Secretariat (CDX), with subsidiary working groups representing federal, state, and local law enforcement.

This curriculum builds on the earlier work of the Generic Intelligence Training Initiative (GITI) developed in 2000-2001 as well as other intelligence training programs, notably from federal agencies. These include the DEA Intelligence Analyst and Intelligence Researcher course, a program developed by the National Drug Intelligence Center, and a course offered by the U.S. Customs Service at FLETC. While CDX does not offer the training itself, the curriculum is available and used by a number of different training entities.

IALEIA Foundations of Intelligence Analysis Training (FIAT)[147]

The five day FIAT program was developed and is offered by the International Association of Law Enforcement Intelligence Analysts. Given the expertise that exists in the IALEIA membership and the extent to which the association has been working on analyst training issues, this course provides a compact yet highly substantive training experience. The program is offered throughout the U.S.

Other Programs and Training Resources

Law enforcement intelligence training continues to evolve, and a number of important initiatives are now underway to deliver improved basic and specialized training at the state and local levels. In addition to the programs described so far, intelligence training initiatives include the

---

146 See http://www.whitehousedrugpolicy.gov/publications/gcip.

147 For the training schedule and enrollment see http://www.ialeia.org/training.html.

> In addition, the State and Local Anti-Terrorism Training (SLATT) program has both DIRECT and INDIRECT intelligence awareness training.

National White Collar Crime Center's (NW3C) Analyst Training Partnership,[148] the Regional Counterdrug Training Academy's "Operational Intelligence" course,[149] the High Intensity Drug Trafficking Areas (HIDTA);[150] and a new intelligence analyst training and certification program offered by the Florida Department of Law Enforcement.[151] In addition, the State and Local Anti-Terrorism Training (SLATT)[152] program has both direct and indirect intelligence awareness training.

While not intelligence training, per se, a program that is essential for all SLTLE agencies is 28 CFR Part 23 training. This section of the Code of Federal Regulations specifies the file guidelines that must be followed for multi-jurisdictional criminal intelligence records systems funded by the federal government. Despite the fact that the regulations only apply to SLTLE agencies meeting those stipulations, the guidelines can be an important tool for minimizing risk to liability and ensuring that all intelligence record keeping is consistent with constitutional standards. A comprehensive training program, funded by the Bureau of Justice Assistance, is available to SLTLE agencies at no charge.[153]

Beyond these programs, several COPS Regional Community Policing Institutes (RCPIs) offer a range of counterterrorism training programs, some of which include components of intelligence awareness training. Agencies should contact the RCPI in their region to determine training program offerings.[154]

INTELLIGENCE COURSES IN HIGHER EDUCATION

In recent years, there has been increasing recognition in the academic community of the need for coursework in law enforcement intelligence that incorporates broad multidisciplinary issues, research, and a philosophical

148 This includes the International Association of Law Enforcement Intelligence Analysts (IALEIA), the Law Enforcement Intelligence Unit (LEIU), and the Regional Information Sharing Systems (RISS). For training opportunities see http://www.nw3c.org/training_courses.html.

149 See http://www.rcta.org/counterdrug/catalog/ifle.htm for a description and enrollment information.

150 A number of the HIDTA initiatives have intelligence-related training programs. See http://www.whitehousedrugpolicy.gov/hidta to find a HIDTA office. In addition, the Washington-Baltimore HIDTA often lists a wide range of training programs, including those that are intelligence related. See http://www.hidta.org/training/law_enforcement.asp.

151 Florida Department of Law Enforcement, Training Division, Post Office Box 1489, Tallahassee, FL 32302, Phone: 850-410-7373.

152 See http://www.iir.com/slatt/training.htm.

153 For the course description, schedule and enrollment, see http://www.iir.com/28cfr/Training.htm.

154 The RCPI for a specific service area and appropriate contact information can be located on the interactive map at http://www.cops.usdoj.gov/default.asp?Item=229.

approach to intelligence issues. While a number of institutions have offered sporadic courses on the topic, there are three degree programs that are worthy of note.

The nation's oldest criminal justice degree program at Michigan State University (MSU) has offered a cross-listed undergraduate/graduate course entitled "Law Enforcement Intelligence Operations" for approximately 15 years. As a result of a partnership created with DEA, MSU will begin offering a master of science degree in criminal justice with an emphasis on Law Enforcement Intelligence in 2005.[155] The degree program, offered completely online, is taught by regular MSU criminal justice faculty members, and is designed as a "terminal" degree, much like a Master of Business Administration. In addition, Michigan State will offer "certificate programs" in different aspects of intelligence, many of which will be available for academic credit.

Mercyhurst College offers a Baccalaureate degree in Research/Intelligence Analysis through its History Department.[156] A Master's degree will be offered in 2004. The degree programs are designed to provide the necessary background for students to pursue careers as research and/or intelligence analysts relating to national security or criminal investigative activities in government agencies and private enterprise.

Established in 1963, the Joint Military Intelligence College (JMIC) is located at Bolling Air Force Base and is attached to the Defense Intelligence Agency (DIA).[157] JMIC is a highly respected institution in the Intelligence Community offering both an accredited baccalaureate and master's degree in intelligence studies. Its mission has been to serve national security and military intelligence needs. Recognizing the integration of law enforcement processes associated with transnational terrorst investigations, JMIC offered a course entitled "Counternarcotics Policy and Intelligence" in spring 2004. The course director was Visiting Professor of Law Enforcement Intelligence Dr. Barry Zulauf who was assigned part time from

155 It is anticipated that the curricular process will approve the degree as a master of science in criminal intelligence effective in the spring of 2005. See http://www.cj.msu.edu.

156 See http://www.mercyhurst.edu/undergraduate/academic-programs/index.php?pt=riap.

157 See http://www.dia.mil/college.

Drug Enforcement Administration. The same course has been offered in fall 2004 at the National Security Agency campus, and will be offered again in spring 2005 at JMIC. A course entitled "Law Enforcement Intelligence Collection and Analysis" is in development for 2005. Moreover, law enforcement personnel – initially from federal agencies – who have at least a Top Secret security clearance with a Sensative Compartmented Information (SCI) designation may now enroll in JMIC degree programs.

CONCLUSION

This chapter provided an overview of critical issues in the management of the law enforcement intelligence function. The author included comprehensive resources in the footnotes so that the reader may monitor changes and current events. The environment of law enforcement intelligence is changing rapidly; hence, published information tends to have a short life. As such, the need to be vigilant in monitoring the online resources becomes even more critical.

Networks and Systems

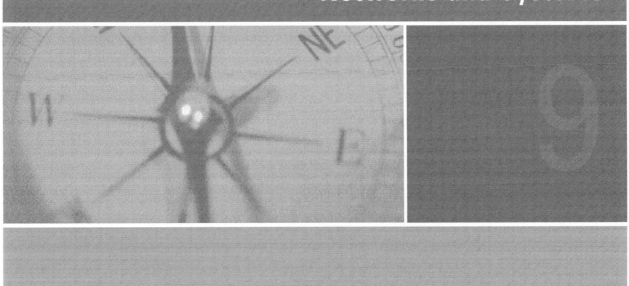

CHAPTER NINE

Networks and Systems

Essential to effective intelligence is the ability to access and share information readily. A number of resources and systems are currently available to state, local, and tribal law enforcement (SLTLE) agencies that permit access to federal intelligence products, regional and local intelligence products, current news and events, and secure email. Many resources are available to law enforcement organizations for a minimal, if any, fee. Regardless of the degree of sophistication of any system, it is essential that a law enforcement organization have some form of secure email and access to a Sensitive But Unclassified (SBU) network to receive current advisories to maximize information sharing.

Regional Information Sharing System (RISS)

RISS has been in operation since 1973 providing services supporting the investigative and prosecution efforts of law enforcement and criminal justice agencies. The network was founded in response to trans-jurisdictional crime problems and the need for cooperation and secure information sharing among law enforcement agencies.

Today, RISS is a national network comprising six multistate centers operating regionally.

- Middle Atlantic-Great Lakes Organized Crime Law Enforcement Network (MAGLOCLEN)[158] (Delaware, Indiana, Maryland, Michigan, New Jersey, New York, Ohio, Pennsylvania, and the District of Columbia. The center also has member agencies in England, the Canadian provinces of Ontario and Quebec, and Australia)
  140 Terry Road, Suite 100
  Newton, PA 18940
  Phone: 215.504.4910
  E-mail: info@magloclen.riss.net

- Mid-States Organized Crime Information Center (MOCIC) (Illinois, Iowa, Kansas, Minnesota, Missouri, Nebraska, North Dakota, South Dakota, and Wisconsin. The center also has member agencies in Canada)
  1610 E. Sunshine Drive, Suite 100
  Springfield, MO 65804
  Phone: 417.883.4383
  Email: info@mocic.riss.net

- New England State Police Information Network (NESPIN) (Connecticut, Maine, Massachusetts, New Hampshire, Rhode Island, and Vermont. The center also has member agencies in Canada)
  124 Grove Street, Suite 305
  Franklin, MA 02038
  Phone: 508.528.8200
  Email: info@nespin.riss.net

158   http://www.iir.com/riss/maglocle.

- Regional Organized Crime Information Center (ROCIC)[159] (Alabama, Arkansas, Florida, Georgia, Kentucky, Louisiana, Mississippi, North Carolina, Oklahoma, South Carolina, Tennessee, Texas, Virginia, and West Virginia, Puerto Rico, and the U.S. Virgin Islands)
    545 Marriott Drive, Suite 850
    Nashville, TN 37214
    Phone: 615.871.0013
    Email: info@rocic.riss.net

- Rocky Mountain Information Network (RMIN)[160] (Arizona, Colorado, Idaho, Montana, Nevada, New Mexico, Utah, and Wyoming. The center also has member agencies in Canada)
    2828 N. Central Avenue, Suite 1000
    Phoenix, AZ 85004
    Phone: 602.351.2320
    Email: info@rmin.riss.net

- Western States Information Network (WSIN) (Alaska, California, Hawaii, Oregon, and Washington. The center also has member agencies in Canada, Australia, and Guam)
    1825 Bell Street, Suite 205
    Sacramento, CA 92403
    Phone: 916.263.1186
    Email: info@wsin.riss.net

The regional approach allows each center to offer support services tailored to the needs of member agencies, though the centers also provide services and products that are national in scope and significance. Typical targets of RISS-member agencies' activities are terrorism, drug trafficking, violent crime, cybercrime, gang activity, and organized crime. While the RISS network is funded by the U.S. Bureau of Justice Assistance, it is controlled by its member agencies. As a result, state and local law enforcement agencies establish priorities as well as decisions related to services, such as secure client email systems.

159   http://www.rocic.com.

160   http://www.iir.com/riss/rmin.

Traditional support services provided to law enforcement member agencies from the RISS centers include the following:

- Information-sharing resources
- Analytical services
- Loan of specialized investigative equipment
- Confidential funds
- Training conferences
- Technical assistance

...it is essential that a LAW ENFORCEMENT organization have some form of SECURE EMAIL and ACCESS to a SENSITIVE BUT UNCLASSIFIED (SBU) network, to receive current advisories in order to MAXIMIZE information sharing.

RISS operates a secure intranet, known as RISS.net, to facilitate law enforcement communications and information sharing nationwide. RISS local, state, federal, and tribal law enforcement member agency personnel have online access to share intelligence and coordinate efforts against criminal networks that operate in many locations across jurisdictional lines. In September 2002, the FBI Law Enforcement Online (LEO) system interconnected with RISS. In October 2003, the RISS/LEO interconnection was recommended in the National Criminal Intelligence Sharing Plan (NCISP) as the initial Sensitive But Unclassified (SBU) communications backbone for implementation of a nationwide criminal intelligence-sharing capability. The plan encourages agencies to connect their systems to RISS/LEO.

Anti-Terrorism Information Exchange (ATIX)

In April 2003, RISS expanded its services and implemented the Anti-Terrorism Information Exchange (ATIX) to provide users with access to homeland security, disaster, and terrorist threat information. RISS member agencies as well as executives and officials from other first-responder agencies and critical infrastructure entities can access the system. ATIX consists of a website and connected services hosted on the RISS network. It is designed for use by officials from government and nongovernment organizations who are responsible for planning and implementing prevention, response, mitigation, and recovery efforts for terrorist attacks and disasters. The ATIX program serves a variety of communities such as state, county, local, and tribal government executives; federal government executives and agencies; regional emergency management; law enforcement and criminal justice organizations; fire departments; agriculture; disaster relief; special rescue units; and telecommunication and transportation.

The website (see Figure 9-1) features secure email and information such as Department of Homeland Security (DHS) bulletins and advisories, terrorist threat-level alerts, advisories from different governmental units such as the Department of Transportation, and areas where users can post and share data specific to their "occupational communities" (e.g., law enforcement, military, emergency services, etc.).

In each individual community section on the website, users can establish collaborative electronic conference services, virtual bulletin boards, and live chat rooms. Member groups also create most of the ATIX site's content and bulletin board posts. Each conference has a live chat feature where users can post conversation threads and discuss topics. An on-screen paging function permits users to notify others if they need to shift a conversation to the telephone or to a face-to-face discussion.

ATIX is informative, user-friendly, and an important resource for law enforcement agencies of any size. The site requires access to the Internet and a Virtual Private Network (VPN) to permit secure communications. To obtain access to ATIX, the potential user must contact the applicable RISS center and request enrollment from the appropriate state coordinator.

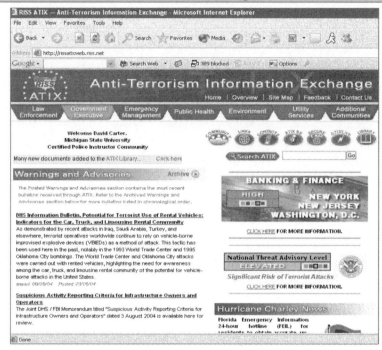

Figure 9-1: Anti-Terrorism Information Exchange (ATIX) Welcome Screen

Law Enforcement Online (LEO)[161]

LEO is an online service operated by the FBI for law enforcement, first responders, and criminal justice officials. Approximately 32,500 members have been on LEO since its inception in1995. All that is required for use is Internet access and the FBI VPN.

After logging on to the LEO site, resources that are available include:

- *Topical Focus Area:* Custom web-type pages that provide a secure community area for general information related to the law enforcement profession using text, graphics, audio, and video.
- *Law Enforcement Special Interest Groups:* Segmented areas with multilevel controlled access for specialized law enforcement groups that have their own members.
- *Email:* Provides the capability to send and receive secure Email/messages electronically between LEO users.

- *News Groups:* Provides general national and state law enforcement and special interest group bulletin boards for posting timely topical information of interest to law enforcement.
- *Chat:* Provides the ability to have a real-time discussion among users (through a keyboard) on three levels; one-to-one, groups, and the Electronic Academy for presentations or question and answer sessions.
- *Feedback:* Provides the capability to survey users for input on various topics.
- *Electronic Calendar:* Provides national, state, and special-interest calendars for posting upcoming dates of interest for conferences, meetings, training courses, seminars, and other important dates.
- *Topical Electronic Library:* Provides an easily accessed repository of a broad range of publications, documents, studies, research, technical bulletins, and reports of interest to the law enforcement community. The library will provide indexed and full-text retrieval capability. Material for this component is expected to come from the entire law enforcement and education communities.
- *Distance Learning:* Provides online topical learning modules that can be used any time of the day or night at the user's own pace with instructional feedback

In addition, FBI *Intelligence Assessments*, FBI *Intelligence Bulletins*, and FBI *Intelligence Information Reports* are available on the LEO website as well as other items of interest related to the FBI intelligence program. To obtain access to LEO, contact the training coordinator at the local FBI Field Office.[162]

162 http://www.fbi.gov/contact/fo/fo.htm.

> … FBI Intelligence ASSESSMENTS, FBI Intelligence BULLETINS, and FBI Intelligence INFORMATION REPORTS are available on the LEO WEBSITE as well as other items of interest related to the FBI intelligence program.

Law Enforcement Intelligence Unit (LEIU)[163]

Founded in 1956, the purpose of LEIU is to gather, record, and exchange confidential information not available through regular law enforcement channels, concerning organized crime and terrorism. It is an association of state and local police departments, similar in many respects to numerous other associations serving professionals. LEIU has no employees and no capability as an entity to conduct any investigation or law enforcement activity. Each member agency is bound by, and acts pursuant to, local law and its own agency regulations.

The organization is divided geographically into four zones: Eastern, Central, Northwestern, and Southwestern. Each zone elects a chair and vice chair to serve as zone officers. Internationally, LEIU elects a general chair, vice general chair, and designates a secretary-treasurer and a legal advisor who serve as international officers. The International Officers, zone officers, past general chair, and two representatives from the Central Coordinating Agency (i.e., the California Department of Justice which houses LEIU data) make up the executive board. The board is the governing body of LEIU, and, as such, establishes policy and passes on the admission of all members, and is governed by a constitution and bylaws.

LEIU membership is limited to law enforcement agencies of general jurisdiction having an intelligence function. To become a member, an agency head submits a written application. The applying agencies must be sponsored by an LEIU member. Each member agency head appoints an LEIU representative as the contact for the Law Enforcement Intelligence Unit.

Virtually any type of information that may be lawfully retained in law enforcement intelligence records may be exchanged as long as the recipient meets the need-to-know and right-to-know standards. Importantly, to keep intelligence records consistent with legal standards, LEIU is not a computer system where members can make queries; rather, it is a network where information is exchanged between members, albeit in electronic form.

163 For more information on LEIU see http://www.leiu-homepage.org/index.html. For contact information concerning LEIU membership, Email leiu@doj.ca.gov. LEIU, California Department of Justice, P.O. Box 163029, Sacramento, CA 95816-3029.

Information Sharing

To submit an inquiry about a suspected criminal to the LEIU automated system, a member agency enters the subject information through a secure intranet, which is stored on RISS.net. The subject information includes, among other items, the person's identity, criminal activity, and criminal associates. All information submitted to the LEIU Automated File must meet LEIU File Guidelines (Appendix D) and comply with 28 CFR Part 23. The submitting agency must certify that the subject meets established criteria, including criminal predicate. The Central Coordinating Agency manages this automated file.

Joint Regional Information Exchange System (JRIES)

The Joint Regional Information Exchange System (JRIES) is the secure collaborative system used by the Department of Homeland Security (DHS) Homeland Security Operations Center (HSOC) to collect and disseminate information between DHS and federal, state, tribal, and local agencies involved in counterterrorism.

- JRIES is focused on information exchange and real-time collaboration among federal, state, tribal, and local authorities.
- JRIES includes information analysis tools and capabilities to support distributed collaborative analysis and reporting across federal, state, tribal and local law enforcement and intelligence.
- JRIES meets all applicable security requirements and has achieved system accreditation by the Intelligence Community.
- JRIES currently is deployed to more than 100 federal, state, and local entities with many more connecting every month.

This communications capability delivers to states and major urban areas real-time interactive connectivity with the DHS Homeland Security Operations Center. This secure system significantly strengthens the flow of real-time threat information at the Sensitive But Unclassified (SBU) level to all users immediately, and provides the platform for future communications classified as Secret to the state level. This collaborative communications environment, developed by state and local authorities, will allow all states and major urban areas to collect and disseminate information among federal, state, and local agencies involved in combating terrorism.

Already in use in the 24/7/365 DHS Watch of the Homeland Security Operations Center, JRIES is an integrated component of the wider DHS information-sharing and collaboration architecture that will help provide situational awareness, information sharing, and collaboration across the 50 states, U.S. territories, and major urban areas. This program helps fulfill the DHS's charge to enable real-time information sharing of threats to the homeland with a variety of homeland security partners throughout the federal, state, and local levels.

JRIES is not just a communications tool but also an analytical tool for its users. Capacity of the system includes the following:

- Collaboration and analysis
- Secure email
- Interactive collaboration tool (live text or voice)
- Supports requests for information
- Link and temporal analysis
- Daily and periodic reporting
- Suspicious incident/pre-incident indicator data
- Data display on maps (national, state, county, city)
- Critical Infrastructure Protection (CIP) repository
- Strategic analysis on terrorist threats, tactics, and weapons.

Homeland Security Information Network

The next generation of JRIES is the Homeland Security Information Network (HSIN). The HSIN will deliver real-time interactive connectivity among state and local partners and with the DHS HSOC through JRIES. This increased connectivity will result in more effective communications and more efficient responses to deter, detect, prevent, or respond to terrorist actions. Information sharing to reduce vulnerabilities is an essential element of the DHS's mission, and this real-time flow of encrypted information among homeland security partners will allow federal, state, and local agencies to better perform their jobs of protecting America's hometowns.

As a foundation of the Homeland Security Information Network initiative, the broadened JRIES community of users will include the State homeland security advisors, state adjutant generals (National Guard), state emergency operations centers, and local emergency services providers including firefighters, law enforcement, and others. The expanded JRIES network will continue to support the law enforcement and intelligence counterterrorism mission, but will also provide communications, collaboration, and information sharing among DHS and federal, state, local, and tribal agencies and private-sector partners.

As a homeland security program focused on monitoring, information sharing, preventing, and responding to potential terrorist threats, the HSIN will connect to other communications tools used by law enforcement agencies. The RISS.net and LEO programs, for example, sponsored by the Department of Justice, address a much wider spectrum of criminal activity. Within the counterterrorism mission, JRIES, RISS.net, and LEO are complementary programs, and DHS will continue to work closely with law enforcement. The HSIN will post its daily reports and warnings directly to RISS.net via a JRIES interface. Combining JRIES' real-time collaboration capability and state-of-the-art portal technology with RISS.net's legacy databases will enhance the capabilities of DHS law enforcement partners.

Priority capabilities of this expanded information exchange system will include the following:

Communications
- Low-cost, always-on connectivity
- End-to-end encrypted communications.

Collaboration / Analysis
- Secure email
- Interactive collaboration tool (real-time text or voice)
- Supports requests for information, exchange, and cross-reference
- Search and link/timeline analysis, map/imagery displays.

Information

- Daily, periodic, and ongoing report sharing
- Suspicious incident/pre-incident indicator data
- Media studies and analysis
- Mapping and imaging (national, state, county, city)
- Critical Infrastructure Protection (CIP) repository
- Strategic analysis of terrorist threats, tactics, and weapons.

Figures 9-2 illustrates the intelligence interrelationship of the HSIN with other networks as well as the integration of intelligence and operations. A long-term goal of the HSIN is to have seamless connectivity among the different portals that serve the law enforcement and homeland security communities.

Figure 9-2: System Integration—HSIN Operations and Intelligence Integration

164 For contact information and more details, see http://www.nlets.org/default.asp.

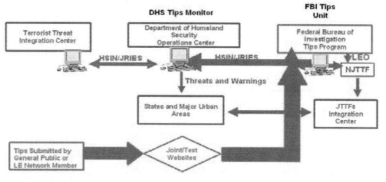

Operations – Complaint information can be addressed by FBI/JTTFs/Nationally via LEO.
Intelligence – Information flows to DHS, TTIC and FBI Tips unit simultaneously via HSIN
Universal Tips Report Number will permit tracking through Operations and Intelligence flow routes.

National Law Enforcement Telecommunications System (NLETS)[164]

The National Law Enforcement Telecommunication System (NLETS) was created by state law enforcement agencies nearly 35 years ago as a primary means of integrating data related to traffic enforcement. Since its founding, the NLETS role has evolved from being primarily an interstate telecommunications service for law enforcement to a more broad-based network servicing the justice community at the local, state, and federal levels. It is now a broad-based interstate law enforcement network for the exchange of law enforcement and related justice information. Its purpose is to provide, within a secure environment, an international criminal justice telecommunications capability that will benefit to the highest degree, the safety, security, and preservation of human life and the protection of property. NLETS will assist those national and international governmental agencies and other organizations with similar missions who enforce or aid in enforcing local, state, federal, or international laws or ordinances.

NLETS is a nonprofit corporation chartered by the states and funded by user fees collected from the membership and managed by a board of directors consisting of state police executives. Primary services include access to key state databases, particularly driver's licenses and motor vehicle records, criminal histories, and sex offender registries. The system also has access to special databases such as Canadian files, hazardous materials archives, U.S. General Services Administration fleet, immigration records, FAA registrations, NDPIX,[165] vehicle impounds, and import/export files. The system also includes terminal-to-terminal messaging and broadcast capabilities (such as an Amber Alert).

Accelerated Information Sharing for Law Enforcement (AISLE)

The next generation of NLETS is Accelerated Information Sharing for Law Enforcement (AISLE). The intent of AISLE is to accelerate information sharing for the entire U.S. law enforcement community by adopting and deploying XML[166] Web Services technology for interstate inquiries and responses. Like the Global Justice Information Sharing Initiative, it also seeks to promote the common XML standard for law enforcement information systems. Essentially, AISLE seeks to move NLETS completely into the most advanced realms of networking to enhance information sharing.

International Criminal Police Organization (INTERPOL)[167]

INTERPOL is the International Criminal Police Organization founded in 1923 to serve as a clearinghouse for information on transnational criminals. It

165   NDPIX is the National Drug Pointer Index, discussed in detail in Chapter 11.

166   Internet web pages are typically written in Hypertext Markup Language (HTML) which aids in formatting and integrating diverse resources. The second generation is XML, Extensible Mark-up Language, which has all the features of HTML and provides significantly increased searching and comparison characteristics.

167   The INTERPOL General Secretariat site is http://www.interpol.int.

receives, stores, analyzes, and disseminates criminal data in cooperation with its 181 member countries on a 24/7/365 basis in its four official languages (English, French, Spanish, and Arabic). INTERPOL deals only with international crimes. INTERPOL's three core functions are to provide member states with the following:

1. A secure global communications system to provide the timely and effective exchange, storage, and processing of important police information to all member countries and provision of other related services including the issuing of international wanted persons notices and similar alerts.
2. Databases and analytical support, which includes the development of programs and services for police including databases on names, fingerprints, DNA, photographs, identification documents, and notices (see figure 9-3).
3. Operational police support enhancing the role of INTERPOL's National Central Bureaus and further integrating Sub Regional Bureaus into overall INTERPOL activity, including the development of relevant law enforcement initiatives in areas such as terrorism, drugs, organized crime, trafficking in human beings, child abuse images on the Internet, and financial and high-tech crime.

Criminal intelligence analysts at INTERPOL are uniquely placed to recognize and detect patterns and criminal trends from a global perspective, as well as having the resources to assist with specific international crime cases.

In the United States, the contact point for INTERPOL is the U.S. National Central Bureau (USNCB) which operates within the guidelines prescribed by the Department of Justice, in conjunction with the DHS. The mission of the USNCB is to facilitate international law enforcement cooperation as the United States representative to INTERPOL.

When INTERPOL is seeking specific information or seeking a person, it issues a color-coded "notice," with each color representing a different type of action from the recipient agencies (Figure 9-3). While these notices are rarely encountered by SLTLE officers, it is nonetheless of value to be familiar with them should the issue arise.

Figure 9-3: INTERPOL Notices[168]

Red Notice
Used to seek the arrest with a view to extradition of subjects wanted and based upon an arrest warrant.

Yellow Notice
Used to help locate missing persons, especially minors, or to help identify persons who are not able to identify themselves; for example, a person suffering from amnesia.

Blue Notice
Used to collect additionnal information about person identity or illegal activities related to a criminal matter. This notice is primarily used for tracing and locating offenders when the decision to extradite has not yet been made, and for locating witnesses to crimes.

Black Notice
Used to seek the true identity of unidentified bodies.

Green Notice
Used to provide warnings and criminal intelligence about persons who have committed criminal offences, and are likely to repeat these crimes in other countries.

U.S. law enforcement officers can gain access to INTERPOL reports and make international inquiries by contacting their state point of contact (usually within the state law enforcement or intelligence agency) who will then query the USNCB. For reference, the USNCB address and website are:

> U.S. Department of Justice
> INTERPOL
> United States National Central Bureau
> Washington, DC 20530
> http://www.usdoj.gov/usncb/index.html

168   http://www.interpol.int/public/Notices/default.asp.

Law Enforcement Information Sharing Program

The U.S. Department of Justice is developing a new initiative called the Law Enforcement Information Sharing Program (LEISP). The initiative is designed not to create a new system, but to integrate systems and relationships that already exist. Too often both systems and initiatives operate independently. The result is that system queries and information dissemination are not comprehensive.

The LEISP plans to implement policies, practices, and technologies to ensure that each component of the Department of Justice share information as a matter of routine across the entire spectrum of the law enforcement community at all levels of government. The intent of the program is to ensure that law enforcement information-sharing practices in the Department of Justice are consistent with the NCISP. Moreover, the program should significantly enhance the amount and quality of intelligence that is shared with SLTLE agencies.

Regional Intelligence Centers[169]

Regional Intelligence Centers (RIC) take many forms throughout the United States. There is currently no one model for what an intelligence center does or how it should be organized. Rather, they have evolved, largely based on local initiatives, as a response to perceived threats related to crime, drug trafficking, and/or terrorism. The intent is to marshal the resources and expertise of multiple agencies within a defined region to deal with cross-jurisdictional crime problems. In some cases, a region is defined as a county (e.g., Rockland County, New York Intelligence Center); as the area surrounding a major city (e.g., Los Angeles Joint Regional Intelligence Center[170]); it may be a portion of a state (e.g., Upstate New York Regional Intelligence Center), or it may encompass an entire state (e.g., Georgia Information Sharing and Analysis Center).

Most RICs were started as the product of counterdrug initiatives starting in the 1980s. Indeed, the High Intensity Drug Trafficking Area (HIDTA) intelligence centers[171] can serve as models for successful structures and initiatives as well as systemic issues that need to be overcome.[172] In the late 1990s, the Bureau of Alcohol, Tobacco and Firearms (ATF) developed a number of programmatic activities to reduce gun violence. Emerging from these initiatives were ATF Regional Crime Gun Centers. The centers, in some cases collocated with the HIDTA RIC, have a number of intelligence-related roles including "…analyzing trace data to identify gun traffickers, disseminate investigative leads, and coordinate with the HIDTA RIC to identify drug traffickers and their sources of guns."[173] In virtually all cases, both the HIDTA and ATF intelligence centers had a great deal of interaction with SLTLE.

169 Regional Intelligence Centers are also sometimes called Fusion Centers. In law enforcement intelligence there is no explicit definition or distinction between the Intelligence Center and Fusion Center.

170 This center serves a five-county region, (Los Angeles, Orange, Riverside, San Bernardino, and Ventura) to collect counter terrorism information for the region and analyze that data that allows 24-hour access for law enforcement.

171 http://www.whitehousedrug policy.gov/hidta.

172 The Counterdrug Intelligence Executive Secretariat (1331 F Street, NW, Suite 700, Washington, DC 20530; Telephone: 202.353.1876/Fax 202.353.1901 has an insightful unpublished report on Metropolitan Area Consolidation/Collocation of Drug Intelligence Elements that describes success and challenges for Regional Intelligence Centers.

173 http://www.atf.gov/field/ newyork/rcgc.

Since 9/11, new regional intelligence centers have been created, or are in the process of being developed, to deal with counterterrorism. In several cases, the RIC is funded by the DHS, yet in other cases local and county governments are bearing the costs. While counterterrorism is what stimulated the growth of RICs, as a general rule these are "all crime centers." That is, the centers perform the intelligence function on trans-jurisdictional and organized crime as well as terrorism. To enhance this function, the FBI Field Intelligence Groups are also supporting the RICs.

The structure of intelligence centers also vary widely from being networks (Figure 9-4) to a physical location staffed by multiple agencies (Figure 9-5). There is no right or wrong way to develop a RIC since it must be driven by needs, resources, and geographic characteristics of the region. While the structure may vary widely, there are some best practices that can help guide the RIC operation. At this writing, the Global Intelligence Working Group (GIWG) is developing a set of minimum standards that should be met when an RIC is developed. The reader should monitor the GIWG website[174] where the standards will be posted.

174 http://it.ojp.gov/topic.jsp?topic_id=56.

175 http://www.state.ia.us/government/dps/intell/lein/main.htm.

Figure 9-4: Law Enforcement Intelligence Network (Iowa)[175]

The Iowa Law Enforcement Intelligence Network (LEIN) is an award-winning program established by the Department of Public Safety in 1984. In August 1994, coordination and administrative responsibilities for LEIN were assigned to the newly created Iowa Department of Public Safety Intelligence Bureau. State, county and local law enforcement agencies from across the state of Iowa provide support to LEIN operations.

LEIN's membership consists of law enforcement officers who have successfully completed a 2-week criminal intelligence course conducted by the Department. LEIN members work together with the department to accomplish two related objectives:

1. To develop and disseminate knowledge about significant criminal conditions that affect the state of Iowa.
2. To use this knowledge to identify, investigate, and remove these criminal conditions.

To achieve the first objective, LEIN serves as a mechanism for the statewide collection and exchange of criminal intelligence information. LEIN members submit information reports to the department's Intelligence Bureau, which in turn, disseminates the information to participating agencies throughout the state.

Figure 9-4: Law Enforcement Intelligence Network (Iowa) (Cont.)

These agencies then use the information to identify and evaluate criminal activity in their area.

LEIN's most effective asset is its members (more than 800 Iowa law enforcement officers and more than 200 agencies) and the trust and personal relationships that are developed to facilitate the sharing of information.

The state is geographically divided into six regions, each of which has a monthly meeting of LEIN members in the region. Information summaries from those meetings are also forwarded to the LEIN Central Coordinating Agency (CCA) for analysis and dissemination.

To further facilitate its mission, LEIN has established relationships with the (MOCIC), Midwest High Intensity Drug Trafficking Area (HIDTA), the LEIU, Iowa Governor's Office of Drug Control Policy (ODCP), U.S. Attorneys' Anti-Terrorism Advisory Councils in both the Northern and Southern Districts of Iowa, and the Iowa Joint Terrorism Task force (JTTF).

Figure 9-5: Georgia Information Sharing and Analysis Center

The Georgia Information Sharing and Analysis Center (GISAC), is responsible for collecting, evaluating, and disseminating intelligence and threat information for Georgia. Its mission is to provide intelligence to law enforcement agencies in Georgia based on the collection, evaluation, and analysis of information that can identify criminal activity. This intelligence can be disseminated the form of either tactical or strategic intelligence.

GISAC is the state's clearinghouse for all terrorism-related intelligence from which it proactively works with the Georgia Bureau of Investigation and other agencies involved in any aspect of counterterrorism.

Multiple state agencies work in the GISAC as outlined in a memorandum of understanding. Federal agencies working in GISAC do so under the provisions of a Participation Agreement between Georgia's Director of Homeland Security and an executive officer for each of the participating federal agencies.

Salary, vehicle, equipment, and supply expenses associated with GISAC personnel are paid for by the employing agency of each GISAC participant. The facilities and furnishings, including computer and communications equipment, are funded by grants and contributions from several of the participating agencies.

CONCLUSION

If effective information sharing is one of the critical goals of contemporary law enforcement intelligence, then networks and systems are the critical tools to reach that goal. As has been seen throughout this chapter, there has been significant growth in the capability for law enforcement agencies to share information. This growth has been a product of new initiatives following 9/11, the availability of new networking technologies that reduce interoperability conflicts, and the commitment of American law enforcement at all levels of government to facilitate information-sharing processes. These factors are in a dynamic state at this writing. Systems and networks will change; therefore, it is incumbent on the intelligence manager to carefully monitor trends to stay current.

Intelligence Requirements and Threat Assessment

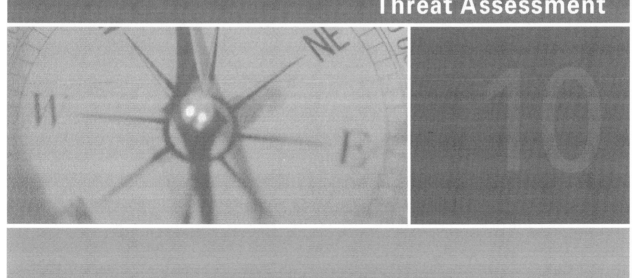

CHAPTER TEN

Intelligence Requirements and Threat Assessment

Information is needed to make decisions — the higher the quality and the more comprehensive the information, the more sound the decision. If an executive is going to make a decision about implementing a new program, he or she needs information on the costs, benefits, and risks of the program as well as the more difficult dimension of what benefits will be lost if a program is not implemented. Typically, the information sought is not conclusive, but based on probability, the experience of others, experimentation, logic or, sometimes, an educated guess. Not having sufficient reliable information makes the decision process more difficult (and risky).

The same phenomenon applies to the operational world of criminal intelligence. To adequately assess the threats from a terrorist group or criminal enterprise, information is needed for a comprehensive analysis. Oftentimes during the course of the analytic process, critical information is missing that prevents a complete and accurate assessment of the issue. This is a gap, an unanswered question related to a criminal or terrorist threat. An intelligence requirement is identified and information needs to aid in answering questions related to criminal or terrorist threats.[177]

In order to adequately ASSESS THE THREATS from a TERRORIST GROUP or CRIMINAL ENTERPRISE, information is needed for a COMPREHENSIVE analysis.

Filling Gaps/Fulfilling Requirements

177 FBI Office of Intelligence. *The FBI Intelligence Cycle: Answering the Questions…*. A desk reference guide for law enforcement. (Pamphlet form). (July 2004).

The information collection process needs to be focused so that specific information needs are fulfilled. This increases efficiency of the process and ensures that the right information needs are being targeted. Too often in the past a "dragnet" approach was used for collecting information, and analysts and investigators would examine the information in hopes of discovering the "pearls" that may emerge. As illustrated in Figure 10-1, there are a number of differences between the traditional approach and the requirements-based approach to information collection. In essence, the requirements-based approach is more scientific; hence, more objective, more efficacious, and less problematic on matters related to civil rights.

Figure 10-1: Traditional Collection vs. Requirements-Based Collection[177]

Tradition-Based	Requirements-Based
• Data-driven	• Analysis-driven
• Exploratory	• Contemplative
• Emphasizes amassing data	• Emphasizes analysis of data
• Infers crimes from suspected persons	• Infers criminal suspects from crimes
• An aggregate approach to information collection (dragnet); even mere suspicion	• Targeting/specificity on information regarding reasonable suspicion of crimes
• Explores all general inferences about potential criminality	• Selectively explores crime leads based on priorities and evidence
• Explores collected information to see if there are questions to answers	• Answers questions by collecting and analyzing information
• Develops intelligence files for contingency needs, (i.e., just in case information is needed)	• Develops intelligence files in support of active crimes and investigations
• Statistics produced for descriptive purposes	• Statistics produced for decision making

Since this is a scientific process, the intelligence function can use a qualitative protocol to collect the information that is needed to fulfill requirements. This protocol is an overlay for the complete information collection processes of the intelligence cycle. The numbered steps in the box below are action items in the protocol, the bulleted points are illustrations. This is not a template, but a process that each agency needs to develop to meet its unique characteristics.

1. Understand your intelligence goal
   • Arrest terrorists and/or criminals
   • Prevent or mitigate terrorists attacks
   • Stop a criminal enterprise from operating
2. Build an analytic strategy
   • What types of information are needed?
   • How can the necessary information be collected?
3. Define the social network
   • Who is in the social circle of the target(s)?
   • Who is in the regular business circle of the target(s)?
   • Who has access to the target(s) for information and observation
   • What hobbies, likes, or characteristics of the target's social behavior are opportunities for information collection, infiltration, and observation?

177 Carter, David L. (2003). *Law Enforcement Intelligence Operations*. Tallahassee, FL: SM&C Sciences, Inc.

4. Define logical networks
   - How does the enterprise operate?
   - Funding sources
   - Communications sources
   - Logistics and supply
5. Define physical networks
   - Homes
   - Offices
   - Storage and staging areas
4. Task the collection process
   - Determine the best methods of getting the information (surveillance, informants, wiretaps, etc.)
   - Get the information

As information sharing becomes more standardized and law enforcement intelligence as a discipline becomes more professional, law enforcement agencies at all levels of government will use the requirements-driven process. In all likelihood, this approach will become a required element for information sharing, particularly with the FBI and the Department of Homeland Security (DHS).

Threat Assessments

Threat assessments are often discussed, but the process remains elusive to many state, local, and tribal law enforcement (SLTLE) agencies (Figure 10-2). There are four key variables in the process:
1. Threat Inventory.
2. Threat Assessment.
3. Target Assessment.
4. Target Vulnerability.

Figure 10-2: Threat Assessment Model for SLTLE[178]

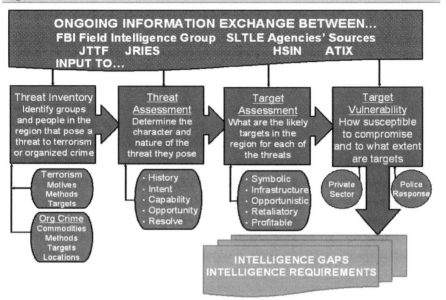

Threat inventory: The threat inventory requires the law enforcement agency to identify groups and individuals within the agency's region[179] that would pose possible threats. These may be international terrorists, domestic extremists, individuals who have an extreme special interest ideology, or a criminal enterprise. The type of information sought centers on identifying answers to certain questions: Who are the people involved? What is their group affiliation, if any, and what do they believe? To understand extremists it also is useful to identify their motives, methods, and targets. With criminal enterprises, the variables are methods, commodities, and locations. In either case, understanding how the criminal entity operates and what it seeks to accomplish can provide significant insight into their ability to act. Care must be taken to collect and retain the information in a manner that is consistent with 28 CFR Part 23 guidelines.

Threat assessment: Each threat identified in the inventory must be assessed with respect to the level of the threat posed. Some individuals make threats, but do not pose a threat. Conversely, some individuals and groups pose threats without ever making a threat. To fully assess their

178   This model was prepared by David L. Carter, Michigan State University, as part of a training program on Intelligence Requirements and Threat Assessment for the Bureau of Justice Assistance (BJA)-funded State and Local Anti-Terrorism Training (SLATT) program.

179   Realistically, the threat assessment must be done on a regional, rather than jurisdictional, basis because a specific threat and/or target will likely have an impact on the jurisdiction.

threat capacity, several factors need to be examined: What is the history of the groups? Have they committed attacks or crimes in the past? If so, what was the modus operandi (MO) and character of the act? Does the group have the capability to actually commit terrorist acts or crimes? If so, how robust is that capability? Are unique opportunities present for the group to commit an act? What appears to be the resolve or the commitment of the group? Factors such as these can develop an image to aid in determining the character of the threat posed by individuals and groups in the inventory.

Target assessment: In light of the nature of the groups in the threat inventory, probable targets can be identified in the region. It is rare that a specific target can be identified, but based on history, statements, threats, and the nature of an extremist group's ideology, the array of targets can be narrowed. Similarly, criminal enterprises tend to have targeted commodities that they traffic or types of frauds they perpetrate.

Target vulnerability: The last variable is to assess each of these targets to determine how vulnerable they are to attack. This often involves working with the private sector and often crime-prevention specialists within the law enforcement agency. Given the difficulty of identifying specific targets, the goal is to ensure that each potential target in the region is hardened against an attack.

When information is not available about the factors in this assessment model, there is an intelligence gap that must be filled by a requirement.

FBI Intelligence Requirements Templates

When going through this threat assessment process, the SLTLE agency will need information from the FBI to aid in fully identifying and assessing threats. As noted by the FBI:

> State and local agencies or entities are served by the FBI and have specific needs for tailored intelligence. ... To appropriately address the information needs of state and local agencies, certain procedures can enhance this process. These include:

- Identifying, prioritizing, and addressing state and local information needs.
- Sharing intelligence, analytical techniques, and tools.
- Timely distribution of appropriate intelligence.
- Seek feedback from state and local [law enforcement concerning the] effectiveness of the support.[180]

To facilitate this information exchange, the FBI Office of Intelligence developed a template (Figure 10-3) expressly for SLTLE agencies to use for logging Intelligence Information Needs (IINs) or intelligence gaps they identify. IINs are questions expressed by customers of the FBI and other intelligence producers, the answers to which support law enforcement functions. IINs are not operational leads or questions on the status of investigations or operations. Intelligence gaps are unanswered questions about a criminal, cyber, or national security issue or threat. To illustrate this further, the FBI developed a sample of "baseline" IINs (Figure 10-4). The SLTLE agency should coordinate its use of IINs and information exchange with the Field Intelligence Group (FIG) of the FBI Field Office servicing it.

180   FBI Office of Intelligence. (2003). *FBI Intelligence Production and Use.* Concept of Operations Report. (unpublished report). Washington, DC: FBI Headquarters Divisions and the Office of Intelligence, p. 18.

> IN ORDER TO FACILITATE THIS INFORMATION EXCHANGE, the FBI Office of Intelligence has developed a template expressly for SLTLE agencies to be used to log Intelligence Information Needs or intelligence gaps they identify.

CONCLUSION

The intent of intelligence requirements and threat assessments is to provide a comprehensive, consistent model for managing the threats to a community. These processes are not necessarily easy; however, the outcomes they provide can be priceless.

Figure 10-3: Intelligence Information Needs (IINs)

Purpose: This form should be used to log IINs or intelligence gaps identified by state, local, or tribal law enforcement agencies in your area of responsibility. IINs are questions expressed by customers of the FBI and other intelligence producers, the answers to which support law enforcement functions. IINs are not operational leads or questions on the status of investigations or operations. Intelligence gaps are unanswered questions about a criminal, cyber, or national security issue or threat.

IIN	Requesting Organization (Agency, department, organization)	Dissemination Instructions (Customer name, position title, mailing address, contact number, LEO or other official e-mail address)

Figure 10-4: "Baseline" Intelligence Information Needs (IINs)

Purpose: This template provides a list of sample IINs that can be presented to state, local, and tribal law enforcement partners as a baseline from which to review intelligence gaps, select issues relevant to their investigative needs, and identify additional intelligence and collection requirements.

IIN	Requesting Organization (Agency, department, organization)	Dissemination Instructions (Customer name, position title, mailing address, contact number, LEO or other official e-mail address)
National and local threat assessment reports. - Reliability of the information received - Group planning attack(s) - Target(s) - Why is the target a target? - Suspected method of attack - Weapons of attack - Time frame of attack - Response of federal entities Global, national and local trend reports regarding organizations and structures of active terrorist, criminal, drug, and hate groups in the US. - Identity of suspects and their roles in the local area - Territorial reach - Decision-making processes; degree of subordinate autonomy - Command-control-communications techniques, equipment, network Global, national and local trend reports regarding capabilities, intentions, MO of suspect groups in the US - Types of weapons, explosives, or WMD - Methods of moving, storing and concealing weapons, contraband and human traffic - Special/technical expertise possessed by groups		

IIN	Requesting Organization	Dissemination Instructions
Illegal activities of suspect groups in local jurisdictions - illegal production/acquisition of CBRNE materials/precursors, illegal drugs or substances, prohibited items or persons - illegal arms trade, theft, diversion, sales; smuggling of aliens, terrorists, or prohibited items; human trafficking - HAZMAT dumping; environmental crimes; trafficking in endangered species - links between criminal groups and terrorist or foreign intelligence organizations; bribery/extortion/corruption of public officials **Identity, roles of US and foreign players sponsoring/supporting criminal, terrorist, espionage activities in local jurisdictions** - criminal function of each operative or entity; extraterritorial reach - associated commercial/charitable entities; front/cover organizations - chain of custody in transport of critical technology, illegal items/persons - overseas connections (official, unofficial, private sources); group sympathizers - financial dependencies; extent of group's reliance on external support, funds **Intelligence/security activities of suspect groups** - surveillance, reconnaissance, concealment, "cover" activities; safe houses - counterintelligence and physical security techniques and tactics - COMSEC operations; ability to monitor LEC communications - informant/mole network available to suspect groups - production of, access to false/counterfeit documents and identification - deception, disinformation operations and techniques		

IIN	Requesting Organization	Dissemination Instructions
Modes of transportation and conveyance (air, maritime, and ground) - use of commercial transport/courier/shipping services and carriers - use of private/non-commercial carriers, couriers - types/identification of cargo containers; modifications - itineraries; favored routes; point of departure/source; nations transited - transshipment nodes; border-crossing techniques - multiple couriers chain-of-custody techniques; arrival/pick-up techniques Finances of suspect groups - support networks; state and private sponsors; shell companies - money-laundering techniques; unconventional financial transfers (e.g., hawalas) - shell companies; charity/humanitarian sponsors and covers - financial crime used to generate income; extortion of vulnerable targets - cooperative, facilitating financial institutions or service providers - financial links between public officials and criminal organizations or enterprises, hate groups, or FIS - criminal control of public, tribal financial assets or property Impact of LE or USG efforts to combat suspect groups' activities - infiltration; compromise; destruction; disruption - which tactics most/least effective; evidence of shift in suspect groups' tactics, techniques, or targets - effectiveness of LE efforts overseas		

IIN	Requesting Organization	Dissemination Instructions
- response of suspect groups to LE efforts (countermeasures) - suspect group efforts at corruption of public/LE officials or employees - evidence of foreign/external LE entities' capabilities to cooperate and collaborate in joint efforts or operations - evidence of change in policies/attitudes overseas that affect tolerance for or freedom of action of suspect groups to operate in foreign environments Recruitment; training; collaboration by suspect groups - recruitment techniques and priority targets - training received: type, location, provider, curriculum, facilities Tactics of intimidation, interference with free exercise of civil rights - targets of hate groups, ethnic supremacist organizations - incidents of violence or incitement against individuals, groups, places of worship, schools, commercial entities identified with ethnic or political minorities Capabilities, plans, intentions, MO of suspect groups to conduct computer intrusion or criminal assault on computer systems and data bases. Locally active hackers.		

Federal Law Enforcement Intelligence

CHAPTER ELEVEN

Federal Law Enforcement Intelligence

Many federal agencies have reengineered their intelligence
function since 9/11. Intelligence products have been
redesigned or new products developed, dissemination
methods have been revised, greater attention has been given
to providing critical information that is unclassified for wide
consumption by state, local, and tribal law enforcement
(SLTLE), and new offices and initiatives have been developed.
More information is being produced and disseminated more
widely than in the history of law enforcement. Among the
challenges that law enforcement now faces is accessing that
needed information and using it with efficacy.

In many instances, federal intelligence initiatives are still in a dynamic state and, as a result, it is virtually impossible to provide an exhaustive discussion of them all. This chapter, therefore, will identify those federal intelligence resources of greatest use to SLTLE, their intelligence products, and the agencies' contact or access information. In addition, the chapter will present a broader discussion of the FBI than of other agencies because of the significant changes that have occurred in the FBI's structure and processes and the importance of the SLTLE/FBI relationship in counterterrorism and control of criminal enterprises.

While federal agencies have attempted to provide more unclassified information to America's law enforcement agencies, a significant amount of classified information remains relating to criminal investigations and terrorism. The FBI, therefore, has made a commitment to increase security clearances for SLTLE officers. Despite this, controversies and questions remain. As a result, dealing with the issue of classified information seems to be the first place to start when discussing intelligence from federal agencies.

Classified Information

There is often a mystique about classified information, leading most people after seeing a collection of classified documents to ask, "That's it?" For the most part, the key distinction between classified and unclassified information is that the former contains "sources and methods."

Some definitions: According to Executive Order 12958[181] issued on March 23, 2003, information at the federal level may be classified at one of three levels:

- "Top Secret" shall be applied to information, the unauthorized disclosure of which reasonably could be expected to cause exceptionally grave damage to the national security that the original classification authority is able to identify or describe.
- "Secret" shall be applied to information, the unauthorized disclosure of which reasonably could be expected to cause serious damage to the national security that the original classification authority is able to identify or describe.

181 http://www.whitehouse.gov/news/releases/2003/03/20030325-11.html which amends a previous Executive Order on classified information.

- "Confidential" shall be applied to information, the unauthorized disclosure of which reasonably could be expected to cause damage to the national security that the original classification authority is able to identify or describe.

When an intelligence analyst from the FBI, Drug Enforcement Administration (DEA), or other federal agency receives raw information, he or she must assess it for its source reliability and content validity. The "weight" of each of these variables and their corollaries provide significant insight into the credibility and importance of the information received. The higher the credibility and the greater the corroboration, the higher the "accuracy" of the information. Collectively, as credibility increases, the greater the need for a policy response.

For example, let us say that the FBI receives information about a possible terrorist attack. If the reliability and validity are very low, little credibility will be placed in the threat, although the FBI will develop corroboration and perhaps plan for a response. As validity and reliability increase, the greater credibility will result in devoting more resources to corroboration and a response. If validity and reliability are high, particularly if corroborated, the FBI will initiate a policy response. Policy responses may include proactive investigations, target hardening, and in the most severe cases, the Department of Homeland Security (DHS) may increase the threat level of the Homeland Security Advisory System (HSAS), triggering a significant string of policy responses at all levels of government. This admittedly oversimplified illustration demonstrates the need for analysts to know the sources and methods of information so that they can make the best judgments in their analysis.

Beyond analysts, it is important for investigators, too, to know sources and methods to work their leads. Members of the Joint Terrorism Task Forces (JTTF) need security clearances to conduct their investigations effectively. Do other members of SLTLE agencies need to have security clearances? Certainly not, but who receives a clearance depends on a number of factors. As a rule, SLTLE executives may apply for a clearance for three reasons:

1. To understand the complete nature of a threat within their jurisdiction.
2. To make management decisions, ranging from the assignment of personnel to investigations to the need for extending shifts and canceling officers' leaves should the threat condition warrant it.
3. As a courtesy to the executive who is contributing staff and resources to counterterrorism. This courtesy is not superficial, but aids the executive on matters of accountability.

For other members of an SLTLE agency, decisions should be made on a case-by-case basis to determine if the security clearance best serves the community's and, hence, national, interests. There are three reasons for not having an "open application" for security clearances. First, security clearance means having access to classified information. Before authorizing the application for a clearance, the agency should assess the applicant's "right to know" and "need to know" classified information should be considered. It may be reasonable to grant a security clearance to a local police detective who works organized crime cases; however, a traffic commander would have virtually no need for a clearance.

Second, the clearance process is labor intensive and expensive. It is simply not prudent fiscal management to authorize clearance investigations in all cases. Third, conducting an excess number of clearance investigations slows the process, thereby taking longer to process clearances for those persons who may be in more critical positions.

In most cases, the FBI will begin consideration of a clearance investigation for an SLTLE officer by examining local issues on a case-by-case basis.[182] For those who seek to apply for a security clearance, the appropriate forms and fingerprint cards can be obtained from the local FBI Field Office. Appendix E describes the process for gaining a clearance and provides a list of frequently asked questions and their answers.[183]

Sensitive But Unclassified (SBU) Information[184]

Since it is not feasible for every law enforcement officer to have a security clearance, there is a mechanism to get critical information into the hands

182 The FBI provides the following guidance: Most information needed by state or local law enforcement can be shared at an unclassified level. In those instances where it is necessary to share classified information, it can usually be accomplished at the Secret level. Local FBI Field Offices can help determine whether or not a security clearance is needed, and if so, what level is appropriate.

183 The National Security Clearance Application (Standard Form SF-86) can be downloaded from http://www.usaid.gov/procurement_bus_opp/procurement/forms/SF-86/sf-86.pdf.

184 As a means to aid in clarity, the FBI is moving away from the SBU label and using/will use Law Enforcement Sensitive in all cases, rather than using both labels.

of officers while not jeopardizing classified information: Declassifying the reports by removing sources and methods and labeling the report as SBU achieves this goal. This process is accomplished in two ways. One way is to use a "tear line" report in which an intelligence report has a segment,

> Intelligence products have been redesigned or new products developed, DISSEMINATION methods have been revised, greater attention has been given to providing CRITICAL INFORMATION that is unclassified for wide consumption by SLTLE…

perhaps at the bottom of the page, where critical information is summarized and sources and methods are excluded. This portion of the report may be "torn off" (at least figuratively) and shared with persons who have a need to know the information but do not have a security clearance. The second method is to write intelligence products in a way that relays all critical information but excludes data that should remain classified. (The FBI Office of Intelligence is working specifically on this process.) Following this process, SLTLE officers receive documents that are labeled "Sensitive But Classified" or "Law Enforcement Sensitive", thereby raising the question, "What does this mean?"

Over time some agencies have established procedures to identify and safeguard SBU information. Generally, this unclassified information is withheld from the public for a variety of reasons, but has to be accessible to law enforcement, private security, or other persons who have a responsibility to safeguard the public. The term SBU has been defined in various presidential-level directives and agency guidelines, but only indirectly in statute. Agencies have discretion to define SBU in ways that serve their particular needs to safeguard information. There is no uniformity in implementing rules throughout the federal government on the use of SBU.[185] There have been even fewer efforts to define and safeguard the information at the state, local, and tribal levels. There is an intuitive

185 For a detailed review of the SBU meaning and how it is defined and used by different statutes and regulations, see: Knezo, Genevieve J. *Sensitive But Unclassified* and Other Federal Security Controls on Scientific and Technical Information. Washington, DC: Congressional Research Service.

understanding, but no formal process to control the information. Perhaps some guidance is being provided by the DHS which issued a directive in 2004 on "For Official Use Only" (FOUO) information.

DHS "For Official Use Only" (FOUO) Information

The FOUO label is used within DHS "…to identify unclassified information of a sensitive nature, not otherwise categorized by statute or regulation, the unauthorized disclosure of which could adversely impact a person's privacy or welfare, the conduct of a federal program, or other programs or operations essential to the national interest."[186] FOUO is not classified information, but information that should be distributed only to persons who need to know the information to be aware of conditions that will help keep the homeland and, hence, the community, secure. Within DHS, the caveat "For Official Use Only" will be used to identify SBU information within the DHS community that is not otherwise governed by statue or regulation. At this point the designation applies only to DHS advisories and bulletins.

Since SLTLE agencies will encounter these labels when receiving federal intelligence products it is useful to know the framework from which they arise. At a practical level, the rule of thumb for law enforcement officers is to use good judgment when handling such materials. This does not mean that SLTLE officers may not disseminate this information further unless prohibited from doing so as indicated on the report. Rather, the officer should use the information in a manner that meets community safety needs, including disseminating portions of the information to those segments of the community that would benefit from the data contained in the report.

FEDERAL INTELLIGENCE PRODUCTS[187]

In light of the perspective regarding classification of federal intelligence reports, the following discussions will describe federal intelligence products, virtually all of which will be SBU.

186 Department of Homeland Security, Management Directive System, MD Number: 11042, Safeguarding Sensitive But Unclassified (For Official Use Only) Information. May 11, 2004.

187 Information in this section is based on interviews with FBI Office of Intelligence personnel, reviews of the Office of Intelligence Concepts of Operations (ConOps) and Congressional testimony of Director Mueller. See http://www.fbi.gov/congress/congress04/mueller022404.htm.

FBI Office of Intelligence

The FBI created the Office of Intelligence (OI) to establish and execute standards for recruiting, hiring, training, and developing the intelligence analytic work force, and ensuring that analysts are assigned to operational and field divisions in line with intelligence priorities. The FBI also established a new position, the executive assistant director for intelligence, who joins the three other executive assistant directors in the top tier of FBI management.[188] However, it is important to recognize that the OI goes far beyond being an analyst work force. Rather, it serves to provide centralized management of the FBI's intelligence capabilities and functions in the form of policy, standards, and oversight. Moreover, it embodies the Intelligence-Led Policing philosophy by serving as the driving force to guide operational activities.

To maximize the effectiveness of the intelligence process, the FBI's Office of Intelligence established a formal "intelligence requirements" process for identifying and resolving intelligence information (or information) needs. This is intended to identify key gaps—unanswered questions about a threat — in the FBI's collection capability that must be filled through targeted collection strategies.

[188] For more information on the FBI Office of Intelligence, see http://www.fbi.gov/intelligence/intell.htm.

> In order to maximize the effectiveness of the intelligence process, the **FBI OI** has established a formal "INTELLIGENCE REQUIREMENTS" process for IDENTIFYING intelligence information (or information) needs and resolving them.

As a means to ensure that FBI-wide collection plans and directives are incorporated into field activities, every FBI Field Office has established a Field Intelligence Group (FIG). The FIG is the centralized intelligence component in each field office that is responsible for the management, execution, and coordination of intelligence functions. FIG personnel gather, analyze, and disseminate the intelligence collected in their field offices. Staffed by both special agents and intelligence analysts, the FIG serves as the primary intelligence contact point for SLTLE agencies.

Field offices are also supporting the "24-hour intelligence cycle" of the FBI by using all appropriate resources to monitor, collect, and disseminate threat information, investigative developments (e.g., urgent reports), and other significant raw intelligence to meet the executive information needs of the field offices, other field offices, FBI Headquarters, Legal Attachés, and other federal or state and local agencies.

The reengineered FBI Office of Intelligence has developed two threat-based joint intelligence products and a third product known as the Intelligence Information Report. All of these products may be accessed by law enforcement at all levels of government.

189   The FIG should be contacted at your local FBI Field Office. Contact information for all field offices is at http://www.fbi.gov/contact/fo/fo.htm.

- *Intelligence Assessment:* A comprehensive report on an intelligence issue related to criminal or national security threats within the service territory of an FBI Field Office. The assessment may be classified at any level or be unclassified depending on the nature of the information contained in the report. In most cases when the report is unclassified, it is Law Enforcement Sensitive.
- *Intelligence Bulletin:* A finished intelligence product in article format that describes new developments and evolving trends. The bulletins typically are SBU and available for distribution to state, local, and tribal law enforcement.
- *Intelligence Information Report:* Raw, unevaluated intelligence concerning "perishable" or time-limited information about criminal or national security issues. While the full IIR may be classified, state, local, and tribal law enforcement agencies will have access to SBU information in the report under the tear line.

An immediate source for FBI intelligence products is the Field Intelligence Group (FIG).[189] In addition, SLTLE agencies are able to gain direct access to these reports by secure email through Law Enforcement Online (LEO), the National Law Enforcement Telecommunications System (NLETS), or the Joint Regional Information Exchange System (JREIS). When circumstances warrant, the FBI and DHS will produce an intelligence product jointly and disseminate it to the appropriate agencies.

FBI Counterterrorism[190]

Designated as the top priority for the FBI, countering terrorists' threats and acts is a responsibility requiring the integration of effective intelligence and operational capabilities. In support of the different intelligence units and activities discussed previously, the FBI has developed or enhanced a number of initiatives that seek to fulfill its counterterrorism mandate. While these are largely not intelligence programs per se, they all contribute to the intelligence cycle and consume intelligence for prevention and apprehension. A brief description of these initiatives will provide a more holistic vision of the FBI's counterterrorism strategy.

Specialized Counterterrorism Units

To improve its system for threat warnings, the FBI established a number of specialized counterterrorism units. They include the following:

- CT Watch, a 24-hour Counterterrorism Watch Center that serves as the FBI's focal point for all incoming terrorist threats
- The Communications Analysis Section analyzes terrorist electronic and telephone communications and identifies terrorist associations and networks
- The Document Exploitation Unit identifies and disseminates intelligence gleaned from million of pages of documents or computers seized overseas by intelligence agencies
- The Special Technologies and Applications Section provides technical support for FBI Field Office investigations requiring specialized computer technology expertise and support
- The interagency Terrorist Financing Operations Section is devoted entirely to the financial aspects of terrorism investigations and liaison with the financial services industry.

Intelligence gleaned from these special information and analysis resources is placed in the appropriate format (i.e., Bulletins, Assessments, IIR, advisories) and distributed to the field through appropriate dissemination avenues.

190   Contact for the various counterterrorism program resources should be coordinated through your local FBI JTTF or FIG   The FBI Counterterrorism Division's comprehensive web page is http://www.fbi.gov/terrorinfo/counterrorism/waronterrorhome.htm.

FBI Information Sharing and Operational Coordination Initiatives

To defeat terrorists and their supporters, a wide range of organizations must work together. The FBI, therefore, has developed or refined both operational and support entities intended to bring the highest possible level of cooperation with SLTLE agencies, the Intelligence Community, and other federal government agencies.

191 On August 28, 2004, President Bush announced: "I have ordered the establishment of a national counterterrorism center. This new center builds on the capabilities of the Terrorist Threat Integration Center, … The center will become our government's central knowledge bank for information about known and suspected terrorists, and will help ensure effective joint action across the government so that our efforts against terrorists are unified in priority and purpose. Center personnel will also prepare the daily terrorism threat report that comes to me and to senior government officials." At this writing, no additional details were available. http://www.whitehouse.gov/news/releases/2004/08/20040828.html.

- Joint Terrorism Task Forces (JTTF). Cooperation has been enhanced with federal, state, local, and tribal law enforcement agencies by significantly expanding the number of JTTFs. The task forces, which are operational in nature, tackle a wide array of potential terrorist threats and conduct investigations related to terrorist activities within the geographic region where the particular JTTF is headquartered.

- The National JTTF (NJTTF). In July 2002, the FBI established the NJTTF at FBI Headquarters and staffed it with representatives from 30 federal, state, and local agencies. The NJTTF acts as a "point of fusion" for terrorism information by coordinating the flow of information between Headquarters and the other JTTFs located across the country and between the agencies represented on the NJTTF and other government agencies.

- The Office of Law Enforcement Coordination (OLEC). The OLEC was created to enhance the ability of the FBI to forge cooperation and substantive relationships with all SLTLE counterparts. The OLEC, which is managed by FBI Assistant Director Louis Quijas, a former chief of police, also has liaison responsibilities with the DHS, COPS Office, Office of Justice Programs, and other federal agencies.

Terrorist Threat Integration Center (TTIC)[191]

The mission of TTIC is to enable full integration of terrorist threat-related information and analysis derived from all information and intelligence sources in the law enforcement and intelligence communities. The center is an interagency joint venture where officers will work together to provide a comprehensive, all-source-based picture of potential terrorist threats to

U.S. interests. TTIC's structure is designed to ensure rapid and unfettered sharing of relevant information across departmental lines by collapsing bureaucratic barriers and closing interjurisdictional seams. Elements of the DHS, FBI, Central Intelligence Agency (CIA), Department of Defense, and other federal government agencies form TTIC.

> The center is an INTERAGENCY joint venture where officers will work together to provide a comprehensive, all-source-based picture of potential TERRORIST THREATS to U.S. interests.

On a daily basis, TTIC's interagency staff sifts through all-source reporting to identify terrorist plans of tactical concern as well as broader threat themes, which together help guide efforts to disrupt terrorist activities and enhance national security. TTIC also plays a key role in establishing a common threat picture by preparing daily threat assessments and updates for the President and the Departments of Defense, State, and Homeland Security, as well as the broader Intelligence Community, and by creating a consolidated website for the counterterrorism community. The center is colocated with counterterrorism elements from the CIA and FBI, further enhancing coordination efforts.

TTIC is not operational and does not collect intelligence; rather, it receives collected intelligence from other agencies (FBI, CIA, etc.) and analyzes the integrated raw information. While not dealing directly with field components of the FBI or SLTLE, the products disseminated by TTIC serve as an important source for threat development and prevention.

Terrorist Screening Center (TSC)[192]

The TSC was created to ensure that government investigators, screeners, agents, and state and local law enforcement officers have ready access to the information and expertise they need to respond quickly when a suspected terrorist is screened or stopped. The TSC consolidates access to terrorist watch lists from multiple agencies and provide 24/7 operational

192   Information for this section was gained from interviews and reviews of various courses, including testimony and press releases at http://www.fbi.gov/congress/congress04/bucella012604.htm. http://www.fbi.gov/pressrel/pressrel03/tscfactsheet091603.htm and http://www.odci.gov/cia/public_affairs/speeches/2003/wiley_speech_02262003.html.

support for thousands of federal screeners and state and local law enforcement officers across the country and around the world. The intent of the TSC is to ensure that federal, state, and local officials are working off of the same unified, comprehensive set of antiterrorist information. Since its implementation on December 1, 2003, the TSC has provided the following:

- A single coordination point for terrorist screening data
- A consolidated 24/7 call center for encounter identification assistance
- A coordinated law enforcement response to federal, state, and local law enforcement
- A formal process for tracking encounters and ensuring that feedback is supplied to the appropriate entities.

The TSC created the terrorist screening database (TSDB), a single, comprehensive source of known or appropriately suspected international and domestic terrorists. These data are available to local, state, and federal law enforcement officers through the National Crime Information Center (NCIC). When a police officer queries the NCIC, he or she may receive a notification that the query resulted in the potential match of a record within the TSDB and the officer is directed to contact the TSC to determine if it is an actual match. If it is an actual match, the TSC transfers the call to the FBI's CT Watch to provide operational guidance to the officer.

Consolidated Terrorist Screening Database

The TSC receives international and domestic terrorist identity records and maintains them in its consolidated TSDB. The TSC reviews each record to determine which are eligible for entry into the NCIC's Violent Gang and Terrorist Organization File (VGTOF) and once the record is entered into NCIC, it is accessible by state, local, and federal law enforcement officers. If a query by a law enforcement officer matches a name in NCIC, the officer will be requested, through the NCIC printout, to contact the TSC. The printout also provides the officer with instructions to arrest, detain, question, or release the subject. If the TSC determines that the person encountered by the officer is a match with a person in the NCIC/VGTOF file, the officer is immediately connected to the FBI's CT Watch for operational guidance. Depending on the situation, the CT Watch may dispatch a local JTTF agent to assist the law enforcement officer. Information that the officer obtained through the encounter is then sent back to the originating agency.

An example will illustrate the TSC's processes. On August 20, 2004, as two off-duty police officers were traveling across the Chesapeake Bay Bridge, they observed individuals filming the structure of the bridge. The officers reported this suspicious activity to the Maryland Transportation Authority (MTA) who then conducted a traffic stop of the vehicle. The MTA officers ran an NCIC check on one of the occupants of the car and learned that the individual may have a record within the TSDB. At the NCIC's request, the officers contacted the TSC and learned that the individual was the subject of the TSDB record. The TSC transferred the call to the FBI's CT Watch who informed the MTA that the individual an alleged coconspirator in a significant terrorism case. The FBI arrested the subject on a material witness warrant, and a search warrant executed at the subject's residence turned up valuable evidence. This new level of information sharing and cooperation among state, local, and federal law enforcement agencies enhances our ability to prevent a terrorist attack within the United States.

Department of Homeland Security[193]

The DHS, through the Directorate of Information Analysis and Infrastructure Protection (IAIP), will merge the capability to identify and assess current and future threats to the homeland, map those threats against our vulnerabilities, issue timely warnings, and take preventive and protective action.

Intelligence Analysis and Alerts

Actionable intelligence, that is, information that can lead to stopping or apprehending terrorists, is essential to the primary mission of DHS. The timely and thorough analysis and dissemination of information about terrorists and their activities will improve the government's ability to disrupt and prevent terrorist acts and to provide useful warning to the private sector and our population. The IAIP Directorate will fuse and analyze

193 The intelligence component of DHS is in the Information Analysis and Infrastructure Protection (IAIP) Directorate: http://www.intelligence.gov/1-members_dhs.shtml. For current information on DHS threats and security, see http://www.dhs.gov/dhspublic/theme_home6.jsp.

information from multiple sources pertaining to terrorist threats. The DHS will be a full partner and consumer of all intelligence-generating agencies, such as the National Security Agency, the CIA, and the FBI.

The DHS's threat analysis and warning functions will support the President and, as he directs, other national decision makers responsible for securing the homeland from terrorism. It will coordinate and, as appropriate, consolidate the federal government's lines of communication with state and local public safety agencies and with the private sector, creating a coherent and efficient system for conveying actionable intelligence and other threat information. The IAIP Directorate also administers the HSAS.

Critical Infrastructure Protection

The attacks of September 11 highlighted the fact that terrorists are capable of causing enormous damage to our country by attacking our critical infrastructure; food, water, agriculture, and health and emergency services; energy sources (electrical, nuclear, gas and oil, dams); transportation (air, road, rail, ports, waterways); information and telecommunications networks; banking and finance systems; postal services; and other assets and systems vital to our national security, public health and safety, economy, and way of life.

Protecting America's critical infrastructure is the shared responsibility of federal, state, and local government, in active partnership with the private sector, which owns approximately 85 percent of our nation's critical infrastructure. The IAIP Directorate will take the lead in coordinating the national effort to secure the nation's infrastructure. This will give state, local, and private entities one primary contact instead of many for coordinating protection activities within the federal government, including vulnerability assessments, strategic planning efforts, and exercises.

Cyber Security

Our nation's information and telecommunications systems are directly connected to many other critical infrastructure sectors, including banking and finance, energy, and transportation. The consequences of an attack on our cyber infrastructure can cascade across many sectors, causing widespread disruption of essential services, damaging our economy, and imperiling public safety. The speed, virulence, and maliciousness of cyber attacks have increased dramatically in recent years. Accordingly, the IAIP Directorate places an especially high priority on protecting our cyber infrastructure from terrorist attack by unifying and focusing the key cyber security activities performed by the Critical Infrastructure Assurance Office (currently part of the Department of Commerce) and the former National Infrastructure Protection Center (FBI). The IAIP Directorate will augment those capabilities with the response functions of the National Cyber Security Division (NCSD) United States Computer Emergency Response Team (US-CERT).[194] Because our information and telecommunications sectors are increasingly interconnected, DHS will also assume the functions and assets of the National Communications System (Department of Defense), which coordinates emergency preparedness for the telecommunications sector.

Indications and Warning Advisories

In advance of real-time crisis or attack, the IAIP Directorate will provide the following:

- Coordinated DHS-FBI threat warnings and advisories against the homeland, including physical and cyber events[195]
- Processes to develop and issue national and sector-specific threat advisories through the HSAS
- Terrorist threat information for release to the public, private industry, or state and local governments.

Figure 11-1 illustrates DHS and intelligence and threat assessment processes. DHS-FBI advisories are produced in several forms. Figures 11-2, 11-3, 11-4, and 11-5 are illustrations of DHS advisory templates. SLTLE agencies have access to these advisories through the various secure law enforcement email systems (i.e., NLETS, LEO, JRIES, Regional Information Sharing Systems [RISS.net], Anti-Terrorism Information Exchange [ATIX]).

194   http://www.us-cert.gov.

195   http://www.dhs.gov/
dhspublic/verify_redirect.jsp
?url=http://www.us-
cert.gov&title=cyber+events.

Figure 11-1: DHS and Intelligence and Threat Assessment Processes

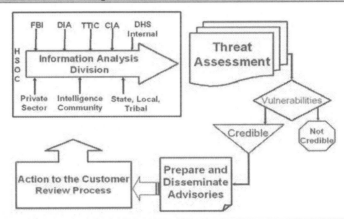

Figure 11-2: DHS Operations Morning Brief

UNCLASSIFIED//FOR OFFICIAL USE ONLY//LAW ENFORCEMENT SENSITIVE

U.S. Department of Homeland Security — Homeland Security Operations Center

WARNING: This document is FOR OFFICIAL USE ONLY. This information shall not be distributed beyond the original addressees without prior authorization of the originator. It contains information that may be exempt from public release under the Freedom of Information Act (5 U.S.C. 552). It is to be controlled, handled, transmitted, distributed, and disposed of in accordance with DHS policy relating to FOUO information and is not to be released to the public or other personnel who do not have a valid "need-to-know" without prior approval of an authorized DHS official.

Homeland Security Operations Morning Brief
DD Month YYYY

Overnight Developments

1. (U//FOUO//LES) STATE: Title. According to CBP reporting, on DD MMM, HSOC initiated name checks. (CBP Morning Report___Mmm YY; ___; HSOC___)

2. (U//FOUO//LES) STATE: Title. According to CBP reporting, on DD MMM, HSOC initiated name checks. (CBP Morning Report___Mmm YY; ___; HSOC___)

3. (U//FOUO//LES) STATE: Title. According to CBP reporting, on DD MMM, HSOC initiated name checks. (CBP Morning Report___Mmm YY; ___; HSOC___)

4. (U//FOUO//LES) STATE: Title. According to CBP reporting, on DD MMM, HSOC initiated name checks. (CBP Morning Report___Mmm YY; ___; HSOC___)

5. (U//FOUO//LES) STATE: Title. According to CBP reporting, on DD MMM, HSOC initiated name checks. (CBP Morning Report___Mmm YY; ___; HSOC___)

Page 1 of 1
Homeland Security Operations Morning Brief   dd Month YYYY
UNCLASSIFIED//FOR OFFICIAL USE ONLY//LAW ENFORCEMENT SENSITIVE
Third Agency Dissemination of This Material is prohibited Without Prior DHS Approval.
This document is for deterring, detecting, and preventing terrorism. It contains law
enforcement sensitive material and may be shared appropriately, but should be
protected from public dissemination.

Figure 11-3: DHS Information Bulletin

Information Bulletin
Title: _____
Date: _____

LIMITED DISTRIBUTION: Any release, dissemination, or sharing of this document, or any information contained herein, is not authorized without the express approval of the Department of Homeland Security (DHS). This information is intended for entities identified on the attention line below. All requests for further distribution must be submitted to the DHS Information Management and Requirements Division at 202-282-8168. After business hours contact the DHS Homeland Security Operations Center at Phone (202) 282-8101.

ATTENTION: Provide guidance as to who within an organization may have primary responsibility for taking action on this product. Examples: Physical Security Officers, Facility Managers, etc.

OVERVIEW
Provide a concise summation of the information in the bulletin, a disclaimer as to the intention of the product, and any limitations as to the further dissemination of this product by the intended recipients.

Homeland Security Information Bulletins are informational in nature and are designed to provide updates on the training, tactics, or strategies of terrorists.

DHS Information Bulletins communicate issues that pertain to the critical national infrastructure and are for informational purposes only.

DETAILS
[This section provides the DHS assessment of the information, any recommendations or resultant changes to procedures or processes, and any other applicable information for the consumer.]

SUGGESTED PROTECTIVE MEASURES
[This section provides the DHS recommended protective actions for immediate implementation, including best practices when available.]

Concluding paragraphs:

DHS encourages recipients of this Information Bulletin to report information concerning suspicious or criminal activity to local law enforcement, local FBI's Joint Terrorism Task Force or the Homeland Security Operations Center (HSOC). The HSOC may be contacted at: Phone: (202) 282-8101.
DHS intends to update this advisory should it receive additional relevant information, including information provided to it by the user community. Based on this notification, no change to the Homeland Security Advisory System (HSAS) level is anticipated; the current HSAS level is _____ .

Information Bulletin

Figure 11-4: DHS Physical Advisory

Advisory
Title _____
Date : _____

LIMITED DISTRIBUTION: Any release, dissemination, or sharing of this document, or any information contained herein, is not authorized without the express approval of the Department of Homeland Security (DHS). This information is intended for entities identified on the attention line below. All requests for further distribution must be submitted to the DHS Information Management and Requirements Division at 202-282-8168. After business hours contact the DHS Homeland Security Operations Center at Phone (202) 282-8101.

ATTENTION: Provide guidance as to who within an organization may have primary responsibility for taking action on this product. Examples: Physical Security Officers, Facility Managers, etc.

OVERVIEW
Provide one or two sentences in the form of an executive summary of the warning. This may be all a recipient reviews upon initial notification due to the limited storage or viewing capacities of electronic paging devices.

DETAILS
This section provides the DHS assessment of the threat, recommendations and solutions for handling the issue, and any other applicable information for the consumer.

SUGGESTED PROTECTIVE MEASURES

This section provides the DHS recommended protective actions for immediate implementation, including best practices when available.

Concluding paragraphs:

DHS encourages recipients of this Advisory to report information concerning suspicious or criminal activity to local law enforcement, local FBI's Joint Terrorism Task Force or the Homeland Security Operations Center (HSOC). The HSOC may be contacted at: Phone: (202) 282-8101.

DHS intends to update this advisory should it receive additional relevant information, including information provided to it by the user community. Based on this notification, no change to the Homeland Security Advisory System (HSAS) level is anticipated; the current HSAS level is _____.

Protecting America's CRITICAL INFRASTRUCTURE is the shared responsibility of FEDERAL, STATE, and LOCAL government, in active PARTNERSHIP with the private sector…

Figure 11-5: DHS Cyber Advisory

Advisory
Title: _____
Date: _____

SYSTEMS AFFECTED [Insert list of systems affected by the threat/vulnerability]

OVERVIEW
[Insert a concise synopsis/summary of the threat/vulnerability.]

IMPACT
[The severity of the threat against the affected system(s) depends upon one or more of the following:
 - widespread use of the affected system(s)
 - mission criticality of the applications running on affected system(s)
 - type(s) of affected system(s).
Available analysis of potential or realized impacts will be inserted here.]

DETAILS
[Insert authorized details on the threat/vulnerability.]

SUGGESTED PROTECTIVE MEASURES
DHS is working with other government agencies, network security experts, and industry representatives to define, prioritize, and mitigate these vulnerabilities. DHS encourages implementation of industry best practices. Additionally, the following suggested workarounds and other mitigation steps are provided:

[Insert detailed threat and vulnerability steps including locations for obtaining patches and vulnerability assessments if available.]

Concluding paragraphs:

DHS encourages recipients of this Advisory to report information concerning suspicious or criminal activity to local law enforcement, local FBI's Joint Terrorism Task Force or the Homeland Security Operations Center (HSOC). The HSOC may be contacted at: Phone: (202) 282-8101.

DHS intends to update this advisory should it receive additional relevant information, including information provided to it by the user community. Based on this notification, no change to the Homeland Security Advisory System (HSAS) level is anticipated; the current HSAS level is _____.

Drug Enforcement Administration[196]

Since its establishment in 1973, the DEA, in coordination with other federal, state, local, and foreign law enforcement organizations, has been responsible for the collection, analysis, and dissemination of drug-related intelligence. The role of intelligence in drug law enforcement is critical. The DEA Intelligence Program helps initiate new investigations of major drug organizations, strengthens ongoing investigations and subsequent prosecutions, develops information that leads to seizures and arrests, and provides policy makers with drug trend information on which they can base programmatic decisions. The specific functions of the DEA's intelligence mission are as follows:

- Collect and produce intelligence in support of the administrator and other federal, state, and local agencies
- Establish and maintain close working relationships with all agencies that produce or use narcotics intelligence
- Increase the efficiency in the reporting, analysis, storage, retrieval, and exchange of such information;
- Undertake a continuing review of the narcotics intelligence effort to identify and correct deficiencies.

The DEA's Intelligence Program has grown significantly since its inception. From only a handful of intelligence analysts (I/A) in the domestic offices and Headquarters in 1973, the total number of intelligence analysts worldwide is now more than 680. DEA's intelligence Program consists of several entities that are staffed by both intelligence analysts and special agents: Intelligence groups and functions in the domestic field divisions, district, resident and foreign offices, the El Paso Intelligence Center, and the Intelligence Division at DEA Headquarters. Program responsibility for the DEA's intelligence mission rests with the DEA assistant administrator for intelligence.

[196] A number of DEA Strategic Intelligence Reports are available online at http://www.dea.gov. For other intelligence reports and related information, contact your nearest DEA Field Office http://www.usdoj.gov/dea/pubs/international/foreign.html.

Legislation and presidential directives and orders have expanded the role of the Intelligence Community and the Department of Defense in the anti-drug effort. DEA interaction with both components occurs on a daily basis in the foreign field and at Headquarters. At the strategic intelligence level, the Intelligence Division participates in a wide range of interagency assessment and targeting groups that incorporate drug intelligence from the antidrug community to provide policymakers with all-source drug trend and trafficking reporting.

With analytical support from the Intelligence Program, DEA has disrupted major trafficking organizations or put them entirely out of business. The DEA Intelligence Division also cooperates a great deal with state and local law enforcement and will soon provide intelligence training for state, local, federal, and foreign agencies. This training will be held at the Justice Training Center in Quantico, Virginia, and will address the full spectrum of drug intelligence training needs. The best practices and theories of all partners in working the drug issue will be solicited and incorporated into the training. Academic programs, the exchange of federal, state, and local drug experience, and the sharing of, and exposure to, new ideas will result in more effective application of drug intelligence resources at all levels. The DEA divides drug intelligence into three broad categories: tactical, investigative, and strategic.

- Tactical intelligence is evaluated information on which immediate enforcement action – arrests, seizures, and interdictions – can be based.
- Investigative intelligence provides analytical support to investigations and prosecutions to dismantle criminal organizations and gain resources.
- Strategic intelligence focuses on the current picture of drug trafficking from cultivation to distribution that can be used for management decision making, resource deployment, and policy planning.

Intelligence Products

Tactical and investigative intelligence is available to SLTLE agencies through the local DEA field office. In addition, intelligence can be shared with state, local, and tribal agencies through secure email. Many strategic intelligence reports are available on the DEA website.[197] Reports that are "Law Enforcement Sensitive" can be obtained through the local DEA office.

197 See http://www.dea.gov/pubs/publications.html.

El Paso Intelligence Center (EPIC)[198]

The El Paso Intelligence Center (EPIC) was established in 1974 in response to a Department of Justice study. The study, which detailed drug and border enforcement strategy and programs, proposed the establishment of a southwest border intelligence service center staffed by representatives of the Immigration and Naturalization Service, the U.S. Customs Service, and the DEA. The original EPIC staff comprised 17 employees from the three founding agencies. Initially, EPIC focused on the U.S.-Mexico border and its primary interest was drug movement and immigration violations.

Today, EPIC still concentrates primarily on drug movement and immigration violations. Because these criminal activities are seldom limited to one geographic area, EPIC's focus has broadened to include all of the United States and the Western Hemisphere where drug and alien movements are directed toward the United States. Staffing at the DEA-led center has increased to more than 300 analysts, agents, and support personnel from 15 federal agencies, the Texas Department of Public Safety, and the Texas Air National Guard. Information-sharing agreements with other federal law enforcement agencies, the Royal Canadian Mounted Police, and each of the 50 states ensure that EPIC support is available to those who need it. A telephone call, fax, or email from any of these agencies provides the requestor with real-time information from different federal databases, plus EPIC's own internal database.

In addition to these services, a number of EPIC programs are dedicated to post-seizure analysis and the establishment of links between recent enforcement actions and ongoing investigations. EPIC also coordinates training for state and local officers in the methods of highway drug and drug currency interdiction through its Operation Pipeline program. In addition, EPIC personnel coordinate and conduct training seminars throughout the United States, covering such topics as indicators of trafficking and concealment methods used by couriers.

In a continuing effort to stay abreast of changing trends, EPIC has developed the National Clandestine Laboratory Seizure Database. EPIC's future course will be driven by the National General Counterdrug

[198] See http://www.dea.gov/programs/epic.htm.

Intelligence Plan, as well. As a major national center in the new drug intelligence architecture, EPIC will serve as a clearinghouse for the High-Intensity Drug Trafficking Areas (HITDA) Intelligence Centers, gathering state and local law enforcement drug information and providing drug intelligence back to the HIDTA Intelligence Centers.

National Drug Pointer Index (NDPIX) and National Virtual Pointer System (NVPS)[199]

For many years, state and local law enforcement envisioned a drug pointer system that would allow them to determine if other law enforcement organizations were investigating the same drug suspect. The DEA was designated by the Office of National Drug Control Policy in 1992 to take the lead in developing a national drug pointer system to assist federal, state, and local law enforcement agencies investigating drug trafficking organizations and to enhance officer safety by preventing duplicate investigations. The DEA drew from the experience of state and local agencies to make certain that their concerns were addressed and that they had extensive input and involvement in the development of the system.

[199] See http://www.dea.gov/programs/ndpix.htm.

> The National Law Enforcement Telecommunications System (NLETS)-a familiar, fast, and effective network that reaches into almost every police entity in the United States-is the backbone of the NDPIX.

The National Drug Pointer Index (NDPIX) became operational across the United States in October 1997. The National Law Enforcement Telecommunications System (NLETS)—a familiar, fast, and effective network that reaches into almost every police entity in the United States—is the backbone of the NDPIX. Participating agencies are required to submit active case-targeting information to NDPIX to receive pointer information from the NDPIX. The greater the number of data elements entered, the greater the likelihood of identifying possible matches. Designed to be a true pointer system, the NDPIX merely serves as a "switchboard" that provides a vehicle for timely notification of common investigative targets. The actual case information is shared only when telephonic contact is made between the officers or agents who have been linked by their entries into the NDPIX.

NDPIX was developed to: (1) promote information sharing; (2) facilitate drug-related investigations; (3) prevent duplicate investigations; (4) increase coordination among federal, state, and local law enforcement agencies; and (5) enhance the personal safety of law enforcement officers. At this writing, NDPIX is being transitioned and upgraded to the National Virtual Pointer System (NVPS). A steering committee—which included DEA, HIDTA, RISS, the National Drug Intelligence Center (NDIC), the National Institute of Justice (NIJ), the National Sheriff's Association (NSA), the International Association of Chiefs of Police (IACP), and the National Alliance of State Drug Enforcement Agencies (NASDEA)—developed the specifications for the system and is overseeing its testing and transition.

Characteristics of the NVPS will include the following:

- It will cover all crimes, not just drugs.
- The system will accept only targets of open investigations with assigned case numbers.
- Transaction formats will contain an identifying field for the NVPS Identifier.
- It will use a secure telecommunications network.
- It will use the NDPIX "Mandatory" data elements.
- A single sign-on from any participant will allow access to all participating pointer databases.
- Each system will provide a userid and password to its respective users.
- Each system will maintain its own data.
- Uniform Crime Reporting (UCR) or the National Incident-Based Reporting System (NIBRS) codes will be used to identify type of crime.
- The system will target deconfliction for all crimes.
- It will rely on web-based communications.
- NVPS will have links with HIDTA and RISS.

An important aspect of the links with NVPS will be that NDPIX participants will continue to use their existing formats and procedures for entries, updates, and renewals and NDPIX notifications will continue in the same formats. The transition to NVPS will be seamless. This change represents an important upgrade to networked intelligence that can be of value to all law enforcement agencies.

National Drug Intelligence Center (NDIC)[200]

The National Drug Intelligence Center (NDIC), established in 1993, is a component of the U.S. Department of Justice and a member of the Intelligence Community. The General Counterdrug Intelligence Plan, implemented in February 2000, designated NDIC as the nation's principal center for strategic domestic counterdrug intelligence. The intent of NDIC is to meet three fundamental missions:

- To support national policymakers and law enforcement decision makers with strategic domestic drug intelligence
- To support Intelligence Community counterdrug efforts
- To produce national, regional, and state drug threat assessments.

The Intelligence Division consists of six geographic units and four specialized units. The six geographic units correspond to the regions of the Department of Justice Organized Crime Drug Enforcement Task Force (OCDETF)[201] program and concentrate on drug trafficking and abuse. The four specialized units include the Drug Trends Analysis Unit, the Organized Crime and Violence Unit, the National Drug Threat Assessment Unit, and the National Interdiction Support Unit.

Within the geographic units, NDIC intelligence analysts cover each state and various U.S. territories. Intelligence analysts maintain extensive contacts with federal, state, and local law enforcement and Intelligence Community personnel in all 50 states, the District of Columbia, Puerto Rico, the Virgin Islands, and the Pacific territories of Guam, American Samoa, and the Northern Mariana Islands. NDIC collaborates with other agencies such as the DEA, FBI, U.S. Coast Guard, Bureau of Alcohol, Tobacco, Firearms and Explosives (ATF), the Bureau of Prisons, and the Office of

200   See http://www.usdoj.gov/ndic.

201   While the OCDETFs are operational, not intelligence entities, they are not only consumers of intelligence, but are also sources for information collection. For more information see http://www.usdoj.gov/dea/programs/ocdetf.htm.

National Drug Control Policy (ONDCP). NDIC is one of four national intelligence centers including the EPIC, the U.S. Department of the Treasury's Financial Crimes Enforcement Network (FinCEN), and the DCI Crime and Narcotics Center (CNC). NDIC also works closely with the High Intensity Drug Trafficking Areas (HIDTAs) and the OCDETF.

Intelligence Products

Threat assessments, NDIC's primary intelligence products, provide policy makers and counterdrug executives with timely, predictive reports of the threat posed by illicit drugs in the United States.

- The *National Drug Threat Assessment*, NDIC's major intelligence product, is a comprehensive annual report on national drug trafficking and abuse trends within the United States. The assessment identifies the primary drug threat to the nation, monitors fluctuations in consumption levels, tracks drug availability by geographic market, and analyzes trafficking and distribution patterns. The report highlights the most current quantitative and qualitative information on availability, demand, production and cultivation, transportation, and distribution, as well as the effects of a particular drug on abusers and society as a whole.
- *State Drug Threat Assessment* provides a detailed threat assessment of drug trends within a particular state. Each report identifies the primary drug threat in the state and gives a detailed overview of the most current trends by drug type.
- *Information Bulletins* are developed in response to new trends or high-priority drug issues. They are relayed quickly to the law enforcement and intelligence communities and are intended to warn law enforcement officials of emerging trends.

High-Intensity Drug Trafficking Areas (HIDTA) Regional Intelligence Centers[202]

The HIDTA Intelligence System has more than 1,500 law enforcement personnel, mostly criminal intelligence analysts, participating full time in more than 60 intelligence initiatives in the 28 HIDTA designated areas

202 See http://www.whitehousedrugpol icy.gov/hidta for HIDTA points of contact.

throughout the United States. While HIDTA is a counterdrug program, the intelligence centers operate in a general criminal intelligence environment, thereby leveraging all criminal intelligence information for the program's primary mission.[203]

The HIDTA Intelligence System, a core element in the creation and growth of many SLTLE intelligence programs, largely depends on HIDTA program mandates. Each HIDTA must establish an intelligence center comanaged by a federal and a state or local law enforcement agency. The core mission of each individual HIDTA Intelligence Center is to provide tactical, operational, and strategic intelligence support to its HIDTA executive board, a group of participating law enforcement agency principals responsible for the daily management of their respective HIDTAs, HIDTA-funded task forces, and other regional HIDTAs. Developing regional threat assessments and providing event and target deconfliction are also among the centers' core missions. These core functions are critical to building trust and breaking down parochialism between and among the local, state, and federal participating law enforcement agencies.

The plan to connect all HIDTA Intelligence Centers through RISS.net was initiated by the HIDTA Program Office at ONDCP in 1999 and completed in mid-2003. The HIDTA Program Office has commissioned interagency and interdisciplinary working committees to develop a national information-sharing plan, focusing on issues relating to legal, agency policy, privacy, technical, and logistical information-sharing matters. HIDTA program and committee personnel are coordinating with, and implementing recommendations made by, other information-sharing initiatives such as Global, Matrix, and federally sponsored intelligence programs.[204]

Bureau of Alcohol, Tobacco, Firearms and Explosives (ATF)[205]

The Intelligence Division of ATF has evolved rapidly as an important tool for the diverse responsibilities of the bureau. Several activities in particular demonstrate the intelligence capability and resources of ATF.

203 http://policechiefmagazine.org/magazine/index.cfm?fuseaction=display_arch&article_id=139&issue_id=11200.

204 As an illustration of the comprehensive and integrated nature of the HIDTA programs and intelligence centers, see http://www.ncjrs.org/ondcppubs/publications/enforce/hidta2001/ca-fs.html.

205 Contact your local ATF Field Office for Intelligence Products and resources. Offices and contact information can be found at http://www.atf.gov/field/index.htm.

The ATF, which is now an agency of the Department of Justice, has developed Field Intelligence Groups at each of its 23 Field Divisions strategically located throughout the United States. These intelligence groups meld the training and experience of special agents, intelligence research specialists, industry operations inspectors, and support staff who focus on providing tactical intelligence support for their respective field divisions and their external law enforcement partners. Each Field Intelligence Group works under the authority of a supervisory special agent. The intelligence group supervisors are coordinated by, and work in conjunction with, the Intelligence Division to form a bureau-wide intelligence infrastructure. The Intelligence Division has provided indoctrination and training for all Field Intelligence Group supervisors, intelligence officers, and intelligence research specialists.

> ... the [ATF] Intelligence Division spearheaded the formulation of an MOU with the FBI to collaborate on investigations conducted by JOINT TERRORISM TASK FORCES located throughout the United States.

ATF maintains intelligence partnerships with the NDIC, EPIC, FinCEN, INTERPOL, the Federal Bureau of Investigation Counter Terrorism Center, (FBI/CTC) and other international intelligence sources. Furthermore, ATF maintains a memorandum of understanding (MOU) with the six Regional Information Sharing Systems (RISS) that represent thousands of SLTLE agencies, pledging to share unique and vital intelligence resources. These external partners are key components of ATF's Strategic Intelligence Plan and the means by which ATF ensures a maximum contribution to the nation's law enforcement and intelligence communities.

During FY 2000, the Intelligence Division spearheaded the formulation of an MOU with the FBI to collaborate on investigations conducted by Joint Terrorism Task Forces located throughout the United States. This MOU brings ATF's unique knowledge and skills of explosives and firearms violations to the FBI's expertise in terrorism.

The Intelligence Division has implemented a state-of-the-art automated case management/ intelligence reporting system called N-FOCIS (National Field Office Case Information System). The system consists of two companion applications: N-FORCE for special agents and N-SPECT for industry operations inspectors. Both eliminate redundant manual data entry on hard copy forms and provide a comprehensive reporting and information management application in a secure electronic environment.

N-FOCIS constitutes an online case management system and electronic central information repository that allows ATF to analyze and fully exploit investigative intelligence. N-FOCIS epitomizes the strength and unique value of ATF's combined criminal and industry operations enforcement missions. The Intelligence Division has provided in-service training to many of the ATF field division special agents, investigative assistants, and inspectors on the use of the N-FOCIS applications. ATF is planning to expand the N-FOCIS functionality and to integrate N-FOCIS with several key ATF applications including the National Revenue Center, the National Tracing Center, National Arson and Explosive Repository, and the Intelligence Division's Text Management System. This integration plan establishes N-FOCIS as the bureau's information backbone.

The Intelligence Division prepares a wide range of strategic intelligence reports related to the ATF mission that are available to SLTLE. In addition, intelligence is shared with state and local agencies through RISS and the JTTFs. In addition, ATF will readily respond to inquiries wherein SBU information may be shared.

ATF has also created a series of Regional Crime Gun Centers. The intent of the centers is to integrate gun tracing with ATF intelligence as well as with the HIDTA Regional Intelligence Centers to suppress gun-related crime.[206]

Financial Crimes Enforcement Network (FinCEN)[207]

The Financial Crimes Enforcement Network (FinCEN) is a network designed to bring agencies, investigators, and information together to fight the complex problem of money laundering. Since its creation in 1990, FinCEN

206   As an illustration see http://www.atf.gov/field/newyork/rcgc/index.htm.

207   See http://www.fincen.gov.

has worked to maximize information sharing among law enforcement agencies and its other partners in the regulatory and financial communities. Through cooperation and partnerships, FinCEN's network approach encourages cost-effective and efficient measures to combat money laundering domestically and internationally.

The network supports federal, state, local, tribal, and international law enforcement by analyzing information required under the Bank Secrecy Act (BSA), one of the nation's most important tools in the fight against money laundering. The BSA's record keeping and reporting requirements establish a financial trail for investigators to follow as they track criminals, their activities, and their assets. Over the years, FinCEN staff has developed its expertise in adding value to the information collected under the BSA by uncovering leads and exposing unknown pieces of information contained in the complexities of money laundering schemes.

Illicit financial transactions can take many routes – some complex, some simple, but all increasingly inventive – with the ultimate goal being to disguise its source. The money can move through banks, check cashers, money transmitters, businesses, casinos, and is often sent overseas to become "clean." The tools of the money launderer can range from complicated financial transactions, carried out through webs of wire transfers and networks of shell companies, to old-fashioned currency smuggling.

Intelligence research specialists and law enforcement support staff research and analyze this information and other critical forms of intelligence to support financial criminal investigations. The ability to network with a variety of databases provides FinCEN with one of the largest repositories of information available to law enforcement in the country. Safeguarding the privacy of the data it collects is an overriding responsibility of the agency and its employees-a responsibility that strongly imprints all of its data management functions and operations.

FinCEN's information sources fall into three categories:

- *Financial Database:* The financial database consists of reports that the BSA requires to be filed, such as data on large currency transactions conducted at financial institutions or casinos, suspicious transactions, and international movements of currency or negotiable monetary instruments. This information often provides invaluable assistance for investigators because it is not readily available from any other source and preserves a financial paper trail for investigators to track criminals' proceeds and their assets.

- *Commercial Databases:* Information from commercially available sources plays an increasingly vital role in criminal investigations. Commercial databases include information such as state, corporation, property, and people locator records, as well as professional licenses and vehicle registrations.
- *Law Enforcement Databases:* FinCEN is able to access various law enforcement databases through written agreements with each agency.

FinCEN works closely with the International Association of Chiefs of Police (IACP), National Association of Attorneys General (NAAG), National White Collar Crime Center (NW3C), and other organizations to inform law enforcement about the information that is available at FinCEN and how to use that information to attack criminal proceeds.

High Risk Money Laundering and Related Financial Crimes Areas (HIFCA)[208]

HIFCAs were first announced in the 1999 National Money Laundering Strategy and were conceived in the Money Laundering and Financial Crimes Strategy Act of 1998 as a means of concentrating law enforcement efforts at the federal, state, and local levels in highintensity money laundering zones. HIFCAs may be defined geographically or they can also be created to address money laundering in an industry sector, a financial institution, or group of financial institutions.

The HIFCA program is intended to concentrate law enforcement efforts at the federal, state, and local levels to combat money laundering in designated high-intensity money laundering zones. To implement this goal, a money laundering action team will be created or identified within each HIFCA to spearhead a coordinated federal, state, and local antimoney laundering effort. Each action team will: (1) be composed of all relevant

208 See http://www.fincen.gov/le_hifca design.html.

federal, state, and local enforcement authorities, prosecutors, and financial regulators; (2) focus on tracing funds to the HIFCA from other areas, and from the HIFCA to other areas so that related investigations can be undertaken; (3) focus on collaborative investigative techniques, both within the HIFCA and between the HIFCA and other areas; (4) ensure a more systemic exchange of information on money laundering between HIFCA participants; and (5) include an asset forfeiture component as part of its work.

Gateway

FinCEN's Gateway system enables federal, state, and local law enforcement agencies to have online access to records filed under the BSA. The system saves investigative time and money by enabling investigators to conduct their own research and analysis of BSA data rather than relying on the resources of an intermediary agency to obtain financial records. A unique feature of Gateway is the "query alert" mechanism that automatically signals FinCEN when two or more agencies have an interest in the same subject. In this way, FinCEN is able to assist participating agencies in coordinating their investigations.

Virtually every criminal enterprise and terrorist organization is involved in some dimension of money laundering. The complexities of forensic accounting, often complicated by jurisdictional barriers, reinforces the need for intelligence personnel to be aware of the resources and expertise available through FinCEN.

CONCLUSION

As demonstrated in this chapter, the amount of information and intelligence being generated by federal law enforcement agencies is significant. If that information is not being used, then its value is lost. Not only are federal agencies responsible for making information available to SLTLE agencies in an accessible and consumable form, nonfederal law enforcement must develop the mechanisms for receiving the information and to be good consumers of it.

One of the ongoing controversies is the problem of dealing with classified information. This chapter explained the classification process as well as the initiatives that are being undertaken to deal with this issue. One measure is to increase the number of security clearances for SLTLE personnel. The other measure is for the FBI to write intelligence reports so that they are unclassified, but remain Law Enforcement Sensitive (LES) in order to give SLTLE personnel access.

By gaining access to secure networking (e.g., LEO, RISS.net, ATIX, JRIES), interacting on a regular basis with the FBI Field Intelligence Group (FIG), and proactively interacting with other federal law enforcement intelligence offices, SLTLE can have access to the types of critical intelligence necessary to protect their communities.

Summary, Conclusions, and Next Steps

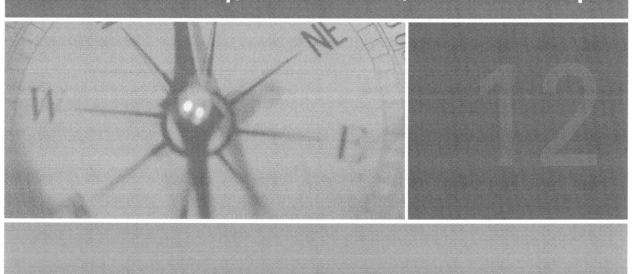

12

Summary, Conclusions, and Next Steps

Effective law enforcement intelligence operations are confusing, controversial, difficult, and effective. Intelligence is confusing because many people do not make the distinction between law enforcement intelligence and national security intelligence. Moreover, the term is used generically to describe a wide body of activities, thereby contributing to the confusion. One purpose of this guide was to provide consistent and clear definitions that are accepted by both law enforcement intelligence professionals and the national standards of the National Criminal Intelligence Sharing Plan, Global Justice Information Sharing Initiative, and the Global Intelligence Working Group.

Law enforcement intelligence operations are controversial both because of the checkered history of intelligence activities as well as the concern of many today that in the zeal to prevent terrorism, citizens' civil rights will be abridged. There is no doubt that law enforcement suffered some setbacks as a result of lawsuits against law enforcement intelligence practices of the 1950s and 1960s. However, with those setbacks important lessons were learned that not only set the stage for 28 CFR Part 23, but helped lay the foundation for law enforcement intelligence as a profession today.

Further controversies face law enforcement today as concerned citizens and civil rights groups, who often do not fully understand the intelligence function, fear that law enforcement agencies will gather and keep information about citizens who have not committed crimes but are exercising their civil rights on controversial issues. The lessons law enforcement has learned from pubic education and community policing initiatives can help eliminate these fears—not only through the practice of ethical policing[209] but also by reaching out to diverse communities to explain police practices, respond to questions, and establishing open, trusted lines of communication.[210]

Intelligence operations are difficult as well. It requires work to establish links with different law enforcement organizations and groups to maximize effective information sharing. It also requires a redistribution of resources to make the intelligence function perform effectively and to meet operational and training standards set out in the National Criminal Intelligence Sharing Plan. A change in culture is required for Intelligence-Led Policing to become a reality and a realignment of priorities may be needed to accomplish new goals. There is always resistance to change and always legitimate competing interests that must be weighed.

Finally, law enforcement intelligence processes can be effective. Intelligence can help identify suspected criminals, targets of terrorists, and activities of criminal enterprises that occur in a community. It takes diverse and often disparate information, integrates it into a cohesive package, and provides insight that might otherwise be lost. Increasingly, law enforcement intelligence is more thorough, of higher quality, and disseminated more broadly as a result of cooperative initiatives such as the

209 The COPS Regional Community Policing Institutes RCPI have a variety of training curricula for executives and line officers on different aspects of ethical policing. Agencies should contact the RCPI in their region for training opportunities. RCPIs can be found by state at: http://www.cops.usdoj.gov/default.asp?Item=229.

210 The COPS Office sponsored an executive session with the Police Executive Research Forum that examined this topic. The resulting white paper, *Working with Diverse Communities*, is a valuable resource. It can be found at: http://www.cops.usdoj.gov/mime/open.pdf?Item=1364.

National Criminal Intelligence Sharing Plan and the Global Justice Information Sharing Initiative, particularly through its subcommittee, the Global Intelligence Working Group. Similarly, there is a greater emphasis on law enforcement intelligence and a renewed spirit of partnership between the FBI and state, local, and tribal law enforcement (SLTLE) agencies that is already bearing fruit. The end result of all of these initiatives is to make our communities safer; hence, the investment pays important dividends for protecting our citizens.

> Similarly, there is a greater emphasis on law enforcement INTELLIGENCE and a renewed SPIRIT of partnership between the FBI and state, local, and tribal law enforcement (SLTLE) agencies that is already bearing fruit.

IMPLEMENTING CHANGE: THE R-CUBED APPROACH[211]

Implementing new intelligence initiatives can be difficult. As a road map to accomplish this, the author recommends a process referred to as "R-cubed": Reassessing, Refocusing, and Reallocating (R3).

The intent of the R3 exercise is to provide a framework for organizational change as related to intelligence responsibilities. It requires a critical self-assessment of responsibilities and resources; objectivity absent special interests; realistic perspectives; both tactical and strategic considerations of traditional and new policing responsibilities; and methods (including financing) of how all police responsibilities will be accomplished. This is a labor-intensive, difficult process that cannot be rushed and should be inclusive, that is, consideration of the inputs of others—employees, community members, elected officials, other agencies—should be included in the process. Final decisions, however, remain with law enforcement administrators to make changes as best determined by their collective judgment of responsibilities, priorities, and available resources.

211 Carter, David L. (2000). The Police and Community. 7th ed. Upper Saddle River, NJ: Prentice-Hall.

A number of factors may be included in each component of the R3 exercise, as described below.

Reassessing

Examine both current priorities and new priorities for intelligence and homeland security to determine what activities need to be continued to maintain community safety and fulfill the police mission related to crime, order maintenance, and terrorism. This assessment should include consideration of a number of variables, such as the following:

- The number of calls for service received by the police department and the ability to handle those calls for service.
- Specialization currently in the police department, e.g., gangs, narcotics, school programs, initiatives directed toward senior citizens, traffic, etc., and the true demand or need for that specialization
  – Objectivity is critical because special interests can skew priorities
- Specialization that needs to be developed, e.g., intelligence capacity; first responder (including weapons of mass destruction); computer crime/cyberterrorism prevention and investigative expertise; investigative capacity for terrorism; obligation to assign personnel to the Joint Terrorism Task Force
- Resources that can be used to help with police responsibilities of all forms, e.g., police reserves, volunteers, expertise in other agencies, community organizations
- Objective assessment of threats and potential targets within the community and within the region (the latter includes how multijurisdictional crime and terrorist threats would affect an agency directly and indirectly, including mutual aid obligations)
- Current intelligence expertise and practices, including information sharing, and the need to modify these practices, including adding a private sector component for critical infrastructure.
- Political mandates from elected officials and/or the community that should not be ignored because expectations and concerns of these groups must be taken into account in any assessment process.

Refocusing

Guided by the results of the reassessment, a department must develop a plan incorporating its new priorities, as appropriate. Virtually all of the department's current tasks will continue in some form, but the amount of emphasis and proportion of resources devoted to those tasks will differ, notably in light of added homeland security needs.

Refocusing first requires the department to establish its new priorities by reassessing and evaluating its responsibilities. From there it can it can refocus on its priorities, if needed. *Reassessment* involves information gathering and analysis. *Refocusing* is implementing policy steps to make the changes operational.

Second, each area of responsibility must be weighted (i.e., weight constitutes the amount of emphasis given to each broad area of tasks and determines which area receives the greatest amount of attention.) The author does not suggest that intelligence should be the top priority; indeed, in most police agencies managing calls for service will remain the top priority. Instead, this is a realistic expectation that priorities will change with the addition of intelligence/homeland security and that all responsibilities will be affected to some degree. Therefore, to determine this realignment, responsibilities and weights must be stipulated.

Third, these changes are actually implemented through the issuance of updated (and new when applicable) policies, procedures, and orders. Implementation also requires communication and, in some cases, in-service training to explain and clarify the changes.

Reallocating

Once refocusing decisions have been made, the department must reallocate its resources to meet adjusted priorities. This includes personnel, operating expenses, equipment (from cars to radios to computers), and office space, as needed. There is always the possibility that the department will receive an increased appropriation for homeland security in its budget. If so, most likely it will be only a proportion of actual resource needs. The difficult process of reallocation is a necessity that will produce some alienation and, in all likelihood, political rifts within the organization. Reallocation, therefore, also requires effective leadership to guide the organization and motivate personnel to understand the necessity of the changes and the concomitant benefits to the community.

There is no explicit recipe for change in an organization. This is particularly true with intelligence where a renewed emphasis is given to a process that is largely not understood by most personnel. There is little guidance and, despite the best plans, time will be needed for experimentation. Agencies should take the time to carefully consider all new responsibilities, balance them with legitimate competing demands within the agency, and make a clear step toward adjusting the organization.

CONCLUSION

As demonstrated throughout this guide, America's law enforcement agencies are facing a new challenge. Throughout the history of policing challenges have been faced, they have been met with resolute determination, and America has been safer as a result. This new challenge is no different. The intent of this guide has been to help America's state, local, and tribal law enforcement agencies make this journey.

Throughout the history of POLICING CHALLENGES have been faced, they have been met with RESOLUTE DETERMINATION, and AMERICA has BEEN SAFER as a result.

Appendices

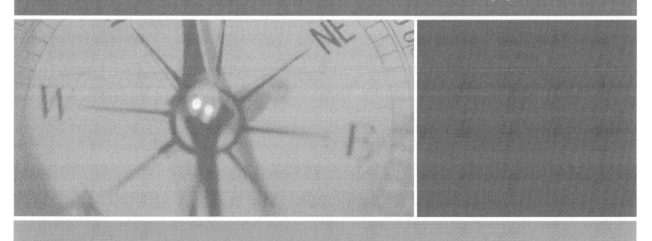

Advisory Board

205

Advisory Board Members

Doug Bodrero
President and CEO
Institute for Intergovernmental Research
Post Office Box 12729
Tallahassee, FL 32317-2729

Theron Bowman, Ph.D.
Chief
Arlington, Texas Police Department
620 West Division Street
Arlington, TX 76011

Michael A. Braun
Acting Assistant Administrator
Intelligence
Drug Enforcement Administration
700 Army-Navy Drive
Arlington, VA 22202

Melvin J. Carraway
Superintendent
Indiana State Police
IGCN - 100 North Senate Avenue
Indianapolis, IN 46204-2259

Robert Casey, Jr.
Deputy Assistant Director
Office of Intelligence, FBI Headquarters
935 Pennsylvania Avenue, NW
Washington, DC 20535

Eileen Garry
Deputy Director
Bureau of Justice Assistance
U.S. Department of Justice
810 Seventh Street, NW
Washington, DC 20531

Ellen Hanson
Chief
Lenexa Police Department
12500 W. 87th St. Parkway
Lenexa, KS 66215

Gil Kerlikowske
Chief
Seattle Police Department
610 Fifth Avenue
Seattle, WA 98124-4986

William Mizner
Chief
Norfolk Police Department
202 N. 7th Street
Norfolk, NE 68701

William Parrish
Senior Representative
Dept. of Homeland Security, Liaison Office
FBI HQ Room 5885
935 Pennsylvania Avenue, NW
Washington, DC 20535

Theodore Quasula
Chief Law Enforcement Officer
Las Vegas Paiute Tribe Police
1 Paiute Drive
Las Vegas, NV 89106

Darrel Stephens
Chief
Charlotte-Mecklenburg Police Department
601 East Trade Street
Charlotte, NC 28202

Bill Young
Sheriff
Las Vegas Metropolitan Police
Department
400 Stewart Avenue
Las Vegas, NV 89101-2984

APPENDIX B

Law Enforcement Intelligence Unit (LEIU) Criminal Intelligence File Guidelines[212]

I. CRIMINAL INTELLIGENCE FILE GUIDELINES

These guidelines were established to provide the law enforcement agency with an information base that meets the needs of the agency in carrying out its efforts to protect the public and suppress criminal operations. These standards are designed to bring about an equitable balance between the civil rights and liberties of citizens and the needs of law enforcement to collect and disseminate criminal intelligence on the conduct of persons and groups who may be engaged in systematic criminal activity.

II. CRIMINAL INTELLIGENCE FILE DEFINED

A criminal intelligence file consists of stored information on the activities and associations of:

A. Individuals who:

    1. Are suspected of being involved in the actual or attempted planning, organizing, financing, or commission of criminal acts; or

    2. Are suspected of being involved in criminal activities with known or suspected crime figures.

B. Organizations, businesses, and groups that:

    1. Are suspected of being involved in the actual or attempted planning, organizing, financing, or commission of criminal acts; or

    2. Are suspected of being operated, controlled, financed, or infiltrated by known or suspected crime figures for use in an illegal manner.

III. FILE CONTENT

Only information with a criminal predicate and which meets the agency's criteria for file input should be stored in the criminal intelligence file. Specifically excluded material includes:

A.   Information on an individual or group merely on the basis that such individual or group supports unpopular causes.

B.   Information on an individual or group merely on the basis of ethnic background.

C.   Information on any individual or group merely on the basis of religious or political affiliations.

D.   Information on an individual or group merely on the basis of non-criminal personal habits.

E.   Criminal Offender Record Information (CORI), should be excluded from an intelligence file. This is because CORI may be subject to specific audit and dissemination restrictions which are designed to protect an individual's right to privacy and to ensure accuracy.

F.   Also excluded are associations with individuals that are not of a criminal nature.

State law or local regulations may dictate whether or not public record and intelligence information should be kept in separate files or commingled. Some agencies believe that separating their files will prevent the release of intelligence information in the event a subpoena is issued. This belief is unfounded, as all information requested in the subpoena (both public and intelligence) must be turned over to the court. The judge then makes the determination on what information will be released.

The decision to commingle or separate public and intelligence documents is strictly a management decision. In determining this policy, administrators should consider the following:

A.   Records relating to the conduct of the public's business that are prepared by a state or local agency, regardless of physical form or characteristics, may be considered public and the public has access to these records.

B. Specific types of records (including intelligence information) may be exempt from public disclosure.

C. Regardless of whether public record information is separated from or commingled with intelligence data, the public may have access to public records.

D. The separation of public information from criminal intelligence information may better protect the confidentiality of the criminal file. If a request is made for public records, an agency can release the public file and leave the intelligence file intact (thus less apt to accidentally disclose intelligence information).

E. Separating of files is the best theoretical approach to maintaining files; however, it is not easy to do. Most intelligence reports either reference public record information or else contain a combination of intelligence and public record data. Thus, it is difficult to isolate them from each other. Maintaining separate public and intelligence files also increases the amount of effort required to index, store, and retrieve information.

IV. FILE CRITERIA

All information retained in the criminal intelligence file should meet file criteria prescribed by the agency. These criteria should outline the agency's crime categories and provide specifics for determining whether subjects involved in these crimes are suitable for file inclusion.

File input criteria will vary among agencies because of differences in size, functions, resources, geographical location, crime problems, etc. The categories listed in the suggested model below are not exhaustive.

A. Permanent Status

1. Information that relates an individual, organization, business, or group is suspected of being involved in the actual or attempted planning, organizing, financing, or committing of one or more of the following criminal acts:

- Narcotic trafficking/manufacturing
- Unlawful gambling
- Loan sharking
- Extortion
- Vice and pornography
- Infiltration of legitimate business for illegitimate purposes
- Stolen securities
- Bribery
- Major crime including homicide, sexual assault, burglary, auto theft, kidnapping, destruction of property, robbery, fraud, fencing stolen property, and arson
- Manufacture, use, or possession of explosive devices for purposes of fraud, intimidation, or political motivation
- Threats to public officials and private citizens.

2. In addition to falling within the confines of one or more of the above criminal activities, the subject/entity to be given permanent status must be identifiable—distinguished by a name and unique identifying characteristics (e.g., date of birth, criminal identification number, driver's license number, address). Identification at the time of file input is necessary to distinguish the subject/entity from existing file entries and those that may be entered at a later time. NOTE: The exception to this rule involves modus operandi (MO) files. MO files describe a unique method of operation for a specific type of crime (homicide, fraud) and may not be immediately linked to an identifiable suspect. MO files may be retained indefinitely while additional identifiers are sought.

B. Temporary Status:

Information that does not meet the criteria for permanent storage but may be pertinent to an investigation involving one of the categories previously listed should be given "temporary" status. It is recommended the retention of temporary information not exceed 1 year unless a compelling reason exists to extend this time period. (An example of a compelling reason is if several pieces of information indicate that a crime has been committed, but more than a year is needed to identify a suspect.) During this period, efforts should be made to identify the subject/entity or validate the information so that its final status may be determined. If the information is still classified temporary at the end of the 1 year period, and a compelling reason for its retention is not evident, the information should be purged. An individual, organization, business, or group may be given temporary status in the following cases:

1. Subject/entity is unidentifiable – subject/entity (although suspected of being engaged in criminal activities) has no known physical descriptors, identification numbers, or distinguishing characteristics available.

2. Involvement is questionable – involvement in criminal activities is suspected by a subject/entity which has either:

   - Possible criminal associations – individual, organization, business, or group (not currently reported to be criminally active) associates with a known criminal and appears to be jointly involved in illegal activities.

   - Criminal history – individual, organization, business, or group (not currently reported to be criminally active) that has a history of criminal conduct, and the circumstances currently being reported (i.e., new position or ownership in a business) indicates they may again become criminally active.

3. Reliability/validity unknown – the reliability of the information sources and/or the validity of the information cannot be determined at the time of receipt; however, the information appears to be significant and merits temporary storage while verification attempts are made.

V. INFORMATION EVALUATION

Information to be retained in the criminal intelligence file should be evaluated and designated for reliability and content validity prior to filing. The bulk of the data an intelligence unit receives consists of unverified allegations or information. Evaluating the information's source and content indicates to future users the information's worth and usefulness. Circulating information which may not have been evaluated, where the source reliability is poor or the content validity is doubtful, is detrimental to the agency's operations and contrary to the individual's right to privacy.

To ensure uniformity with the intelligence community, it is strongly recommended that stored information be evaluated according to the criteria set forth below.

Source Reliability:

(A) Reliable – The reliability of the source is unquestioned or has been well tested in the past.

(B) Usually Reliable – The reliability of the source can usually be relied upon as factual. The majority of information provided in the past has proven to be reliable.

(C) Unreliable – The reliability of the source has been sporadic in the past.

(D) Unknown –The reliability of the source cannot be judged. Its authenticity or trustworthiness has not yet been determined by either experience or investigation.

Content Validity:

(1) Confirmed – The information has been corroborated by an investigator or another independent, reliable source.

(2) Probable – The information is consistent with past accounts.

(3) Doubtful – The information is inconsistent with past accounts.

(4) Cannot Be Judged – The information cannot be judged. Its authenticity has not yet been determined by either experience or investigation.

VI. INFORMATION CLASSIFICATION

Information retained in the criminal intelligence file should be classified in order to protect sources, investigations, and the individual's right to privacy. Classification also indicates the internal approval which must be completed prior to the release of the information to persons outside the agency. However, the classification of information in itself is not a defense against a subpoena duces tecum.

The classification of criminal intelligence information is subject to continual change. The passage of time, the conclusion of investigations, and other factors may affect the security classification assigned to particular documents. Documents within the intelligence files should be reviewed on an ongoing basis to ascertain whether a higher or lesser degree of document security is required to ensure that information is released only when and if appropriate.

Classification systems may differ among agencies as to the number of levels of security and release authority. In establishing a classification system, agencies should define the types of information for each security level, dissemination criteria, and release authority. The system listed below classifies data maintained in the Criminal Intelligence File according to one of the following categories:

Sensitive

1. Information pertaining to significant law enforcement cases currently under investigation.

2. Corruption (police or other government officials), or other sensitive information.

3. Informant identification information.

4. Criminal intelligence reports which require strict dissemination and release criteria.

Confidential

1. Criminal intelligence reports not designated as sensitive.

2. Information obtained through intelligence unit channels that is not classified as sensitive and is for law enforcement use only.

Restricted

1. Reports that at an earlier date were classified sensitive or confidential and the need for high-level security no longer exists.

2. Nonconfidential information prepared for/by law enforcement agencies.

Unclassified

1. Civic-related information to which, in its original form, the general public had direct access (i.e., public record data).

2. News media information — newspaper, magazine, and periodical clippings dealing with specified criminal categories.

VII. INFORMATION SOURCE

In all cases, source identification should be available in some form. The true identity of the source should be used unless there is a need to protect the source. Accordingly, each law enforcement agency should establish criteria that would indicate when source identification would be appropriate.

The value of information stored in a criminal intelligence file is often directly related to the source of such information. Some factors to consider in determining whether source identification is warranted include:

- The nature of the information reported.
- The potential need to refer to the source's identity for further or prosecutorial activity.
- The reliability of the source.

Whether or not confidential source identification is warranted, reports should reflect the name of the agency and the reporting individual. In those cases when identifying the source by name is not practical for internal security reasons, a code number may be used. A confidential listing of coded sources of information can then be retained by the intelligence unit commander. In addition to identifying the source, it may be appropriate in a particular case to describe how the source obtained the information (for example "S- 60, a reliable police informant heard" or "a reliable law enforcement source of the police department saw" a particular event at a particular time).

VIII. INFORMATION QUALITY CONTROL

Information to be stored in the criminal intelligence file should undergo a thorough review for compliance with established file input guidelines and agency policy prior to being filed. The quality control reviewer is responsible for seeing that all information entered into the criminal intelligence files conforms with the agency's file criteria and has been properly evaluated and classified.

IX. FILE DISSEMINATION

Agencies should adopt sound procedures for disseminating stored information. These procedures will protect the individual's right to privacy as well as maintain the confidentiality of the sources and the file itself.

Information from a criminal intelligence report can only be released to an individual who has demonstrated both a "need-to-know" and a "right-to-know."

"Right-to-know" Requestor has official capacity and statutory authority to the information being sought.

"Need-to-know" Requested information is pertinent and necessary to the requestor agency in initiating, furthering, or completing an investigation.

No "original document" which has been obtained from an outside agency is to be released to a third agency. Should such a request be received, the requesting agency will be referred to the submitting agency for further assistance.

Information classification and evaluation are, in part, dissemination controls. They denote who may receive the information as well as the internal approval level(s) required for release of the information. In order to encourage conformity within the intelligence community, it is recommended that stored information be classified according to a system similar to the following.

The integrity of the criminal intelligence file can be maintained only by strict adherence to proper dissemination guidelines. To eliminate unauthorized use and abuses of the system, a department should utilize a dissemination control form that could be maintained with each stored document. This control form would record the date of the request, the name of the agency and individual requesting the information, the need-to-know, the information provided, and the name of the employee handling the request. Depending upon the needs of the agency, the control form also may be designed to record other items useful to the agency in the management of its operations. This control form also may be subject to discovery.

Security Level	Dissemination Criteria	Release Authority
Sensitive	Restricted to law enforcement personnel having a specific need-to-know and right-to-know	Intelligence Unit Commander
Confidential	Same as for Sensitive	Intelligence Unit Manager or Designee
Restricted	Same as for Sensitive	Intelligence Unit Supervisor or Designee
Unclassified	Not Restricted	Intelligence Unit Personnel

X.   FILE REVIEW AND PURGE

Information stored in the criminal intelligence file should be reviewed periodically for reclassification or purge in order to: ensure that the file is current, accurate, and relevant to the needs and objective of the agency; safeguard the individual's right of privacy as guaranteed under federal and state laws; and, ensure that the security classification level remains appropriate.

Law enforcement agencies have an obligation to keep stored information on subjects current and accurate. Reviewing of criminal intelligence should be done on a continual basis as agency personnel use the material in carrying out day-to-day activities. In this manner, information that is no longer useful or that cannot be validated can immediately be purged or reclassified where necessary.

To ensure that all files are reviewed and purged systematically, agencies should develop purge criteria and schedules. Operational procedures for the purge and the method of destruction for purged materials should be established.

A.   Purge Criteria:

General considerations for reviewing and purging of information stored in the criminal intelligence file are as follows:

1.   Utility

   – How often is the information used?
   – For what purpose is the information being used?
   – Who uses the information?

2.   Timeliness and Appropriateness

   – Is this investigation still ongoing?
   – Is the information outdated?
   – Is the information relevant to the needs and objectives of the agency?
   – Is the information relevant to the purpose for which it was collected and stored?

3.   Accuracy and Completeness

   Is the information still valid?
   Is the information adequate for identification purposes?
   Can the validity of the data be determined through investigative techniques?

B.   Review and Purge Time Schedule:

Reclassifying and purging information in the intelligence file should be done on an ongoing basis as documents are reviewed. In addition, a complete review of the criminal intelligence file for purging purposes should be undertaken periodically. This review and purge schedule can vary from once each year for documents with temporary status to once every 5 years for permanent documents. Agencies should develop a schedule best suited to their needs and should contact their legal counsel for guidance.

C.   Manner of Destruction:

Material purged from the criminal intelligence file should be destroyed. Disposal is used for all records or papers that identify a person by name. It is the responsibility of each agency to determine that their obsolete records are destroyed in accordance with applicable laws, rules, and state or local policy.

XI.   FILE SECURITY

The criminal intelligence file should be located in a secured area with file access restricted to authorized personnel.

Physical security of the criminal intelligence file is imperative to maintain the confidentiality of the information stored in the file and to ensure the protection of the individual's right to privacy.

GLOSSARY

Public Record

Public record includes any writing containing information relating to the conduct of the public's business prepared, owned, used, or retained by any state or local agency regardless of physical form or characteristics.

"Member of the public" means any person, except a member, agent, officer, or employee of a federal, state, or local agency acting within the scope of his or her membership in an agency, office, or employment.

For purposes of these guidelines, public record information includes only that information to which the general public normally has direct access, (i.e., birth or death certificates, county recorder's information, incorporation information, etc.)

Criminal Offender Record Information (CORI)

CORI is defined as summary information to arrests, pretrial proceedings, sentencing information, incarcerations, parole, and probation.

a. Summary criminal history records are commonly referred to as "rap sheets." Data submitted on fingerprint cards, disposition of arrest and citation forms and probation flash notices create the entries on the rap sheet.

APPENDIX C

Intelligence Unit Management Audit

Audit Factors for the Law Enforcement Intelligence Function[213]

213   Prepared by David L. Carter, Michigan State University, for an audit of the Denver, Colorado Police Department Intelligence Bureau in compliance with a U.S. District Court settlement. Copyright © 2004 by David L. Carter. All rights reserved.

214   http://it.ojp.gov/topic.jsp ?topic_id=8.

215   http://it.ojp.gov/topic.jsp? topic_id=93.

216   http://www.ojp.usdoj.gov/ odp/docs/ODPPrev1.pdf.

217   http://www.calea.org/new web/accreditation%20Info/ descriptions_of_standards _approv.htm.

218   http://it.ojp.gov/process_ links.jsp?link_id=3774.

219   http://it.ojp.gov/process_ links.jsp?link_id=3773.

220   http://www.theiacp.org/ documents/index.cfm? fuseaction=document& document_type_id=1& document_id=95.

221   http://www.theiacp.org/ documents/index.cfm? fuseaction=document& document_type_id=1& document_id=94.

222   As one good example, see the Santa Clara, CA Police Department's Value Statements at http://www.scpd.org/value_sta tement.html.

223   http://www.iir.com/28cfr.

Section A. Meeting National Standards

1.   Does the police department subscribe to the tenets and standards of the *Global Justice Information Sharing Initiative*?[214]
     ❑   Yes   ❑   No

2.   Does the police department subscribe to the standards of the *National Criminal Intelligence Sharing Plan*?[215]
     ❑   Yes   ❑   No

3.   Does the police department subscribe to the guidelines for information and intelligence sharing of the Office of Domestic Preparedness *Guidelines for Homeland Security*?[216]
     ❑   Yes   ❑   No

4.   Does the police department subscribe to the guidelines of the Commission on Accreditation for Law Enforcement Agencies (CALEA) Standard 51.1.1 *Criminal Intelligence*?[217]
     ❑   Yes   ❑   No

5.   Does the police department subscribe to the provisions of the International Association of Chiefs of Police (IACP) *Model Criminal Intelligence Policy*?[218]
     ❑   Yes   ❑   No

6.   Does the police department subscribe to the standards of the Law Enforcement Intelligence Unit (LEIU) *Criminal Intelligence File Guidelines*?[219]
     ❑   Yes   ❑   No

7.   Does the police department subscribe to the IACP *Code of Ethics*[220] or have an articulated Code of Ethics?
     ❑   Yes   ❑   No

8.   Does the police department subscribe to the IACP *Code of Conduct*[221] or have an articulated Code of Conduct?
     ❑   Yes   ❑   No

9.   Does the police department have an articulated Statement of Values?[222]
     ❑   Yes   ❑   No

10. Does the police department adhere to the regulations of 28 CFR Part 23[223] for its Criminal Intelligence Records System?
     ❑   Yes   ❑   No

a. Does the police department operate a federally funded multi-jurisdictional criminal intelligence records system?

❑ Yes ❑ No

11. Does the police department subscribe to the tenets of the *Justice Information Privacy Guidelines*?[224]

❑ Yes ❑ No

12. Does the police department subscribe to the tenets for information system security defined in the report, *Applying Security Practices to Justice Information Sharing*?[225]

❑ Yes ❑ No

13. Does the law enforcement agency subscribe to the philosophy of *Intelligence-Led Policing*?[226]

❑ Yes ❑ No

14. Are defined activities for the intelligence unit designed exclusively to prevent and control crime with no political, religious or doctrinal purpose?

❑ Yes ❑ No

Section B: Management Issues

1. Has a mission statement been written for the Intelligence Unit?

❑ Yes ❑ No

2. Is the purpose and role of the Unit clearly articulated and related to the Police Department's Mission Statement?

❑ Yes ❑ No

3. Have priorities been established for the types of crimes the Unit will address?

❑ Yes ❑ No

a. Is any written rationale provided for these priorities?

❑ Yes ❑ No

4. Are expected activities of the unit articulated?[227]

❑ Yes ❑ No

5. Does the mission statement express ethical standards?

❑ Yes ❑ No

6. Does the mission statement express the importance of protecting citizens' rights?

❑ Yes ❑ No

224 http://www.ncja.org/pdf/privacyguideline.pdf.

225 http://it.ojp.gov/documents/asp.

226 http://www.theiacp.org/documents/pdfs/Publications/intelsharingreport%2Epdf.

227 E.g., collection, analysis, collation, dissemination, contact point for other agencies, clearinghouse, etc.

1. Policies and Procedures

228 The questions in this audit outline the parameters of 28 CFR Part 23 as of the date of this writing. This guideline specifies standards that are required for state and local law enforcement agencies that are operating a federally funded multijurisdictional criminal intelligence system. While the guideline does not apply to all state and local Intelligence Records Systems, the law enforcement intelligence community considers it good practice that all law enforcement agencies should adhere to the standards regardless of whether or not it is formally applicable.

1. Are there written and officially articulated policies and procedures for management of the intelligence function?
    ❏ Yes   ❏ No

2. Have intelligence policies been formed to minimize the discretion of information collectors?
    ❏ Yes   ❏ No
    If Yes, Describe:

3. Is there a policy and procedures on "Information Collection"?
    ❏ Yes   ❏ No
    If Yes, Describe:

2. Management of Information:[228] Definitional Standards (see chart on next page)

1. Are there standard terms used in intelligence activities that have been operationally defined in writing so that all persons in the department know the explicit meaning and implications of the terms?
    ❏ Yes   ❏ No

2. What is the source of the definitions?
    ❏ NCISP   ❏ Federal Agency
    ❏ Mixed   ❏ N/A

3. Has the department articulated standards for classifying information in the Intelligence Unit?
    ❏ Yes   ❏ No

Priority	Classification	Description	Release Authority
Highest Level	Sensitive	Current corruption case; complex criminality; confidential informants	Dept Executive or Intelligence Cmdr.
Medium Level	Confidential	Non-sensitive information through intelligence channels; Law Enforcement only	Intelligence Unit Cmdr or Supervisor
Lowest Level	Restricted	LE use but no need for high security	Intell Unit Personnel
Unclassified	Public Access	Information that may be released to public and media	Intell Unit Personnel

4. How are those standards monitored and enforced?
   ❑ Supervisor   ❑ Other

5. Does the department have a system for assessing the reliability of sources that provide information that will be retained in the Intelligence Records System?
   ❑ Yes   ❑ No

6. Are there standardized definitions of the reliability scale?
   ❑ Yes   ❑ No

7. Does the department have a system for assessing the validity of the information that will be retained in the Intelligence Records System?
   ❑ Yes   ❑ No

8. Are there standardized definitions of the validity scale?
   ❑ Yes   ❑ No

9. Does the Intelligence Unit have operational definitions that can be applied to a person under investigation or a series of related crimes where the perpetrator is not identifiable in order to classify the case file as either a "permanent file" or a "temporary file"?
   ❑ Yes   ❑ No
   If Yes...
   a. Are the types of identifying information that should be placed in the file articulated?
   ❑ Yes   ❑ No
   b. Is there a procedure for requiring the articulation of the criminal predicate for the permanent file?
   ❑ Yes   ❑ No

c.	Is there a procedure articulating the conditions wherein a temporary file may be created?

❑ Yes	❑ No

d.	Does the procedure specify a time limit that the temporary file can be kept?

❑ Yes	❑ No

e.	Is there an operational definition of "Non-Criminal Identifying Information" and procedures for recording and retaining this information?

❑ Yes	❑ No

f.	Are there clear procedures that *describe* the types of information that should not be entered into the Intelligence Records System?

❑ Yes	❑ No

3. Management of Information: Source Documents

1.	Does the department have a written directive explaining the different types of source documents that will be entered in the Intelligence Records System?

❑ Yes	❑ No

2.	What types of source documents are entered into the Intelligence Records System?[229]
Describe:

3.	Does the police department have a written directive that the rationale for each source document entered into the Intelligence Records System must be articulated in a report or notation?

❑ Yes	❑ No

229 For example, Intelligence reports generated by the police department; intelligence reports generated by other agencies; offense reports; arrest reports; criminal history checks; output from consolidated data bases; field interview reports, newspaper and open-source materials, informant statements, etc.

4. Management of Information: Data Entry

1. Who is responsible for entering information into the Intelligence
    Records System?
    Position/Classification:

2. Who supervises the information entry process?
    Position/Classification:

5. Management of Information: Accountability

1. Who is the Custodian of the Intelligence Records System that ensures
    all regulations, law, policy and procedures are being followed?
    Position/Classification:

2. Is there a person external to the Intelligence Unit who is designated to
    monitor the Intelligence Records System and related processes?
    ❏ Yes   ❏ No
    If Yes, Position/Classification):

3. Does the department have written procedures for the retention of
    records in the Intelligence Records System?
    ❏ Yes   ❏ No

6. Management of Information: Retention and Purging of Records

1. Does the retention process adhere to the guidelines of 28 CFR Part 23?
    ❏ Yes   ❏ No

2. Does the retention policy and procedure include written criteria for
    purging information?
    ❏ Yes   ❏ No

3.	How often does a review and purge process occur?
	Frequency:

4.	What is the purge process?
	Describe:

5.	Does the purge process include a system review of information to confirm its continuing propriety, accuracy and relevancy?
	❑ Yes ❑ No

6.	Does the purge process require destruction of the source document and removal of all references to the document to be purged if the information is no longer appropriate for retention?
	❑ Yes ❑ No

7.	What is the destruction process for purged "hard copy" records?
	Describe:

8.	After information has been purged from a computerized Intelligence Records System, is free space on the hard drive and/or specific purged files electronically "wiped"?
	❑ Yes ❑ No
	a.	Are back-ups wiped?
	❑ Yes ❑ No

b. What is the accountability system for purging back-ups?
    Describe:

9. Does the purge process require the elimination of partial information that is no longer appropriate if the source document is to be kept because the remaining information in the source documents merits retention?
    ❑ Yes   ❑ No

10. What is the process for purging partial information from "hard copy" source documents?
    Describe:

11. Who is responsible for ensuring compliance of the purge process?
    Position/Classification:

7. Management of Information: Personal/Individually-Held Records and Files

1. Is there an intelligence unit policy and procedures concerning the retention of individual notes and records that identifies persons wherein criminality is suspected but is not in either a temporary or permanent file and is not entered into any formal records system or database?
    ❑ Yes   ❑ No

a. How is the possession of personal records monitored?

❑ Yes   ❑ No

b. How is the policy enforced?

❑ Yes   ❑ No

8. Management of Information: Accessing Intelligence Records

1. Is access to the Intelligence Records limited?

❑ Yes   ❑ No

2. If yes, who may access the Intelligence Records System?
Describe:

3. What security controls exist for accessing computerized records?
Describe:

4. Can the computerized records system be accessed through remote access?

❑ Yes   ❑ No

a. If so, what security controls exist for remote access?
Describe:

5. How are physical records stored?
   Describe:

6. Who grants access privileges to Intelligence Records?
   Position/Classification:

7. Who has access to records?
   Position/Classification:

8. Does the police department apply the Third Agency Rule to information
   that is shared with other agencies?
   ❑ Yes   ❑ No

9. What audit process is in place for access to computerized records?
   Describe:

10. What audit process is in place for access to physical records?
    Describe:

11. How are physical records secured?
     Describe:

12. What process is in place to handle unauthorized access to intelligence
     physical records?
     Describe:

13. What sanctions are in place for a police department employee who
     accesses and/or disseminates intelligence records without
     authorization?
     Describe:

9. Physical Location of the Intelligence Unit and Records

1.   Sufficiency: Is the Intelligence Unit in a physical location that has
     sufficient space to perform all of its responsibilities?
     ❑ Yes   ❑ No
2.   Security: Is the Intelligence Unit in a physical location wherein the
     entire workspace may be completely secured?
     ❑ Yes   ❑ No

a. Is there adequate secured storage cabinets (or a vault) for (1) documents classified by the Intelligence Unit and (2) sensitive records storage within the Intelligence Unit's physical location?

❑ Yes   ❑ No

b. Is there adequate security and segregated storage for federally classified documents within the Intelligence Unit?

❑ Yes   ❑ No

1) Is that storage accessible only by persons with a federal top secret security clearance?

❑ Yes   ❑ No

3. Convenience: Is the Intelligence Unit in a physical location that is convenient to the people, equipment, and resources necessary to maximize efficiency and effectiveness of operations?

❑ Yes   ❑ No

10. Tangential Policy Issues: Criminal Informants and Undercover Operations[230]

1. Is there a formally articulated policy and procedures for managing criminal informants?

❑ Yes   ❑ No

a. Is a background investigation conducted and a comprehensive descriptive file completed on each confidential informant?

❑ Yes   ❑ No

b. Are informant files secured separately from intelligence files?

❑ Yes   ❑ No

2. Is there a formally articulated policy and procedures concerning undercover operations that apply to members of the Intelligence Unit?

❑ Yes   ❑ No

3. Does the police department have a policy on alcohol consumption for officers working undercover?

❑ Yes   ❑ No

a. Does the police department have a policy requiring designated drivers for undercover officers who have consumed alcohol?

❑ Yes   ❑ No

230   The use of criminal informants and undercover operations varies between law enforcement agencies. In some cases these resources may be a functional part of the Intelligence Unit, in other cases they are relied on by the unit for information collection. Understanding the management and control of these activities can be important for the intelligence commander for they can reflect the validity, reliability, and constitutional admissibility of the information collected.

4. Does the police department have a "narcotics simulation" policy and training for undercover officers?
    ☐ Yes   ☐ No

5. Does the police department have a policy for the issuance of fictitious identification for undercover officers and the proper use of such fictitious identification?
    ☐ Yes   ☐ No

6. Do undercover officers receive training specifically related to proper conduct and information collection while working in an undercover capacity?
    ☐ Yes   ☐ No

7. With respect to undercover operating funds:
    a. Is there a 1-tier or 2-tier process to approve use of the funds?
        ☐ 1 Tier   ☐ 2 Tier
    b. Is a written report required to document expenditure of the funds?
        ☐ Yes   ☐ No
    c. What is the maximum time that may pass between the expenditure of funds and personnel accountability for the funds?
        Days   ☐ No Set Time
    d. Is there a regular external audit of undercover funds?
        ☐ Yes [How Often?   ] ☐ No

Section C: Personnel

1. Is a position classification plan in place that provides a clear job description for each position in the unit?
    ☐ Yes   ☐ No

2. Is a position classification plan in place that articulates Knowledge, Skills and Abilities (KSAs) for each position?
    ☐ Yes   ☐ No

3. Is there sufficient hierarchical staff (managers/supervisors) assigned to the unit to effectively perform supervisory responsibilities?
    ☐ Yes   ☐ No

4. Is there sufficient functional staff (analysts and/or investigators) to effectively fulfill defined unit responsibilities?
    ☐ Yes   ☐ No

5. Is there sufficient support staff (secretaries, clerks) to effectively support the unit's activities?
   ❑ Yes   ❑ No
6. Does the screening process for nonsworn employees of the intelligence unit require:
   a. Fingerprint check?
   ❑ Yes   ❑ No
   b. Background investigation
   ❑ Yes   ❑ No
7. If the Intelligence Unit has non-PD employees assigned to it – e.g., National Guard analysts, personnel from the state or local law enforcement agencies – would there be a screening process for those persons?
   ❑ Yes   ❑ No
   If Yes, Describe:

1. Training

1. What types of training do preservice and newly assigned personnel receive?
   ❑ None   ❑ Some–Describe:

   a. Are newly assigned sworn employees to the Intelligence Unit required to attend 28 CFR Part 23 training?
   ❑ Yes   ❑ No
   b. Are newly hired or assigned non-sworn employees required to attend 28 CFR Part 23 training?
   ❑ Yes   ❑ No

2. What types of training do in-service personnel receive?[231]
    ❑ None   ❑ Some
    Describe:

3. Have members of the Intelligence Unit attended any of the following
    federal government intelligence training programs which are open to
    state and local law enforcement officers?
    a. DEA Federal Law Enforcement Analyst Training (FLEAT)?
        ❑   Yes   ❑ No
    b. FBI College of Analytic Studies?
        ❑   Yes   ❑ No
    c. Federal Law Enforcement Training Center (FLETC) Criminal
        Intelligence Analysis Training Course?
        ❑   Yes   ❑ No
    d. National Drug Intelligence Center Basic Intelligence Analysis
        Course?
        ❑   Yes   ❑ No
    e. National White Collar Crime Center Foundations of Intelligence
        Analysis?
        ❑ Yes   ❑ No
    f. Regional Counterdrug Training Academy Intelligence Operations
        Course?
        ❑ Yes   ❑ No

2. Supervision

1. Does supervision effectively monitor adherence to written procedures?
    ❑ Yes   ❑ No
2. Does supervision effectively monitor adherence to guidelines adopted
    by the department?
    ❑ Yes   ❑ No

231 Note: Training should go
     beyond "the basics" and
     include updates of law,
     current crime issues, and
     trends; new technologies,
     new resources, etc.

3. Are performance evaluations tied directly to the job descriptions?[232]
   ❑ Yes ❑ No
4. Does supervision effectively monitor the performance of required duties (Including the quality of performance)?
   ❑ Yes ❑ No
5. Is supervision effectively monitoring personnel to ensure civil rights allegations cannot be made with respect to negligent:
   a. Failure to train?
      ❑ Yes ❑ No
   b. Hiring?
      ❑ Yes ❑ No
   c. Failure to supervise?
      ❑ Yes ❑ No
   d. Assignment?
      ❑ Yes ❑ No
   e. Failure to direct?
      ❑ Yes ❑ No
   f. Failure to discipline?
      ❑ Yes ❑ No
   g. Entrustment?
      ❑ Yes ❑ No
6. Is there effective supervision of the Intelligence Unit throughout the chain of command external to the Intelligence Unit?
   ❑ Yes ❑ No

Section D: Fiscal Management

1. Is the budget sufficient to fulfill the stated mission?
   ❑ Yes ❑ No
2. Does the Intelligence Commander have input into the budget planning process?
   ❑ Yes ❑ No

232 Intelligence Unit staff responsibilities are sufficiently different from other police positions that standard performance evaluations typically do not apply (particularly those evaluations that have a quantitative component.

3. Is there over-reliance on "soft money" to operate the unit?[233]
   ❑ Yes   ❑ No
4. Are equipment and personnel line items assigned directly to the Intelligence Unit?[234]
   ❑ Yes   ❑ No
5. Is there an established process for reliably monitoring credit cards assigned to personnel?
   ❑ Yes   ❑ No   ❑ NA

Section E: Unit Evaluation

1. As a whole, is the unit effective with respect to:
   a. Providing information to prevent crime?
      ❑   Yes   ❑ No
   b. Providing information to apprehend criminals?
      ❑   Yes   ❑ No
   c. Effectively analyzing information to identify criminal enterprises, crime trends, criminal anomalies, etc.?
      ❑   Yes   ❑ No
2. Are data collected on the following factors and reported in an annual report as indicators of the intelligence unit's productivity as an organizational entity?
   a. Number and type of analytic products delivered for investigative purposes?
      ❑   Yes   ❑ No   ❑ NA
   b. Number and type of analytic products that led to arrest?
      ❑   Yes   ❑ No   ❑ NA
   c. Assets seized from illegal activities wherein intelligence contributed to the arrest and/or seizure?
      ❑   Yes   ❑ No   ❑ NA
   d. Number and types of strategic intelligence products delivered to the command staff?
      ❑   Yes   ❑ No   ❑ NA
   e. Number of intelligence-sharing meetings attended by unit staff?
      ❑   Yes   ❑ No   ❑ NA
   f. Number of briefings provided by the intelligence staff?
      ❑   Yes   ❑ No   ❑ NA

233 For example, grants, cooperative agreements, contracts with other agencies, etc.

234 N.B.: If they are not specifically assigned, then they can be withdrawn more easily.

g. Total number of queries into the intelligence data base?
    ❏   Yes   ❏ No   ❏ NA
h. Number of permanent files opened?
    ❏   Yes   ❏ No   ❏ NA
i. Number of temporary files investigated?
    ❏   Yes   ❏ No   ❏ NA
j. Number of requests for information to the unit from outside agencies?
    ❏   Yes   ❏ No   ❏ NA

3. Are products produced by the Intelligence Unit:
    a. In a consistent format?
        ❏   Yes   ❏ No
    b. Easily consumed and used (i.e., understandable and actionable)?
        ❏   Yes   ❏ No
    c. Contain timely information and disseminated in a timely manner?
        ❏   Yes   ❏ No
    d. Have substantive contact to aid in preventing or controlling crime?
        ❏   Yes   ❏ No

4. Given the confidential nature of the information contained in the Intelligence Unit, is there a policy and procedures if a city, county, state, or federal fiscal or program auditor seeks to audit the Intelligence Unit?
    ❏ Yes   ❏ No
    If Yes, Describe:

Section F. Collection

1. Is there an articulated collection plan for the Intelligence Unit?
   ❑ Yes ❑ No
   If Yes, Describe:

   a. How often and when is the plan updated?
      Describe:

2. Have the following activities been performed by the Intelligence Unit:
   a. An inventory of threats in the region posed by criminal enterprises, terrorists, and criminal extremists?
      ❑ Yes ❑ No
   b. An assessment of the threats with respect to their probability of posing a criminal or terrorist threat to the region?
      ❑ Yes ❑ No
   c. A target or criminal commodity analysis of the region?
      ❑ Yes ❑ No
   d. A target or criminal commodity vulnerability assessment in the region?
      ❑ Yes ❑ No
3. For each identified threat, have intelligence requirements been articulated?
   ❑ Yes ❑ No

a. If Yes, Describe the methods of collection that will be used to fulfill those intelligence requirements.

Section G: Technology and Networking

1. Are any members of the Intelligence Unit subscribed members to the FBI's secure Email system Law Enforcement Online (LEO)?
   ❑ Yes-All   ❑ Yes-Some   ❑ No

2. Are any members of the Intelligence Unit subscribed members to the secure Regional Information Sharing System (RISS) email system riss.net?
   ❑ Yes-All   ❑ Yes-Some   ❑ No

   a. If yes, are the RISS databases (e.g., RISS.gang, ATIX, etc.) regularly used?
   ❑ Yes   ❑ No

3. Is the police department a member of the Regional Information Sharing System?[235]
   ❑ Yes   ❑ No

4. Is a systematic procedure in place to ensure that advisories and notifications transmitted via the National Law Enforcement Teletype System (NLETS) are forwarded to the Intelligence Unit?
   ❑ Yes   ❑ No

5. Are you connected to any state-operated intelligence or information networks?
   ❑ Yes   ❑ No
   If Yes, Describe:

[235] The six Regional Information Sharing System centers are: MAGLOCLEN, MOCIC, NESPIN, RMIN, ROCIC, WSIN. See http://www.iir.com/riss/RISS_centers.htm.

6. Are you connected to any regional intelligence or information networks (including HIDTA)?

   ❑ Yes   ❑ No

   If Yes, Describe:

7. Does the intelligence have access and use the National Virtual Pointer[236] System (NVPS)?[237]

   ❑ Yes   ❑ No

8. Is there a formal approval process for entering into a memorandum of understanding (MOU) for information and intelligence sharing with other law enforcement agencies or law enforcement intelligence entities?

   ❑ Yes   ❑ No

   If Yes, Describe the process:

   Who must approve the MOU?

Section H: Legal Issues

1. Is there a designated person in the police department who reviews Freedom of Information Act requests directed to the intelligence unit?

   ❑ Yes   ❑ No

2. Is there a designated person in the police department who responds to Privacy Act inquiries directed to the intelligence unit?

   ❑ Yes   ❑ No

236 A Pointer System – also known as a deconfliction center – determines when two different agencies are investigating the same criminal incident to same person. Since two agencies are investigating the same entity, they are possibly in conflict. In order to "deconflict", the pointer system notifies both agencies of their mutual interest in a case/person in order to avoid duplication of effort, conflicting approaches, and increasing efficiency and effectiveness.

237 NVPS integrates HIDTA, NDPIX, and RISS pointers via secure web-based communications.

3. Is there a designated person the police department contacts in response to a subpoena for a file in the Intelligence Records System?
   ❑ Yes ❑ No

4. Does the Intelligence Unit Commander have a legal resource for advice to help protect intelligence records from objectionable access?
   ❑ Yes ❑ No

5. Does the Intelligence Unit Commander have a legal resource for advice on matters related to criminal procedure and civil rights?
   ❑ Yes ❑ No

6. Does the Intelligence Unit Commander have a legal resource for advice on matters related to questions of civil liability as it relates to all aspects of the intelligence function?
   ❑ Yes ❑ No

7. Has legal counsel reviewed and approved all policies and procedures of the intelligence unit?
   ❑ Yes ❑ No

28 CFR Part 23

28 CFR Part 23
Criminal Intelligence Systems
Operating Policies[238]

1. Purpose.
2. Background.
3. Applicability.
4. Operating principles.
5. Funding guidelines.
6. Monitoring and auditing of grants for the funding of intelligence systems.

Authority: 42 U.S.C. 3782(a); 42 U.S.C. 3789g(c).

§ 23.1 Purpose.

The purpose of this regulation is to assure that all criminal intelligence systems operating through support under the Omnibus Crime Control and Safe Streets Act of 1968, 42 U.S.C. 3711, et seq., as amended (Pub. L. 90-351, as amended by Pub. L. 91-644, Pub. L. 93-83, Pub. L. 93-415, Pub. L. 94-430, Pub. L. 94-503, Pub. L. 95-115, Pub. L. 96-157, Pub. L. 98-473, Pub. L. 99-570, Pub. L. 100-690, and Pub. L. 101-647), are utilized in conformance with the privacy and constitutional rights of individuals.

§ 23.2 Background.

It is recognized that certain criminal activities including but not limited to loan sharking, drug trafficking, trafficking in stolen property, gambling, extortion, smuggling, bribery, and corruption of public officials often involve some degree of regular coordination and permanent organization involving a large number of participants over a broad geographical area. The exposure of such ongoing networks of criminal activity can be aided by the pooling of information about such activities. However, because the collection and exchange of intelligence data necessary to support control of serious criminal activity may represent potential threats to the privacy of individuals to whom such data relates, policy guidelines for Federally funded projects are required.

[238] Based on Executive Order 12291, February 17, 1981. The list of executive orders can be found at the National Archive website: http://www.archives.gov. The most current text of 28 CFR Part 23 can be found at the Library of Congress website by retrieving the regulation from the Code of Federal Regulations (CFR) search engine at: http://www.gpoaccess.gov/cfr/index.html.

§ 23.3 Applicability.

(a) These policy standards are applicable to all criminal intelligence systems operating through support under the Omnibus Crime Control and Safe Streets Act of 1968, 42 U.S.C. 3711, et seq., as amended (Pub. L. 90-351, as amended by Pub. L. 91-644, Pub. L. 93-83, Pub. L. 93-415, Pub. L. 94-430, Pub. L. 94-503, Pub. L. 95-115, Pub. L. 96-157, Pub. L. 98-473, Pub. L. 99-570, Pub. L. 100-690, and Pub. L. 101-647).

(b) As used in these policies: (1) Criminal Intelligence System or Intelligence System means the arrangements, equipment, facilities, and procedures used for the receipt, storage, interagency exchange or dissemination, and analysis of criminal intelligence information; (2) Interjurisdictional Intelligence System means an intelligence system which involves two or more participating agencies representing different governmental units or jurisdictions; (3) Criminal Intelligence Information means data which has been evaluated to determine that it: (i) is relevant to the identification of and the criminal activity engaged in by an individual who or organization which is reasonably suspected of involvement in criminal activity, and (ii) meets criminal intelligence system submission criteria; (4) Participating Agency means an agency of local, county, State, Federal, or other governmental unit which exercises law enforcement or criminal investigation authority and which is authorized to submit and receive criminal intelligence information through an interjurisdictional intelligence system. A participating agency may be a member or a nonmember of an interjurisdictional intelligence system; (5) Intelligence Project or Project means the organizational unit which operates an intelligence system on behalf of and for the benefit of a single agency or the organization which operates an interjurisdictional intelligence system on behalf of a group of participating agencies; and (6) Validation of Information means the procedures governing the periodic review of criminal intelligence information to assure its continuing compliance with system submission criteria established by regulation or program policy.

§ 23.20 Operating principles.

(a) A project shall collect and maintain criminal intelligence information concerning an individual only if there is reasonable suspicion that the individual is involved in criminal conduct or activity and the information is relevant to that criminal conduct or activity.

(b) A project shall not collect or maintain criminal intelligence information about the political, religious or social views, associations, or activities of any individual or any group, association, corporation, business, partnership, or other organization unless such information directly relates to criminal conduct or activity and there is reasonable suspicion that the subject of the information is or may be involved in criminal conduct or activity.

(c) Reasonable Suspicion or Criminal Predicate is established when information exists which establishes sufficient facts to give a trained law enforcement or criminal investigative agency officer, investigator, or employee a basis to believe that there is a reasonable possibility that an individual or organization is involved in a definable criminal activity or enterprise. In an interjurisdictional intelligence system, the project is responsible for establishing the existence of reasonable suspicion of criminal activity either through examination of supporting information submitted by a participating agency or by delegation of this responsibility to a properly trained participating agency which is subject to routine inspection and audit procedures established by the project.

(d) A project shall not include in any criminal intelligence system information which has been obtained in violation of any applicable Federal, State, or local law or ordinance. In an interjurisdictional intelligence system, the project is responsible for establishing that no information is entered in violation of Federal, State, or local laws, either through examination of supporting information submitted by a participating agency or by delegation of this responsibility to a properly trained participating agency which is subject to routine inspection and audit procedures established by the project.

(e) A project or authorized recipient shall disseminate criminal intelligence information only where there is a need to know and a right to know the information in the performance of a law enforcement activity.

(f) (1) Except as noted in paragraph (f) (2) of this section, a project shall disseminate criminal intelligence information only to law enforcement authorities who shall agree to follow procedures regarding information receipt, maintenance, security, and dissemination which are consistent with these principles.

(2) Paragraph (f) (1) of this section shall not limit the dissemination of an assessment of criminal intelligence information to a government official or to any other individual, when necessary, to avoid imminent danger to life or property.

(g) A project maintaining criminal intelligence information shall ensure that administrative, technical, and physical safeguards (including audit trails) are adopted to insure against unauthorized access and against intentional or unintentional damage. A record indicating who has been given information, the reason for release of the information, and the date of each dissemination outside the project shall be kept. Information shall be labeled to indicate levels of sensitivity, levels of confidence, and the identity of submitting agencies and control officials. Each project must establish written definitions for the need to know and right to know standards for dissemination to other agencies as provided in paragraph (e) of this section. The project is responsible for establishing the existence of an inquirer's need to know and right to know the information being requested either through inquiry or by delegation of this responsibility to a properly trained participating agency which is subject to routine inspection and audit procedures established by the project. Each intelligence project shall assure that the following security requirements are implemented:

(1) Where appropriate, projects must adopt effective and technologically advanced computer software and hardware designs to prevent unauthorized access to the information contained in the system;

(2) The project must restrict access to its facilities, operating environment and documentation to organizations and personnel authorized by the project;

(3) The project must store information in the system in a manner such that it cannot be modified, destroyed, accessed, or purged without authorization;

(4) The project must institute procedures to protect criminal intelligence information from unauthorized access, theft, sabotage, fire, flood, or other natural or manmade disaster;

(5) The project must promulgate rules and regulations based on good cause for implementing its authority to screen, reject for employment, transfer, or remove personnel authorized to have direct access to the system; and

(6) A project may authorize and utilize remote (off-premises) system data bases to the extent that they comply with these security requirements.

(h) All projects shall adopt procedures to assure that all information which is retained by a project has relevancy and importance. Such procedures shall provide for the periodic review of information and the destruction of any information which is misleading, obsolete or otherwise unreliable and shall require that any recipient agencies be advised of such changes which involve errors or corrections. All information retained as a result of this review must reflect the name of the reviewer, date of review and explanation of decision to retain. Information retained in the system must be reviewed and validated for continuing compliance with system submission criteria before the expiration of its retention period, which in no event shall be longer than five (5) years.

(i) If funds awarded under the Act are used to support the operation of an intelligence system, then:

(1) No project shall make direct remote terminal access to intelligence information available to system participants, except as specifically approved by the Office of Justice Programs (OJP) based on a determination that the system has adequate policies and procedures in place to insure that it is accessible only to authorized systems users; and

(2) A project shall undertake no major modifications to system design without prior grantor agency approval.

(j) A project shall notify the grantor agency prior to initiation of formal information exchange procedures with any Federal, State, regional, or other information systems not indicated in the grant documents as initially approved at time of award.

(k) A project shall make assurances that there will be no purchase or use in the course of the project of any electronic, mechanical, or other device for surveillance purposes that is in violation of the provisions of the Electronic Communications Privacy Act of 1986, Public Law 99-508, 18 U.S.C. 2510-2520, 2701-2709 and 3121-3125, or any applicable State statute related to wiretapping and surveillance.

(l) A project shall make assurances that there will be no harassment or interference with any lawful political activities as part of the intelligence operation.

(m) A project shall adopt sanctions for unauthorized access, utilization, or disclosure of information contained in the system.

(n) A participating agency of an interjurisdictional intelligence system must maintain in its agency files information which documents each submission to the system and supports compliance with project entry criteria. Participating agency files supporting system submissions must be made available for reasonable audit and inspection by project representatives. Project representatives will conduct participating agency inspection and audit in such a manner so as to protect the confidentiality and sensitivity of participating agency intelligence records.

(o) The Attorney General or designee may waive, in whole or in part, the applicability of a particular requirement or requirements contained in this part with respect to a criminal intelligence system, or for a class of submitters or users of such system, upon a clear and convincing showing that such waiver would enhance the collection, maintenance or dissemination of information in the criminal intelligence system, while ensuring that such system would not be utilized in violation of the privacy and constitutional rights of individuals or any applicable state or federal law.

§ 23.30 Funding guidelines.

The following funding guidelines shall apply to all Crime Control Act funded discretionary assistance awards and Bureau of Justice Assistance (BJA) formula grant program subgrants, a purpose of which is to support the operation of an intelligence system. Intelligence systems shall only be funded where a grantee/subgrantee agrees to adhere to the principles set forth above and the project meets the following criteria:

(a) The proposed collection and exchange of criminal intelligence information has been coordinated with and will support ongoing or proposed investigatory or prosecutorial activities relating to specific areas of criminal activity.

(b) The areas of criminal activity for which intelligence information is to be utilized represent a significant and recognized threat to the population and:

> (1) Are either undertaken for the purpose of seeking illegal power or profits or pose a threat to the life and property of citizens; and
> (2) Involve a significant degree of permanent criminal organization; or
>
> (3) Are not limited to one jurisdiction.

(c) The head of a government agency or an individual with general policy making authority who has been expressly delegated such control and supervision by the head of the agency will retain control and supervision of information collection and dissemination for the criminal intelligence system. This official shall certify in writing that he or she takes full responsibility and will be accountable for the information maintained by and disseminated from the system and that the operation of the system will be in compliance with the principles set forth in § 23.20.

(d) Where the system is an interjurisdictional criminal intelligence system, the governmental agency which exercises control and supervision over the operation of the system shall require that the head of that agency or an individual with general policymaking authority who has been expressly delegated such control and supervision by the head of the agency:

(1) assume official responsibility and accountability for actions taken in the name of the joint entity, and

(2) certify in writing that the official takes full responsibility and will be accountable for insuring that the information transmitted to the interjurisdictional system or to participating agencies will be in compliance with the principles set forth in § 23.20.

The principles set forth in § 23.20 shall be made part of the by-laws or operating procedures for that system. Each participating agency, as a condition of participation, must accept in writing those principles which govern the submission, maintenance and dissemination of information included as part of the interjurisdictional system.

(e) Intelligence information will be collected, maintained and disseminated primarily for State and local law enforcement efforts, including efforts involving Federal participation.

§ 23.40 Monitoring and auditing of grants for the funding of intelligence systems.

(a) Awards for the funding of intelligence systems will receive specialized monitoring and audit in accordance with a plan designed to insure compliance with operating principles as set forth in § 23.20. The plan shall be approved prior to award of funds.

(b) All such awards shall be subject to a special condition requiring compliance with the principles set forth in § 23.20.

(c) An annual notice will be published by OJP which will indicate the existence and the objective of all systems for the continuing interjurisdictional exchange of criminal intelligence information which are subject to the 28 CFR Part 23 Criminal Intelligence Systems Policies.

28 CFR Part 23: 1993 Revision and Commetary Criminal Intelligence Systems Operating Policies

AGENCY: Office of Justice Programs, Justice.

ACTION: Final Rule

SUMMARY: The regulation governing criminal intelligence systems operating through support under Title I of the Omnibus Crime Control and Safe Streets Act of 1968, as amended, is being revised to update basic authority citations and nomenclature, to clarify the applicability of the regulation, to define terms, and to modify a number of the regulation's operating policies and funding guidelines.

EFFECTIVE DATE: September 16, 1993

FOR FURTHER INFORMATION CONTACT: Paul Kendall, Esquire, General Counsel, <u>Office of Justice Programs</u>, 633 Indiana Ave., NW, Suite 1245-E, Washington, DC 20531, Telephone (202) 307-6235.

SUPPLEMENTARY INFORMATION: The rule which this rule supersedes had been in effect and unchanged since September 17, 1980. A notice of proposed rulemaking for 28 CFR part 23, was published in the Federal Register on February 27, 1992, (57 FR 6691).

The statutory authorities for this regulation are section 801(a) and section 812(c) of title I of the Omnibus Crime Control and Safe Streets Act of 1968, as amended, (the Act), 42 U.S.C. 3782(a) and 3789g(c). 42 U.S.C. 3789g (c) and (d) provide as follows:

CONFIDENTIALITY OF INFORMATION
Sec. 812....
(c) All criminal intelligence systems operating through support under this title shall collect, maintain, and disseminate criminal intelligence information in conformance with policy standards which are prescribed by the Office of Justice Programs and which are written to assure that the

funding and operation of these systems furthers the purpose of this title and to assure that such systems are not utilized in violation of the privacy and constitutional rights of individuals.

(d) Any person violating the provisions of this section, or of any rule, regulation, or order issued thereunder, shall be fined not to exceed $10,000, in addition to any other penalty imposed by law.

28 CFR Part 23: 1998 Policy Clarification Criminal Intelligence Systems Operating Policies

[Federal Register: December 30, 1998 (Volume 63, Number 250)]
[Page 71752-71753]
From the Federal Register Online via GPO Access [wais.access.gpo.gov]
DEPARTMENT OF JUSTICE
28 CFR Part 23
[OJP(BJA)-1177B]
RIN 1121-ZB40

CRIMINAL INTELLIGENCE SHARING SYSTEMS; POLICY CLARIFICATION

AGENCY: Bureau of Justice Assistance (BJA), Office of Justice Programs (OJP), Justice.

ACTION: Clarification of policy.

SUMMARY: The current policy governing the entry of identifying information into criminal intelligence sharing systems requires clarification. This policy clarification is to make clear that the entry of individuals, entities and organizations, and locations that do not otherwise meet the requirements of reasonable suspicion is appropriate when it is done solely for the purposes of criminal identification or is germane to the criminal subject's criminal activity. Further, the definition of "criminal intelligence system" is clarified.

EFFECTIVE DATE: This clarification is effective December 30, 1998.

FOR FURTHER INFORMATION CONTACT: Paul Kendall, General Counsel, Office of Justice Programs, 810 7th Street N.W, Washington, DC 20531, (202) 307-6235.

SUPPLEMENTARY INFORMATION: The operation of criminal intelligence information systems is governed by 28 CFR Part 23. This regulation was written to both protect the privacy rights of individuals and to encourage and expedite the exchange of criminal intelligence information between and among law enforcement agencies of different jurisdictions. Frequent interpretations of the regulation, in the form of policy guidance and correspondence, have been the primary method of ensuring that advances in technology did not hamper its effectiveness.

COMMENTS

The clarification was opened to public comment. Comments expressing unreserved support for the clarification were received from two Regional Intelligence Sharing Systems (RISS) and five states. A comment from the Chairperson of a RISS, relating to the use of identifying information to begin new investigations, has been incorporated. A single negative comment was received, but was not addressed to the subject of this clarification.

Use of Identifying Information

28 CFR 23.3(b)(3) states that criminal intelligence information that can be put into a criminal intelligence sharing system is "information relevant to the identification of and the criminal activity engaged in by an individual who or organization which is reasonably suspected of involvement in criminal activity, and *** [m]eets criminal intelligence system submission criteria." Further, 28 CFR 23.20(a) states that a system shall only collect information on an individual if "there is reasonable suspicion that the individual is involved in criminal conduct or activity and the information is relevant to that criminal conduct or activity." 28 CFR 23.20(b) extends that limitation to collecting information on groups and corporate entities.

In an effort to protect individuals and organizations from the possible taint of having their names in intelligence systems (as defined at 28 C.F.R. Sec. 23.3(b)(1)), the Office of Justice Programs has previously interpreted this section to allow information to be placed in a system only if that information independently meets the requirements of the regulation. Information that might be vital to identifying potential criminals, such as favored locations and companions, or names of family members, has been excluded from the systems. This policy has hampered the effectiveness of many criminal intelligence sharing systems.

Given the swiftly changing nature of modern technology and the expansion of the size and complexity of criminal organizations, the Bureau of Justice Assistance (BJA) has determined that it is necessary to clarify this element of 28 CFR Part 23. Many criminal intelligence databases are now employing "Comment" or "Modus Operandi" fields whose value would be greatly enhanced by the ability to store more detailed and wide-ranging identifying information. This may include names and limited data about people and organizations that are not suspected of any criminal activity or involvement, but merely aid in the identification and investigation of a criminal suspect who independently satisfies the reasonable suspicion standard.

Therefore, BJA issues the following clarification to the rules applying to the use of identifying information. Information that is relevant to the identification of a criminal suspect or to the criminal activity in which the suspect is engaged may be placed in a criminal intelligence database, provided that (1) appropriate disclaimers accompany the information noting that is strictly identifying information, carrying no criminal connotations; (2) identifying information may not be used as an independent basis to meet the requirement of reasonable suspicion of involvement in criminal activity necessary to create a record or file in a criminal intelligence system; and (3) the individual who is the criminal suspect identified by this information otherwise meets all requirements of 28 CFR Part 23. This information may be a searchable field in the intelligence system.

For example: A person reasonably suspected of being a drug dealer is known to conduct his criminal activities at the fictional "Northwest Market." An agency may wish to note this information in a criminal intelligence database, as it may be important to future identification of the suspect. Under the previous interpretation of the regulation, the entry of

"Northwest Market" would not be permitted, because there was no reasonable suspicion that the "Northwest Market" was a criminal organization. Given the current clarification of the regulation, this will be permissible, provided that the information regarding the "Northwest Market" was clearly noted to be non-criminal in nature. For example, the data field in which "Northwest Market" was entered could be marked "Non-Criminal Identifying Information," or the words "Northwest Market" could be followed by a parenthetical comment such as "This organization has been entered into the system for identification purposes only-it is not suspected of any criminal activity or involvement." A criminal intelligence system record or file could not be created for "Northwest Market" solely on the basis of information provided, for example, in a comment field on the suspected drug dealer. Independent information would have to be obtained as a basis for the opening of a new criminal intelligence file or record based on reasonable suspicion on "Northwest Market." Further, the fact that other individuals frequent "Northwest Market" would not necessarily establish reasonable suspicion for those other individuals, as it relates to criminal intelligence systems.

THE DEFINITION OF A "CRIMINAL INTELLIGENCE SYSTEM"

The definition of a "criminal intelligence system" is given in 28 CFR 23.3(b)(1) as the "arrangements, equipment, facilities, and procedures used for the receipt, storage, interagency exchange or dissemination, and analysis of criminal intelligence information ***." Given the fact that cross-database searching techniques are now common-place, and given the fact that multiple databases may be contained on the same computer system, BJA has determined that this definition needs clarification, specifically to differentiate between criminal intelligence systems and non-intelligence systems.

The comments to the 1993 revision of 28 CFR Part 23 noted that "[t]he term 'intelligence system' is redefined to clarify the fact that historical telephone toll files, analytical information, and work products that are not either retained, stored, or exchanged and criminal history record information or identification (fingerprint) systems are excluded from the definition, and hence are not covered by the regulation ***." 58 FR 48448-48449 (Sept. 16, 1993.) The comments further noted that materials that "may assist an agency to produce investigative or other information for an intelligence system ***" do not necessarily fall under the regulation. Id.

The above rationale for the exclusion of non-intelligence information sources from the definition of "criminal intelligence system," suggests now that, given the availability of more modern non-intelligence information sources such as the Internet, newspapers, motor vehicle administration records, and other public record information on-line, such sources shall not be considered part of criminal intelligence systems, and shall not be covered by this regulation, even if criminal intelligence systems access such sources during searches on criminal suspects. Therefore, criminal intelligence systems may conduct searches across the spectrum of non-intelligence systems without those systems being brought under 28 CFR Part 23. There is also no limitation on such non-intelligence information being stored on the same computer system as criminal intelligence information, provided that sufficient precautions are in place to separate the two types of information and to make it clear to operators and users of the information that two different types of information are being accessed.

Such precautions should be consistent with the above clarification of the rule governing the use of identifying information. This could be accomplished, for example, through the use of multiple windows, differing colors of data or clear labeling of the nature of information displayed.

APPENDIX E

FBI Security Clearance

Federal Security Clearance Process for the FBI

It is the policy of the Federal Bureau of Investigation (FBI) to share with Law Enforcement personnel pertinent information regarding terrorism. In the past, the primary mechanism for such information sharing was the Joint Terrorism Task Force (JTTF). In response to the terrorist attack on America on September 11, 2001, the FBI established the State and Local Law Enforcement Executives and Elected Officials Security Clearance Initiative. This program was initiated to brief officials with an established "need-to-know" on classified information that would or could affect their area of jurisdiction.

Most information needed by state or local law enforcement can be shared at an unclassified level. In those instances where it is necessary to share classified information, it can usually be accomplished at the Secret level. This brochure describes when security clearances are necessary and the notable differences between clearance levels. It also describes the process involved in applying and being considered for a clearance. State and local officials who require access to classified material must apply for a security clearance through their local FBI Field Office. The candidate should obtain from their local FBI Field Office a Standard Form 86 (SF 86), Questionnaire for National Security Positions; and two FD-258 (FBI applicant fingerprint cards). One of two levels of security clearance, Secret or Top Secret, may be appropriate.

The background investigation and records checks for Secret and Top Secret security clearance are mandated by Presidential Executive Order (EO). The EO requires these procedures in order for a security clearance to be granted; the FBI does not have the ability to waive them.

Secret Clearances

A Secret security clearance may be granted to those persons that have a "need-to-know" national security information, classified at the Confidential or Secret level. It is generally the most appropriate security clearance for state and local law enforcement officials that do not routinely work on an FBI Task Force or in an FBI facility. A Secret security clearance takes the least amount of time to process and allows for escorted access to FBI facilities.

The procedure is as follows:

FBI performs record checks with various Federal agencies and local law enforcement, as well as, a review of credit history.

Candidate completes forms SF-86 and FD-258. Once favorably adjudicated for a Secret security clearance, the candidate will be required to sign a Non-Disclosure Agreement.

Top Secret Clearances

A Top Secret clearance may be granted to those persons who have a "need-to-know" national security information, classified up to the Top Secret level, and who need unescorted access to FBI facilities, when necessary. This type of clearance will most often be appropriate for law enforcement officers assigned to FBI Task Forces housed in FBI facilities. In addition to all the requirements at the Secret level, a background investigation, covering a 10-year time period, is required. Once favorably adjudicated for a Top Secret security clearance, the candidate will be required to sign a Non-Disclosure Agreement.

Questions and Answers (Q&A)

Q: Who should apply for a security clearance?
A: State or local officials whose duties require that they have access to classified information, and who are willing to undergo a mandatory background investigation.
Q: What is the purpose of a background investigation?
A: The scope of the investigation varies with the level of the clearance being sought. It is designed to allow the government to assess whether a candidate is sufficiently trustworthy to be granted access to classified information. Applicants must meet certain criteria, relating to

their honesty, character, integrity, reliability, judgment, mental health, and association with undesirable persons or foreign nationals.

Q: If an individual occupies an executive position with a law enforcement agency, must he or she still undergo a background investigation in order to access classified information?

A: An Executive Order (EO), issued by the President, requires background investigations for all persons entrusted with access to classified information. The provisions of the EO are mandatory, cannot be waived, and apply equally to all federal, state, and local law enforcement officers. This is true of both Secret and Top Secret security clearances.

Q: How long does it normally take to obtain a Secret security clearance?

A: It is the goal of the FBI to complete the processing for Secret security clearances within 45 to 60 days, once a completed application is submitted. The processing time for each individual case will vary depending upon its complexity.

Q: How long does it normally take to obtain a Top Secret security clearance?

A: It is the goal of the FBI to complete the processing for Top Secret security clearances within 6 to 9 months, once a completed application is submitted. The processing time for each individual case will vary depending upon its complexity

Q: What kind of inquiries will the FBI make into my background?

A: Credit and criminal history checks will be conducted on all applicants. For a Top Secret security clearance, the background investigation includes additional record checks which can verify citizenship for the applicant and family members, verification of birth, education, employment history, and military history. Additionally, interviews will be conducted of persons who know the candidate, and of any spouse divorced within the past ten years. Additional interviews will be conducted, as needed, to resolve any inconsistencies. Residences will be confirmed, neighbors interviewed, and public records queried for information about bankruptcies, divorces, and criminal or civil litigation. The background investigation may be expanded if an applicant has resided abroad, or has a history of mental disorders, or drug or alcohol abuse. A personal interview will be conducted of the candidate.

Q: If I have a poor credit history, or other issues in my background, will this prevent me from getting a security clearance?

A: A poor credit history, or other issues, will not necessarily disqualify a candidate from receiving a clearance, but resolution of the issues will likely take additional time. If the issues are significant, they may prevent a clearance from being approved.

Q: If I choose not to apply for a security clearance, will I still be informed about counterterrorism issues important to my jurisdiction?

A: Absolutely. If the FBI receives information relevant to terrorism which may impact your jurisdiction, you will be informed by your local Field Office, through the Law Enforcement On- Line network, via NLETS, and through other available mechanisms which are approved for the transmission of unclassified information. Most terrorism-related information can be provided in an unclassified form.

Q: Are there any other advantages or disadvantages to receiving unclassified or classified terrorism related information?

A: An additional advantage of receiving unclassified terrorism-related information is that there may be fewer restrictions on your ability to further disseminate it within your jurisdiction. Classified information may only be disseminated to other cleared persons, who also have a need-to-know.

Q: What is the difference between an interim and a full security clearance?

A: Interim clearances are granted in exceptional circumstances where official functions must be performed before completion of the investigative and adjudicative processes associated with the security clearance procedure. There is no difference between an interim and a full security clearance as it relates to access to classified information. However, when such access is granted, the background investigation must be expedited, and, if unfavorable information is developed at anytime, the interim security clearance may be withdrawn.

If you have any additional questions, and/or wish to apply for a security clearance, please contact your local FBI field office. (See http://www.fbi.gov/contact/fo/fo.htm to locate the nearest field office.)

Biography of David L. Carter, Ph.D.

David L. Carter (Ph.D., Sam Houston State University) is a professor in the School of Criminal Justice and director of the Intelligence Program at Michigan State University. A former Kansas City, Missouri police officer, Dr. Carter was chairman of the Department of Criminal Justice at the University of Texas-Pan American in Edinburg, Texas for 9 years prior to his appointment at Michigan State in 1985. He has served as a trainer, consultant, and advisor to many law enforcement agencies throughout the U.S., Europe, and Asia on matters associated with officer behavior, community policing, law enforcement intelligence, and computer crime. In addition, he has presented training sessions at the FBI National Academy, the FBI Law Enforcement Executive Development Seminar (LEEDS); the International Law Enforcement Academy in Budapest, Hungary; the United Nations Asia and Far East Institute (UNAFEI) in Tokyo; police "command colleges" of Texas, Florida, Ohio, Massachusetts, Wisconsin, and Kentucky; and served at the FBI Academy's Behavioral Science Services Unit the first academic faculty exchange with the Bureau. Dr. Carter is also an instructor in the Bureau of Justice Assistance SLATT program, author of the COPS-funded publication, *Law Enforcement Intelligence: A Guide for State, Local, and Tribal Law Enforcement*, and project director of the managerial intelligence training program funded by the Department of Homeland Security. He is a fellowship recipient from the Foundation for Defending Democracies where he studied terrorism in Israel. In addition to teaching graduate and undergraduate courses at Michigan State, Dr. Carter is director of the Criminal Justice Overseas Study Program to England. He is the author or co-author of five books and numerous articles and monographs on policing issues and is a member of the editorial boards of various professional publications. His most recent book is the seventh edition of the widely-used community relations textbook, *The Police and Community*, (published by Prentice-Hall). He has another book forthcoming from Prentice-Hall entitled *Homeland Security for State and Local Police*.

APPENDIX G

Intelligence Unit Management Audit (Tear-Out Section)

Audit Factors for the Law Enforcement Intelligence Function

Section A. Meeting National Standards

1. Does the police department subscribe to the tenets and standards of the *Global Justice Information Sharing Initiative*?
   ❏ Yes ❏ No

2. Does the police department subscribe to the standards of the *National Criminal Intelligence Sharing Plan*?
   ❏ Yes ❏ No

3. Does the police department subscribe to the guidelines for information and intelligence sharing of the Office of Domestic Preparedness *Guidelines for Homeland Security*?
   ❏ Yes ❏ No

4. Does the police department subscribe to the guidelines of the Commission on Accreditation for Law Enforcement Agencies (CALEA) Standard 51.1.1 *Criminal Intelligence*?
   ❏ Yes ❏ No

5. Does the police department subscribe to the provisions of the International Association of Chiefs of Police (IACP) *Model Criminal Intelligence Policy*?
   ❏ Yes ❏ No

6. Does the police department subscribe to the standards of the Law Enforcement Intelligence Unit (LEIU) *Criminal Intelligence File Guidelines*?
   ❏ Yes ❏ No

7. Does the police department subscribe to the IACP *Code of Ethics* or have an articulated Code of Ethics?
   ❏ Yes ❏ No

8. Does the police department subscribe to the IACP *Code of Conduct* or have an articulated Code of Conduct?
   ❏ Yes ❏ No

9. Does the police department have an articulated Statement of Values?
   ❏ Yes ❏ No

Law Enforcement Intelligence:
A Guide for State, Local, and Tribal Law Enforcement Agencies

David L. Carter, Ph.D.
School of Criminal Justice
Michigan State University

10. Does the police department adhere to the regulations of 28 CFR Part 23 for its Criminal Intelligence Records System?
    ❑ Yes   ❑ No
    a. Does the police department operate a federally funded multi-jurisdictional criminal intelligence records system?
    ❑ Yes   ❑ No
11. Does the police department subscribe to the tenets of the *Justice Information Privacy Guidelines*?
    ❑ Yes   ❑ No
12. Does the police department subscribe to the tenets for information system security defined in the report, *Applying Security Practices to Justice Information Sharing*?
    ❑ Yes   ❑ No
13. Does the law enforcement agency subscribe to the philosophy of *Intelligence-Led Policing*?
    ❑ Yes   ❑ No
14. Are defined activities for the intelligence unit designed exclusively to prevent and control crime with no political, religious or doctrinal purpose?
    ❑ Yes   ❑ No

Section B: Management Issues

1. Has a mission statement been written for the Intelligence Unit?
   ❑ Yes   ❑ No
2. Is the purpose and role of the Unit clearly articulated and related to the Police Department's Mission Statement?
   ❑ Yes   ❑ No
3. Have priorities been established for the types of crimes the Unit will address?
   ❑ Yes   ❑ No
   a. Is any written rationale provided for these priorities?
   ❑ Yes   ❑ No
4. Are expected activities of the unit articulated?
   ❑ Yes   ❑ No
5. Does the mission statement express ethical standards?
   ❑ Yes   ❑ No

Law Enforcement Intelligence:
A Guide for State, Local, and Tribal Law Enforcement Agencies

David L. Carter, Ph.D.
School of Criminal Justice
Michigan State University

6. Does the mission statement express the importance of protecting citizens' rights?
   ❑ Yes   ❑ No

1. Policies and Procedures

1. Are there written and officially articulated policies and procedures for management of the intelligence function?
   ❑ Yes   ❑ No
2. Have intelligence policies been formed to minimize the discretion of information collectors?
   ❑ Yes   ❑ No
   If Yes, Describe:

3. Is there a policy and procedures on "Information Collection"?
   ❑ Yes   ❑ No
   If Yes, Describe:

2. Management of Information: Definitional Standards

1. Are there standard terms used in intelligence activities that have been operationally defined in writing so that all persons in the department know the explicit meaning and implications of the terms?
   ❑ Yes   ❑ No
2. What is the source of the definitions?
   ❑ NCISP   ❑ Federal Agency
   ❑ Mixed   ❑ N/A

Law Enforcement Intelligence:
A Guide for State, Local, and Tribal Law Enforcement Agencies

David L. Carter, Ph.D.
School of Criminal Justice
Michigan State University

3. Has the department articulated standards for classifying information in the Intelligence Unit?

❑ Yes   ❑ No

Priority	Classification	Description	Release Authority
Highest Level	Sensitive	Current corruption case; complex criminality; confidential informants	Dept Executive or Intelligence Cmdr.
Medium Level	Confidential	Non-sensitive information through intelligence channels; Law Enforcement only	Intelligence Unit Cmdr or Supervisor
Lowest Level	Restricted	LE use but no need for high security	Intell Unit Personnel
Unclassified	Public Access	Information that may be released to public and media	Intell Unit Personnel

4. How are those standards monitored and enforced?

❑ Supervisor   ❑ Other

5. Does the department have a system for assessing the reliability of sources that provide information that will be retained in the Intelligence Records System?

❑ Yes   ❑ No

6. Are there standardized definitions of the reliability scale?

❑ Yes   ❑ No

7. Does the department have a system for assessing the validity of the information that will be retained in the Intelligence Records System?

❑ Yes   ❑ No

8. Are there standardized definitions of the validity scale?

❑ Yes   ❑ No

9. Does the Intelligence Unit have operational definitions that can be applied to a person under investigation or a series of related crimes where the perpetrator is not identifiable in order to classify the case file as either a "permanent file" or a "temporary file"?

❑ Yes   ❑ No

If Yes...

a. Are the types of identifying information that should be placed in the file articulated?

❑   Yes   ❑ No

b. Is there a procedure for requiring the articulation of the criminal predicate for the permanent file?

❑   Yes   ❑ No

c. Is there a procedure articulating the conditions wherein a temporary file may be created?

❑ Yes ❑ No

d. Does the procedure specify a time limit that the temporary file can be kept?

❑ Yes ❑ No

e. Is there an operational definition of "Non-Criminal Identifying Information" and procedures for recording and retaining this information?

❑ Yes ❑ No

f. Are there clear procedures that *describe* the types of information that should not be entered into the Intelligence Records System?

❑ Yes ❑ No

3. Management of Information: Source Documents

1. Does the department have a written directive explaining the different types of source documents that will be entered in the Intelligence Records System?

❑ Yes ❑ No

2. What types of source documents are entered into the Intelligence Records System?

Describe:

3. Does the police department have a written directive that the rationale for each source document entered into the Intelligence Records System must be articulated in a report or notation?

❑ Yes ❑ No

Law Enforcement Intelligence:
A Guide for State, Local, and Tribal Law Enforcement Agencies

David L. Carter, Ph.D.
School of Criminal Justice
Michigan State University

4. Management of Information: Data Entry

1.   Who is responsible for entering information into the Intelligence Records System?
     Position/Classification:

2.   Who supervises the information entry process?
     Position/Classification:

5. Management of Information: Accountability

1.   Who is the Custodian of the Intelligence Records System that ensures all regulations, law, policy and procedures are being followed?
     Position/Classification:

Law Enforcement Intelligence:
A Guide for State, Local, and Tribal Law Enforcement Agencies

David L. Carter, Ph.D.
School of Criminal Justice
Michigan State University

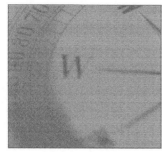

2.   Is there a person external to the Intelligence Unit who is designated to monitor the Intelligence Records System and related processes?
     ❑ Yes   ❑ No
     If Yes, Position/Classification):

3.   Does the department have written procedures for the retention of records in the Intelligence Records System?
     ❑ Yes   ❑ No

6. Management of Information: Retention and Purging of Records

1.   Does the retention process adhere to the guidelines of 28 CFR Part 23?
     ❑ Yes   ❑ No
2.   Does the retention policy and procedure include written criteria for purging information?
     ❑ Yes   ❑ No

3. How often does a review and purge process occur?
   Frequency:

4. What is the purge process?
   Describe:

5. Does the purge process include a system review of information to
   confirm its continuing propriety, accuracy and relevancy?
   ❑ Yes ❑ No

6. Does the purge process require destruction of the source document
   and removal of all references to the document to be purged if the
   information is no longer appropriate for retention?
   ❑ Yes ❑ No

7. What is the destruction process for purged "hard copy" records?
   Describe:

8. After information has been purged from a computerized Intelligence
   Records System, is free space on the hard drive and/or specific
   purged files electronically "wiped"?
   ❑ Yes ❑ No
   a. Are back-ups wiped?
   ❑ Yes ❑ No

**Law Enforcement
Intelligence:**
A Guide for State, Local,
and Tribal Law
Enforcement Agencies

David L. Carter, Ph.D.
School of Criminal Justice
Michigan State University

b. What is the accountability system for purging back-ups?
   Describe:

9. Does the purge process require the elimination of partial information that is no longer appropriate if the source document is to be kept because the remaining information in the source documents merits retention?
   ❏ Yes   ❏ No

10. What is the process for purging partial information from "hard copy" source documents?
    Describe:

Law Enforcement Intelligence:
A Guide for State, Local, and Tribal Law Enforcement Agencies

David L. Carter, Ph.D.
School of Criminal Justice
Michigan State University

11. Who is responsible for ensuring compliance of the purge process?
    Position/Classification:

7. Management of Information: Personal/Individually-Held Records and Files

1. Is there an intelligence unit policy and procedures concerning the retention of individual notes and records that identifies persons wherein criminality is suspected but is not in either a temporary or permanent file and is not entered into any formal records system or database?
   ❏ Yes   ❏ No

a. How is the possession of personal records monitored?
    ☐   Yes   ☐   No
b. How is the policy enforced?
    ☐   Yes   ☐   No

8. Management of Information: Accessing Intelligence Records

1. Is access to the Intelligence Records limited?
    ☐ Yes   ☐ No
2. If yes, who may access the Intelligence Records System?
    Describe:

3. What security controls exist for accessing computerized records?
    Describe:

4. Can the computerized records system be accessed through remote access?
    ☐ Yes   ☐ No
    a. If so, what security controls exist for remote access?
    Describe:

Law Enforcement Intelligence:
A Guide for State, Local, and Tribal Law Enforcement Agencies

David L. Carter, Ph.D.
School of Criminal Justice
Michigan State University

5. How are physical records stored?
   Describe:

6. Who grants access privileges to Intelligence Records?
   Position/Classification:

7. Who has access to records?
   Position/Classification:

**Law Enforcement
Intelligence:**
A Guide for State, Local,
and Tribal Law
Enforcement Agencies

David L. Carter, Ph.D.
School of Criminal Justice
Michigan State University

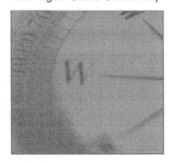

8. Does the police department apply the Third Agency Rule to information
   that is shared with other agencies?
   ❏ Yes   ❏ No

9. What audit process is in place for access to computerized records?
   Describe:

10. What audit process is in place for access to physical records?
    Describe:

11. How are physical records secured?
    Describe:

12. What process is in place to handle unauthorized access to intelligence
    physical records?
    Describe:

13. What sanctions are in place for a police department employee who
    accesses and/or disseminates intelligence records without
    authorization?
    Describe:

Law Enforcement
Intelligence:
A Guide for State, Local,
and Tribal Law
Enforcement Agencies

David L. Carter, Ph.D.
School of Criminal Justice
Michigan State University

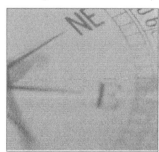

9. Physical Location of the Intelligence Unit and Records

1. Sufficiency: Is the Intelligence Unit in a physical location that has
   sufficient space to perform all of its responsibilities?
   ❏ Yes   ❏ No
2. Security: Is the Intelligence Unit in a physical location wherein the
   entire workspace may be completely secured?
   ❏ Yes   ❏ No
   a. Is there adequate secured storage cabinets (or a vault) for (1)
      documents classified by the Intelligence Unit and (2) sensitive
      records storage within the intelligence unit's physical location?
      ❏   Yes   ❏ No

b.	Is there adequate security and segregated storage for federally classified documents within the intelligence unit?
❑	Yes	❑	No

1)	Is that storage accessible only by persons with a federal top secret security clearance?
❑	Yes	❑	No

3.	Convenience: Is the Intelligence Unit in a physical location that is convenient to the people, equipment, and resources necessary to maximize efficiency and effectiveness of operations?
❑	Yes	❑	No

## 10.	Tangential Policy Issues:	Criminal Informants and Undercover Operations

1.	Is there a formally articulated policy and procedures for managing criminal informants?
❑	Yes	❑	No

a.	Is a background investigation conducted and a comprehensive descriptive file completed on each confidential informant?
❑	Yes	❑	No

b.	Are informant files secured separately from intelligence files?
❑	Yes	❑	No

2.	Is there a formally articulated policy and procedures concerning undercover operations that apply to members of the Intelligence Unit?
❑	Yes	❑	No

3.	Does the police department have a policy on alcohol consumption for officers working undercover?
❑	Yes	❑	No

a.	Does the police department have a policy requiring designated drivers for undercover officers who have consumed alcohol?
❑	Yes	❑	No

4.	Does the police department have a "narcotics simulation" policy and training for undercover officers?
❑	Yes	❑	No

5.	Does the police department have a policy for the issuance of fictitious identification for undercover officers and the proper use of such fictitious identification?
❑	Yes	❑	No

Law Enforcement Intelligence:
A Guide for State, Local, and Tribal Law Enforcement Agencies

David L. Carter, Ph.D.
School of Criminal Justice
Michigan State University

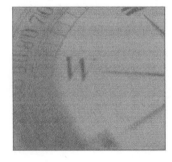

6. Do undercover officers receive training specifically related to proper conduct and information collection while working in an undercover capacity?
    ❑ Yes ❑ No
7. With respect to undercover operating funds:
    a. Is there a 1-tier or 2-tier process to approve use of the funds?
        ❑ 1 Tier ❑ 2 Tier
    b. Is a written report required to document expenditure of the funds?
        ❑ Yes ❑ No
    c. What is the maximum time that may pass between the expenditure of funds and personnel accountability for the funds?
        Days   ❑ No Set Time
    d. Is there a regular external audit of undercover funds?
        ❑ Yes [How Often?]   ❑ No

Section C: Personnel

1. Is a position classification plan in place that provides a clear job description for each position in the unit?
    ❑ Yes ❑ No
2. Is a position classification plan in place that articulates Knowledge, Skills and Abilities (KSAs) for each position?
    ❑ Yes ❑ No
3. Is there sufficient hierarchical staff (managers/supervisors) assigned to the unit to effectively perform supervisory responsibilities?
    ❑ Yes ❑ No
4. Is there sufficient functional staff (analysts and/or investigators) to effectively fulfill defined unit responsibilities?
    ❑ Yes ❑ No
5. Is there sufficient support staff (secretaries, clerks) to effectively support the unit's activities?
    ❑ Yes ❑ No
6. Does the screening process for nonsworn employees of the intelligence unit require:
    a. Fingerprint check?
        ❑   Yes ❑ No
    b. Background investigation
        ❑   Yes ❑ No

7. If the Intelligence Unit has non-PD employees assigned to it – e.g., National Guard analysts, personnel from the state or local law enforcement agencies – would there be a screening process for those persons?

❏ Yes   ❏ No

If Yes, Describe:

Law Enforcement
Intelligence:
A Guide for State, Local,
and Tribal Law
Enforcement Agencies

David L. Carter, Ph.D.
School of Criminal Justice
Michigan State University

1. Training

1. What types of training do preservice and newly assigned personnel receive?

❏ None   ❏ Some–Describe:

a. Are newly assigned sworn employees to the Intelligence Unit required to attend 28 CFR Part 23 training?

❏   Yes   ❏ No

b. Are newly hired or assigned non-sworn employees required to attend 28 CFR Part 23 training?

❏   Yes   ❏ No

2. What types of training do in-service personnel receive?

❏ None   ❏ Some

Describe:

3. Have members of the Intelligence Unit attended any of the following federal government intelligence training programs which are open to state and local law enforcement officers?
   a. DEA Federal Law Enforcement Analyst Training (FLEAT)?
      ❑ Yes   ❑ No
   b. FBI College of Analytic Studies?
      ❑ Yes   ❑ No
   c. Federal Law Enforcement Training Center (FLETC) Criminal Intelligence Analysis Training Course?
      ❑ Yes   ❑ No
   d. National Drug Intelligence Center Basic Intelligence Analysis Course?
      ❑ Yes   ❑ No
   e. National White Collar Crime Center Foundations of Intelligence Analysis?
      ❑ Yes   ❑ No
   f. Regional Counterdrug Training Academy Intelligence Operations Course?
      ❑ Yes   ❑ No

2. Supervision

1. Does supervision effectively monitor adherence to written procedures?
   ❑ Yes   ❑ No
2. Does supervision effectively monitor adherence to guidelines adopted by the department?
   ❑ Yes   ❑ No
3. Are performance evaluations tied directly to the job descriptions?
   ❑ Yes   ❑ No
4. Does supervision effectively monitor the performance of required duties (Including the quality of performance)?
   ❑ Yes   ❑ No
5. Is supervision effectively monitoring personnel to ensure civil rights allegations cannot be made with respect to negligent:
   a. Failure to train?
      ❑ Yes   ❑ No

Law Enforcement Intelligence:
A Guide for State, Local, and Tribal Law Enforcement Agencies

David L. Carter, Ph.D.
School of Criminal Justice
Michigan State University

b. Hiring?
    ☐   Yes   ☐   No
c. Failure to supervise?
    ☐   Yes   ☐   No
d. Assignment?
    ☐   Yes   ☐   No
e. Failure to direct?
    ☐   Yes   ☐   No
f. Failure to discipline?
    ☐   Yes   ☐   No
g. Entrustment?
    ☐   Yes   ☐   No

6. Is there effective supervision of the Intelligence Unit throughout the chain of command external to the Intelligence Unit?
    ☐   Yes   ☐   No

Section D: Fiscal Management

1. Is the budget sufficient to fulfill the stated mission?
    ☐   Yes   ☐   No

2. Does the Intelligence Commander have input into the budget planning process?
    ☐   Yes   ☐   No

3. Is there over-reliance on "soft money" to operate the unit?
    ☐   Yes   ☐   No

4. Are equipment and personnel line items assigned directly to the Intelligence Unit?[235]
    ☐   Yes   ☐   No

5. Is there an established process for reliably monitoring credit cards assigned to personnel?
    ☐   Yes   ☐   No   ☐   NA

Section E: Unit Evaluation

1. As a whole, is the unit effective with respect to:
    a. Providing information to prevent crime?
        ☐   Yes   ☐   No

Law Enforcement Intelligence:
A Guide for State, Local, and Tribal Law Enforcement Agencies

David L. Carter, Ph.D.
School of Criminal Justice
Michigan State University

b. Providing information to apprehend criminals?

❑ Yes ❑ No

c. Effectively analyzing information to identify criminal enterprises, crime trends, criminal anomalies, etc.?

❑ Yes ❑ No

2. Are data collected on the following factors and reported in an annual report as indicators of the intelligence unit's productivity as an organizational entity?

a. Number and type of analytic products delivered for investigative purposes?

❑ Yes ❑ No ❑ NA

b. Number and type of analytic products that led to arrest?

❑ Yes ❑ No ❑ NA

c. Assets seized from illegal activities wherein intelligence contributed to the arrest and/or seizure?

❑ Yes ❑ No ❑ NA

d. Number and types of strategic intelligence products delivered to the command staff?

❑ Yes ❑ No ❑ NA

e. Number of intelligence-sharing meetings attended by unit staff?

❑ Yes ❑ No ❑ NA

f. Number of briefings provided by the intelligence staff?

❑ Yes ❑ No ❑ NA

g. Total number of queries into the intelligence data base?

❑ Yes ❑ No ❑ NA

h. Number of permanent files opened?

❑ Yes ❑ No ❑ NA

i. Number of temporary files investigated?

❑ Yes ❑ No ❑ NA

j. Number of requests for information to the unit from outside agencies?

❑ Yes ❑ No ❑ NA

3. Are products produced by the Intelligence Unit:

a. In a consistent format?

❑ Yes ❑ No

b. Easily consumed and used (i.e., understandable and actionable)?

❑ Yes ❑ No

Law Enforcement
Intelligence:
A Guide for State, Local,
and Tribal Law
Enforcement Agencies

David L. Carter, Ph.D.
School of Criminal Justice
Michigan State University

c. Contain timely information and disseminated in a timely manner?
❑   Yes   ❑   No

d. Have substantive contact to aid in preventing or controlling crime?
❑   Yes   ❑   No

4. Given the confidential nature of the information contained in the Intelligence Unit, is there a policy and procedures if a city, county, state, or federal fiscal or program auditor seeks to audit the Intelligence Unit?
❑   Yes   ❑   No
If Yes, Describe:

Section F. Collection

1. Is there an articulated collection plan for the Intelligence Unit?
❑   Yes   ❑   No
If Yes, Describe:

    a. How often and when is the plan updated?
      Describe:

2. Have the following activities been performed by the Intelligence Unit:
    a. An inventory of threats in the region posed by criminal enterprises, terrorists, and criminal extremists?
❑   Yes   ❑   No
    b. An assessment of the threats with respect to their probability of posing a criminal or terrorist threat to the region?
❑   Yes   ❑   No
    c. A target or criminal commodity analysis of the region?
❑   Yes   ❑   No
    d. A target or criminal commodity vulnerability assessment in the region?
❑   Yes   ❑   No

3. For each identified threat, have intelligence requirements been articulated?
❑   Yes   ❑   No

Law Enforcement Intelligence:
A Guide for State, Local, and Tribal Law Enforcement Agencies

David L. Carter, Ph.D.
School of Criminal Justice
Michigan State University

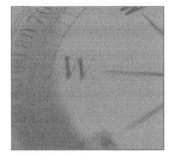

a.   If Yes, Describe the methods of collection that will be used to fulfill those intelligence requirements.

Section G: Technology and Networking

1.   Are any members of the Intelligence Unit subscribed members to the FBI's secure Email system Law Enforcement Online (LEO)?
     ❏ Yes–All   ❏ Yes–Some   ❏ No

2.   Are any members of the Intelligence Unit subscribed members to the secure Regional Information Sharing System (RISS) email system riss.net?
     ❏ Yes–All   ❏ Yes–Some   ❏ No
     a.   If yes, are the RISS databases (e.g., RISS.gang, ATIX, etc.) regularly used?
          ❏ Yes   ❏ No

3.   Is the police department a member of the Regional Information Sharing System?
     ❏ Yes   ❏ No

4.   Is a systematic procedure in place to ensure that advisories and notifications transmitted via the National Law Enforcement Teletype System (NLETS) are forwarded to the Intelligence Unit?
     ❏ Yes   ❏ No

5.   Are you connected to any state-operated intelligence or information networks?
     ❏ Yes   ❏ No
     If Yes, Describe:

Law Enforcement Intelligence:
A Guide for State, Local, and Tribal Law Enforcement Agencies

David L. Carter, Ph.D.
School of Criminal Justice
Michigan State University

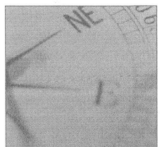

6. Are you connected to any regional intelligence or information networks (including HIDTA)?

    ❑ Yes   ❑ No

    If Yes, Describe:

7. Does the intelligence have access and use the National Virtual Pointer System (NVPS)?

    ❑ Yes   ❑ No

8. Is there a formal approval process for entering into a memorandum of understanding (MOU) for information and intelligence sharing with other law enforcement agencies or law enforcement intelligence entities?

    ❑ Yes   ❑ No

    If Yes, Describe the process:

Who must approve the MOU?

Section H: Legal Issues

1. Is there a designated person in the police department who reviews Freedom of Information Act requests directed to the intelligence unit?

    ❑ Yes   ❑ No

2. Is there a designated person in the police department who responds to Privacy Act inquiries directed to the intelligence unit?

    ❑ Yes   ❑ No

3. Is there a designated person the police department contacts in response to a subpoena for a file in the Intelligence Records System?
   ❑ Yes   ❑ No
4. Does the Intelligence Unit Commander have a legal resource for advice to help protect intelligence records from objectionable access?
   ❑ Yes   ❑ No
5. Does the Intelligence Unit Commander have a legal resource for advice on matters related to criminal procedure and civil rights?
   ❑ Yes   ❑ No
6. Does the Intelligence Unit Commander have a legal resource for advice on matters related to questions of civil liability as it relates to all aspects of the intelligence function?
   ❑ Yes   ❑ No
7. Has legal counsel reviewed and approved all policies and procedures of the intelligence unit?
   ❑ Yes   ❑ No

Law Enforcement Intelligence:
A Guide for State, Local, and Tribal Law Enforcement Agencies

David L. Carter, Ph.D.
School of Criminal Justice
Michigan State University

27480020R00180

Made in the USA
Charleston, SC
15 March 2014

1.

Year	Total Dividends	Preferred Dividends		Common Dividends	
		Total	Per Share	Total	Per Share
1996					
1997					
1998					
1999					
2000					
2001					

2.

3.

Name _____

PROBLEM 12 - 2 ___

JOURNAL

PAGE _____

	DATE		DESCRIPTION	POST. REF.	DEBIT	CREDIT	
1							1
2							2
3							3
4							4
5							5
6							6
7							7
8							8
9							9
10							10
11							11
12							12
13							13
14							14
15							15
16							16
17							17
18							18
19							19
20							20
21							21
22							22
23							23
24							24
25							25
26							26
27							27
28							28
29							29
30							30
31							31
32							32
33							33

PROBLEM 12 - 2 ___ , Concluded

JOURNAL

PAGE

	DATE		DESCRIPTION	POST. REF.	DEBIT	CREDIT	
1							1
2							2
3							3
4							4
5							5
6							6
7							7
8							8
9							9
10							10
11							11
12							12
13							13
14							14
15							15
16							16
17							17
18							18
19							19
20							20
21							21
22							22
23							23
24							24
25							25
26							26
27							27
28							28
29							29
30							30
31							31
32							32
33							33

JOURNAL

PAGE

	DATE		DESCRIPTION	POST. REF.	DEBIT	CREDIT	
1							1
2							2
3							3
4							4
5							5
6							6
7							7
8							8
9							9
10							10
11							11
12							12
13							13
14							14
15							15
16							16
17							17
18							18
19							19
20							20
21							21
22							22
23							23
24							24
25							25
26							26
27							27
28							28
29							29
30							30
31							31
32							32
33							33

PROBLEM 12 - 3 ___ , Concluded

JOURNAL

PAGE

	DATE		DESCRIPTION	POST. REF.	DEBIT	CREDIT	
1							1
2							2
3							3
4							4
5							5
6							6
7							7
8							8
9							9
10							10
11							11
12							12
13							13
14							14
15							15
16							16
17							17
18							18
19							19
20							20
21							21
22							22
23							23
24							24
25							25
26							26
27							27
28							28
29							29
30							30
31							31
32							32
33							33

1. and 2.

Common Stock

Paid-In Capital in Excess of Stated Value

Retained Earnings

Treasury Stock

Paid-In Capital from Sale of Treasury Stock

Donated Capital

Stock Dividends Distributable

Stock Dividends

Cash Dividends

Name _____

PROBLEM 12 - 4 ___ , Continued

2.

JOURNAL   PAGE

	DATE		DESCRIPTION	POST. REF.	DEBIT	CREDIT	
1							1
2							2
3							3
4							4
5							5
6							6
7							7
8							8
9							9
10							10
11							11
12							12
13							13
14							14
15							15
16							16
17							17
18							18
19							19
20							20
21							21
22							22
23							23
24							24
25							25
26							26
27							27
28							28
29							29
30							30
31							31
32							32
33							33

JOURNAL

PAGE

	DATE		DESCRIPTION	POST. REF.	DEBIT	CREDIT	
1							1
2							2
3							3
4							4
5							5
6							6
7							7
8							8
9							9
10							10
11							11
12							12
13							13
14							14
15							15
16							16
17							17
18							18
19							19
20							20
21							21
22							22
23							23
24							24
25							25
26							26
27							27
28							28
29							29

3.

Name _____

JOURNAL

PAGE _____

	DATE		DESCRIPTION	POST. REF.	DEBIT	CREDIT	
1							1
2							2
3							3
4							4
5							5
6							6
7							7
8							8
9							9
10							10
11							11
12							12
13							13
14							14
15							15
16							16
17							17
18							18
19							19
20							20
21							21
22							22
23							23
24							24
25							25
26							26
27							27
28							28
29							29
30							30
31							31
32							32
33							33

PROBLEM 12 - 5 ___ , Concluded

JOURNAL

PAGE

	DATE		DESCRIPTION	POST. REF.	DEBIT	CREDIT	
1							1
2							2
3							3
4							4
5							5
6							6
7							7
8							8
9							9
10							10
11							11
12							12
13							13
14							14
15							15
16							16
17							17
18							18
19							19
20							20
21							21
22							22
23							23
24							24
25							25
26							26
27							27
28							28
29							29
30							30
31							31
32							32
33							33

1. and 2.

Year	Income Tax Deducted on Income Statement	Income Tax Payments for the Year	Deferred Income Tax Payable	
			Year's Addition (Deduction)	Year-End Balance
First				
Second				
Third				
Fourth				
Total				

Page not used.

Name _____

Omit "00" in the cents columns.

1.

2.

3.

PROBLEM 13 - 3 ___ , Concluded

JOURNAL   PAGE

	DATE		DESCRIPTION	POST. REF.	DEBIT	CREDIT	
1							1
2							2
3							3
4							4
5							5
6							6
7							7
8							8
9							9
10							10
11							11
12							12
13							13
14							14
15							15
16							16
17							17
18							18
19							19
20							20
21							21
22							22
23							23
24							24
25							25
26							26
27							27
28							28
29							29
30							30
31							31
32							32
33							33

JOURNAL

PAGE

	DATE	DESCRIPTION	POST. REF.	DEBIT	CREDIT	
1						1
2						2
3						3
4						4
5						5
6						6
7						7
8						8
9						9
10						10
11						11
12						12
13						13
14						14
15						15
16						16
17						17
18						18
19						19
20						20
21						21
22						22
23						23
24						24
25						25
26						26
27						27
28						28
29						29
30						30
31						31
32						32
33						33

1.

	Plan 1	Plan 2	Plan 3
Earnings before interest and income tax			
Deduct interest on bonds			
Income before income tax			
Deduct income tax			
Net income			
Dividends on preferred stock			
Available for dividends on common stock			
Shares of common stock outstanding			
Earnings per share on common stock			

2.

	Plan 1	Plan 2	Plan 3
Earnings before interest and income tax			
Deduct interest on bonds			
Income before income tax			
Deduct income tax			
Net income			
Dividends on preferred stock			
Available for dividends on common stock			
Shares of common stock outstanding			
Earnings per share on common stock			

3.

1. and 2.

JOURNAL

PAGE

	DATE		DESCRIPTION	POST. REF.	DEBIT	CREDIT	
1							1
2							2
3							3
4							4
5							5
6							6
7							7
8							8
9							9
10							10
11							11
12							12
13							13
14							14
15							15
16							16
17							17
18							18
19							19
20							20
21							21
22							22
23							23
24							24
25							25
26							26
27							27
28							28
29							29
30							30
31							31
32							32
33							33

PROBLEM 14 - 2 ___ , Concluded

JOURNAL

PAGE _____

	DATE	DESCRIPTION	POST. REF.	DEBIT	CREDIT	
1						1
2						2
3						3
4						4
5						5
6						6
7						7
8						8
9						9
10						10
11						11
12						12
13						13
14						14
15						15
16						16
17						17
18						18
19						19

3.

4.

1. and 2.

JOURNAL

PAGE _____

	DATE		DESCRIPTION	POST. REF.	DEBIT	CREDIT	
1							1
2							2
3							3
4							4
5							5
6							6
7							7
8							8
9							9
10							10
11							11
12							12
13							13
14							14
15							15
16							16
17							17
18							18
19							19
20							20
21							21
22							22
23							23
24							24
25							25
26							26
27							27
28							28
29							29
30							30
31							31
32							32
33							33

JOURNAL PAGE

	DATE		DESCRIPTION	POST. REF.	DEBIT	CREDIT	
1							1
2							2
3							3
4							4
5							5
6							6
7							7
8							8
9							9
10							10
11							11
12							12
13							13
14							14
15							15
16							16
17							17
18							18
19							19

3.

4.

1.

JOURNAL

PAGE _____

	DATE		DESCRIPTION	POST. REF.	DEBIT	CREDIT	
1							1
2							2
3							3
4							4
5							5
6							6
7							7
8							8
9							9
10							10
11							11
12							12
13							13
14							14
15							15
16							16
17							17
18							18
19							19
20							20
21							21
22							22
23							23
24							24
25							25
26							26
27							27
28							28
29							29
30							30
31							31
32							32
33							33

JOURNAL

PAGE

	DATE		DESCRIPTION	POST. REF.	DEBIT	CREDIT	
1							1
2							2
3							3
4							4
5							5
6							6
7							7
8							8
9							9
10							10
11							11
12							12
13							13
14							14
15							15
16							16
17							17
18							18
19							19

2.

3.

JOURNAL

PAGE _____

	DATE		DESCRIPTION	POST. REF.	DEBIT	CREDIT	
1							1
2							2
3							3
4							4
5							5
6							6
7							7
8							8
9							9
10							10
11							11
12							12
13							13
14							14
15							15
16							16
17							17
18							18
19							19
20							20
21							21
22							22
23							23
24							24
25							25
26							26
27							27
28							28
29							29
30							30
31							31
32							32
33							33

JOURNAL   PAGE

	DATE		DESCRIPTION	POST. REF.	DEBIT	CREDIT	
1							1
2							2
3							3
4							4
5							5
6							6
7							7
8							8
9							9
10							10
11							11
12							12
13							13
14							14
15							15
16							16
17							17
18							18
19							19
20							20
21							21
22							22
23							23
24							24
25							25
26							26
27							27
28							28
29							29
30							30
31							31
32							32
33							33

Name _____

APPENDIX PROBLEM 14 - 6 ___

1.

JOURNAL   PAGE

	DATE	DESCRIPTION	POST. REF.	DEBIT	CREDIT	
1						1
2						2
3						3
4						4
5						5
6						6
7						7
8						8
9						9
10						10
11						11
12						12
13						13
14						14
15						15
16						16
17						17
18						18
19						19

2.

325

1.

JOURNAL   PAGE

	DATE		DESCRIPTION	POST. REF.	DEBIT	CREDIT	
1							1
2							2
3							3
4							4
5							5
6							6
7							7
8							8
9							9
10							10
11							11
12							12
13							13
14							14
15							15
16							16
17							17
18							18
19							19

2.

1.

JOURNAL

PAGE _____

	DATE		DESCRIPTION	POST. REF.	DEBIT	CREDIT	
1							1
2							2
3							3
4							4
5							5
6							6
7							7
8							8
9							9
10							10
11							11
12							12
13							13
14							14
15							15
16							16
17							17
18							18
19							19
20							20
21							21
22							22
23							23
24							24
25							25
26							26
27							27
28							28
29							29
30							30
31							31
32							32
33							33

JOURNAL

PAGE

	DATE	DESCRIPTION	POST. REF.	DEBIT	CREDIT	
1						1
2						2
3						3
4						4
5						5
6						6
7						7
8						8
9						9
10						10
11						11
12						12
13						13
14						14
15						15
16						16
17						17
18						18
19						19
20						20
21						21
22						22
23						23
24						24
25						25
26						26
27						27
28						28
29						29
30						30
31						31
32						32
33						33

2. a. *Omit "00" in the cents columns.*

Income Statement

Income Statement (Concluded)

Name _____

COMPREHENSIVE PROBLEM 4, Continued

2.b. *Omit "00" in the cents columns.*

Retained Earnings Statement

COMPREHENSIVE PROBLEM 4, Continued

2.c. *Omit "00" in the cents columns.*

Balance Sheet

332

Balance Sheet (Concluded)

Page not used.

Name _____

Omit "00" in the cents columns.

The use of this form is not required unless so indicated by the instructor.

Work Sheet for Statement of Cash Flows

ACCOUNTS	BALANCE, _____ , 1999	TRANSACTIONS DEBIT	CREDIT	BALANCE, _____ , 2000

ACCOUNTS	BALANCE, _____ , 1999	TRANSACTIONS		BALANCE, _____ , 2000
		DEBIT	CREDIT	

Omit "00" in the cents columns.

The use of this form is not required unless so indicated by the instructor.

Work Sheet for Statement of Cash Flows

ACCOUNTS	BALANCE, DEC. 31, 1999	TRANSACTIONS		BALANCE, DEC. 31, 2000
		DEBIT	CREDIT	

ACCOUNTS	BALANCE, DEC. 31, 1999	TRANSACTIONS		BALANCE, DEC. 31, 2000
		DEBIT	CREDIT	

Name _____

Omit "00" in the cents columns.

The use of this form is not required unless so indicated by the instructor.

Work Sheet for Statement of Cash Flows

ACCOUNTS	BALANCE, DEC. 31, 1999	TRANSACTIONS		BALANCE, DEC. 31, 2000
		DEBIT	CREDIT	

PROBLEM 15 - 3 ___ , Concluded

ACCOUNTS	BALANCE, DEC. 31, 1999	TRANSACTIONS		BALANCE, DEC. 31, 2000
		DEBIT	CREDIT	

Name _____

Omit "00" in the cents columns.

PROBLEM 15 - 4 ___ , Continued

The use of this form is not required unless so indicated by the instructor.

Work Sheet for Statement of Cash Flows

ACCOUNTS	BALANCE, DEC. 31, 2000	TRANSACTIONS		BALANCE, DEC. 31, 2001
		DEBIT	CREDIT	

PROBLEM 15 - 4 ___ , Concluded

ACCOUNTS	BALANCE, DEC. 31, 2000	TRANSACTIONS		BALANCE, DEC. 31, 2001
		DEBIT	CREDIT	

Name _____

PROBLEM 15 - 5 ___

Omit "00" in the cents columns.

351

The use of this form is not required unless so indicated by the instructor.

Work Sheet for Statement of Cash Flows

ACCOUNTS	BALANCE, _____, 1999	TRANSACTIONS		BALANCE, _____, 2000
		DEBIT	CREDIT	

PROBLEM 15 - 5 ___ , Concluded

ACCOUNTS	BALANCE, _____, 1999	TRANSACTIONS		BALANCE, _____, 2000
		DEBIT	CREDIT	

1.

Comparative Income Statement

	2000	1999	INCREASE (DECREASE)	
			AMOUNT	PERCENT

2.

1.

Comparative Income Statement

	2000		1999	
	AMOUNT	PERCENT	AMOUNT	PERCENT

2.

1.a.

1.b.

1.c.

2.

Transaction	Working Capital	Current Ratio	Acid-Test Ratio
a.			
b.			
c.			
d.			
e.			
f.			
g.			
h.			
i.			
j.			

1. through 19.

1. a.

1. b.

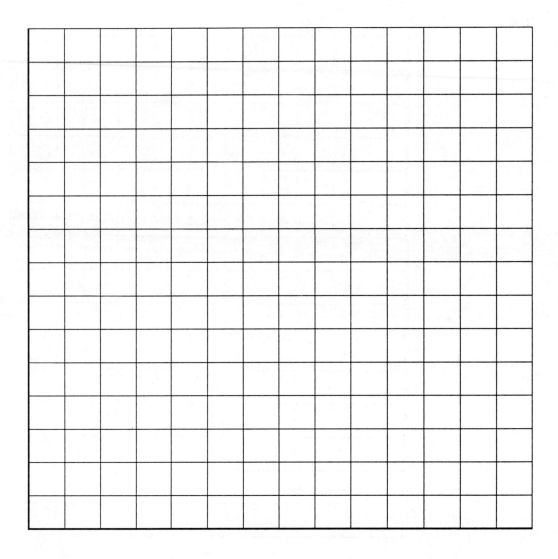

1. c.

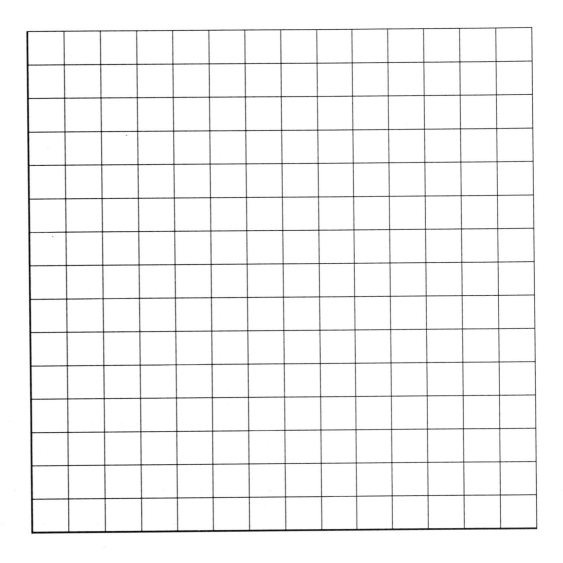

1. d.

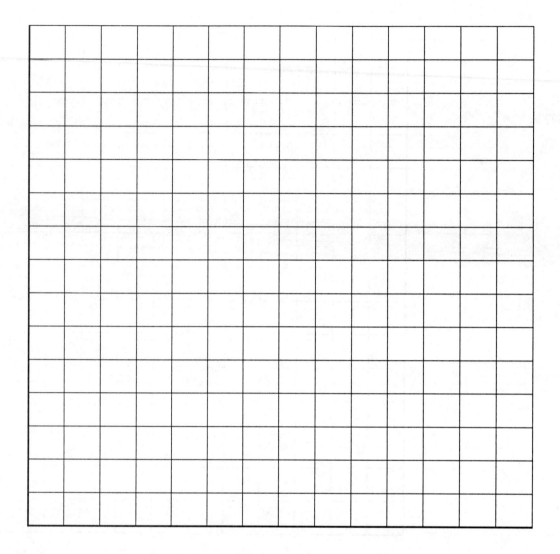

2.

PROBLEM 16 - 5 ___ , Concluded

1. a. through r. _____

_____

_____

_____

_____

_____

_____

_____

_____

_____

_____

_____

_____

_____

_____

_____

_____

_____

_____

_____

_____

_____

_____

_____

_____

_____

_____

_____

_____

_____

_____

_____

_____

_____

_____

_____

_____

_____

_____

_____

_____

_____

_____

_____

_____

_____

_____

2. _____

_____

_____

_____

_____

_____

_____

_____

_____

_____

_____

_____

_____

_____

_____

_____

_____

_____

_____

_____

_____

_____

_____

_____

_____

_____

_____

_____

_____

_____

_____

_____

_____

_____

_____

_____

_____

_____

_____

_____

_____

Cost	Product Costs			Period Costs	
	Direct Materials Cost	Direct Labor Cost	Factory Overhead Cost	Selling Expense	Administrative Expense
a.					
b.					
c.					
d.					
e.					
f.					
g.					
h.					
i.					
j.					
k.					
l.					
m.					
n.					
o.					
p.					
q.					
r.					
s.					
t.					
u.					
v.					
w.					
x.					
y.					
z.					

Page Not Used.

JOURNAL

PAGE ___

	DATE	DESCRIPTION	POST. REF.	DEBIT	CREDIT	
1						1
2						2
3						3
4						4
5						5
6						6
7						7
8						8
9						9
10						10
11						11
12						12
13						13
14						14
15						15
16						16
17						17
18						18
19						19
20						20
21						21
22						22
23						23
24						24
25						25
26						26
27						27
28						28
29						29
30						30
31						31
32						32
33						33

JOURNAL

PAGE

	DATE		DESCRIPTION	POST. REF.	DEBIT	CREDIT	
1							1
2							2
3							3
4							4
5							5
6							6
7							7
8							8
9							9
10							10
11							11
12							12
13							13
14							14
15							15
16							16
17							17
18							18
19							19
20							20
21							21
22							22
23							23
24							24
25							25
26							26
27							27
28							28
29							29
30							30
31							31
32							32
33							33

Name _____

1.

JOURNAL

PAGE _____

	DATE		DESCRIPTION	POST. REF.	DEBIT	CREDIT	
1							1
2							2
3							3
4							4
5							5
6							6
7							7
8							8
9							9
10							10
11							11
12							12
13							13
14							14
15							15
16							16
17							17
18							18
19							19
20							20
21							21
22							22
23							23
24							24
25							25
26							26
27							27
28							28
29							29
30							30
31							31
32							32
33							33

PROBLEM 17 - 3 ___ , Concluded

2.

Work in Process

Finished Goods

3.

Schedule of Unfinished Jobs

	DIRECT MATERIALS	DIRECT LABOR	FACTORY OVERHEAD	TOTAL

4.

Schedule of Completed Jobs

	DIRECT MATERIALS	DIRECT LABOR	FACTORY OVERHEAD	TOTAL

JOB ORDER COST SHEET

Customer _____	Date _____
Address _____	Date wanted _____
_____	Date completed _____
Item _____	Job No. _____

ESTIMATE

Direct Materials		Direct Labor		Summary	
	Amount		Amount		Amount
____meters at $ ____	_____	____hours at $ ____	_____	Direct materials	_____
____meters at ____	_____	____hours at ____	_____	Direct labor	_____
____meters at ____	_____	____hours at ____	_____	Factory overhead	_____
____meters at ____	_____	____hours at ____	_____	Total cost	_____
Total	_____	Total	_____		

ACTUAL

Direct Materials			Direct Labor			Summary	
Mat. Req. No.	Description	Amount	Time Ticket No.	Description	Amount	Item	Amount
____	_____	_____	____	_____	_____	Direct materials	_____
____	_____	_____	____	_____	_____	Direct labor	_____
____	_____	_____	____	_____	_____	Factory overhead	_____
____	_____	_____	____	_____	_____	Total cost	_____
Total		_____	Total		_____		

Comments:

Page not used.

PROBLEM 17 - 5 ___ , Concluded

1.

2.

1.

JOURNAL

PAGE _____

	DATE		DESCRIPTION	POST. REF.	DEBIT	CREDIT	
1							1
2							2
3							3
4							4
5							5
6							6
7							7
8							8
9							9
10							10
11							11
12							12
13							13
14							14
15							15
16							16
17							17
18							18
19							19
20							20
21							21
22							22
23							23
24							24
25							25
26							26
27							27
28							28
29							29
30							30
31							31
32							32
33							33

JOURNAL

PAGE

	DATE	DESCRIPTION	POST. REF.	DEBIT	CREDIT	
1						1
2						2
3						3
4						4
5						5
6						6

2. and 3.

JOURNAL

PAGE _____

	DATE		DESCRIPTION	POST. REF.	DEBIT	CREDIT	
1							1
2							2
3							3
4							4
5							5
6							6
7							7
8							8
9							9
10							10
11							11
12							12
13							13
14							14
15							15
16							16
17							17
18							18
19							19
20							20
21							21
22							22
23							23
24							24
25							25
26							26
27							27
28							28
29							29
30							30
31							31
32							32
33							33

JOURNAL

PAGE

	DATE	DESCRIPTION	POST. REF.	DEBIT	CREDIT	
1						1
2						2
3						3
4						4
5						5
6						6
7						7
8						8
9						9
10						10
11						11
12						12
13						13
14						14
15						15
16						16
17						17
18						18
19						19
20						20
21						21
22						22
23						23
24						24
25						25
26						26
27						27
28						28
29						29
30						30
31						31
32						32
33						33

UNITS	WHOLE UNITS	EQUIVALENT UNITS	
		DIRECT MATERIALS	CONVERSION

COSTS	COSTS		
	DIRECT MATERIALS	CONVERSION	TOTAL COSTS

Name _____

1.

UNITS	WHOLE UNITS	EQUIVALENT UNITS	
		DIRECT MATERIALS	CONVERSION

COSTS	COSTS		
	DIRECT MATERIALS	CONVERSION	TOTAL COSTS

2.

JOURNAL

PAGE _____

	DATE		DESCRIPTION	POST. REF.	DEBIT	CREDIT	
1							1
2							2
3							3
4							4
5							5
6							6
7							7
8							8
9							9
10							10
11							11
12							12
13							13
14							14
15							15
16							16
17							17
18							18
19							19
20							20
21							21
22							22
23							23
24							24
25							25
26							26
27							27
28							28
29							29
30							30
31							31
32							32
33							33

PROBLEM 18 - 4 ___ , Concluded

3.

Name _____

1. and 2.

ACCOUNT   *Work in Process—_____ Department*   ACCOUNT NO. _____

DATE	ITEM	POST. REF.	DEBIT	CREDIT	BALANCE	
					DEBIT	CREDIT

1.

UNITS	WHOLE UNITS	EQUIVALENT UNITS	
		DIRECT MATERIALS	CONVERSION

COSTS	COSTS		
	DIRECT MATERIALS	CONVERSION	TOTAL COSTS

PROBLEM 18 - 5 ___ , Continued

2.

UNITS	WHOLE UNITS	EQUIVALENT UNITS	
		DIRECT MATERIALS	CONVERSION

COSTS	COSTS		
	DIRECT MATERIALS	CONVERSION	TOTAL COSTS

Page Not Used.

Name _____

Cost	Fixed Cost	Variable Cost	Mixed Cost
a.			
b.			
c.			
d.			
e.			
f.			
g.			
h.			
i.			
j.			
k.			
l.			
m.			
n.			
o.			
p.			
q.			
r.			
s.			
t.			

Page not used.

1. *Omit "00" in the cents columns.*

	FIXED COSTS	VARIABLE COSTS

2. through 8. _____

PROBLEM 19 - 2 ___ , Concluded

1. and 2.

3.

Sales and Costs

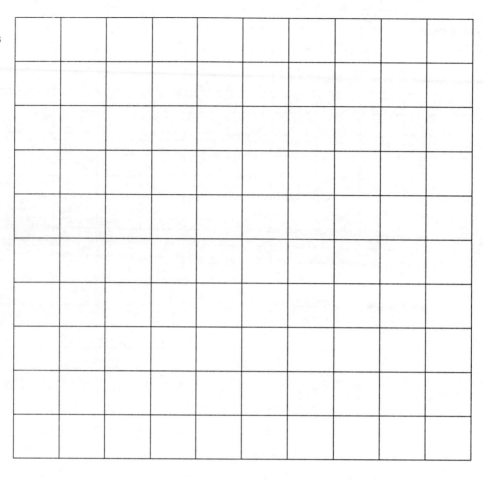

Units of Sales

4. _____

_____

_____

_____

_____

_____

_____

_____

_____

_____

_____

_____

_____

_____

_____

_____

_____

_____

1.

Sales and Costs

Units of Sales

2.a. _____

   b. _____

3.

Sales and Costs

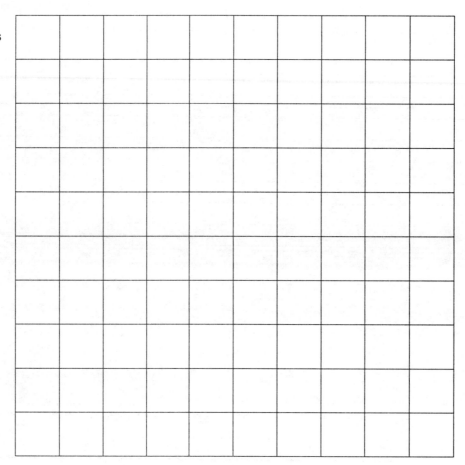

Units of Sales

4.a. _____

b. _____

Name _____

PROBLEM 19 - 5 ___

_____
_____
_____
_____
_____
_____
_____
_____
_____
_____
_____
_____
_____
_____
_____
_____
_____
_____
_____
_____
_____
_____
_____
_____
_____
_____
_____
_____
_____
_____
_____
_____
_____
_____
_____
_____
_____
_____
_____
_____

PROBLEM 19 - 5 ___ , Concluded

Name _____

1. *Omit "00" in the cents columns.*

	Estimated Income Statement					
	For Year Ending December 31, 2000					

PROBLEM 19 - 6 ___ , Continued

2. and 3.

4.

Sales and Costs

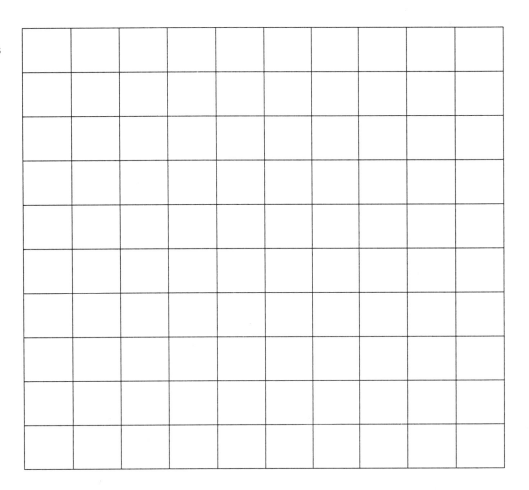

Units of Sales

5. and 6.

1.

	UNIT SALES, YEAR ENDED 2000		INCREASE (DECREASE) ACTUAL OVER BUDGET	
	BUDGET	ACTUAL	AMOUNT	PERCENT

2.

	2000 BUDGETED UNITS	PERCENTAGE INCREASE (DECREASE)	2001 BUDGETED UNITS

3.

	Sales Budget		
	For Year Ending December 31, 2001		
PRODUCT AND AREA	UNIT SALES VOLUME	UNIT SELLING PRICE	TOTAL SALES

Name _____

1.

Sales Budget

PRODUCT AND AREA	UNIT SALES VOLUME	UNIT SELLING PRICE	TOTAL SALES	

2.

Production Budget

	UNITS	

PROBLEM 20 - 2 ___ , Concluded

3.

Direct Materials Purchases Budget

	DIRECT MATERIALS				TOTAL

4.

Direct Labor Cost Budget

				TOTAL

1.

Sales Budget

PRODUCT	UNIT SALES VOLUME	UNIT SELLING PRICE	TOTAL SALES

2.

Production Budget

	UNITS	

PROBLEM 20 - 3 ___ , Continued

3.

Direct Materials Purchases Budget

	DIRECT MATERIALS		TOTAL

4.

Direct Labor Cost Budget

			TOTAL

5.

Factory Overhead Cost Budget						

6.

Cost of Goods Sold Budget

Name _____

PROBLEM 20 - 3 ___ , Continued

7.

Selling and Administrative Expenses Budget

PROBLEM 20 - 3 ___ , Continued

8.

	Budgeted Income Statement																

Name _____

1. *Omit "00" in the cents columns.*

Cash Budget

PROBLEM 20 - 4 ___ , Concluded

Computations

2.

Name _____

1. *Omit "00" in the cents columns.*

Budgeted Income Statement

PROBLEM 20 - 5 ___ , Concluded

2. *Omit "00" in the cents columns.*

Budgeted Balance Sheet				

1. a. *Omit "00" in the cents columns.*

			TOTAL	

1. b.   *Omit "00" in the cents columns.*

			TOTAL	

2.

a.

b.

PROBLEM 21 - 3 ___ , Concluded

c.

Factory Overhead Cost Variance Report—

Normal capacity for the month:

Actual production for the month:

	BUDGET	ACTUAL	VARIANCES	
			FAVORABLE	UNFAVORABLE

Page not used.

Name _____

1.

2.

1.

2.

3.

1.

2.

3.

1.

2.

3.

4.

5.

1.

2.

3.

4.

1.

2.

3.

			TOTAL	

4. _____

_____
_____
_____
_____
_____
_____
_____
_____
_____
_____
_____
_____
_____
_____
_____
_____
_____
_____
_____
_____
_____
_____
_____
_____
_____
_____
_____
_____
_____
_____
_____

5. _____

_____
_____
_____
_____
_____
_____
_____
_____
_____

PROBLEM 22 - 6 ___ , Concluded

PROBLEM 22 - 6 ___ , Concluded

Name _____

1. *Omit "00" in the cents column.*

Proposal to Operate Warehouse

2.

3.

PROBLEM 23 - 1 ___ , Concluded

1. *Omit "00" in the cents column.*

Proposal to Replace Machine

2.

1. *Omit "00" in the cents column.*

Proposals for Sales Promotion Campaign

PROBLEM 23 - 3 ___ , Concluded

2.

1. *Omit "00" in the cents column.*

Proposal to Process _____ Further

2. _____

Page not used.

1.

2.

3.

4.

5.

6. a. *Omit "00" in the cents column.*

Proposal to Sell to

6. b.

1. *Omit "00" in the cents column.*

2.

PROBLEM 23 - 6 ___ , Concluded

3.

1. a. _____

_____

_____

_____

_____

b.

Year	Present Value of $1 at _____%	Net Cash Flow		Present Value of Net Cash Flow	
		Project _____	Project _____	Project _____	Project _____
1					
2					
3					
4					
5					
Total					
Amount to be invested					
Net present value					

2. _____

_____

_____

_____

_____

_____

_____

_____

_____

_____

_____

_____

_____

_____

_____

_____

_____

_____

_____

_____

_____

PROBLEM 24 - 1 ___ , Concluded

1. a. _____

_____

_____

_____

_____

b.

Year	Present Value of $1 at _____%	Net Cash Flow		Present Value of Net Cash Flow	
		Project _____	Project _____	Project _____	Project _____
1					
2					
3					
4					
5					
Total					
Amount to be invested					
Net present value					

2. _____

_____

_____

_____

_____

_____

_____

_____

_____

_____

_____

_____

_____

_____

_____

_____

_____

_____

1. Proposal (Project) _____ :

Year	Present Value of $1 at _____%	Net Cash Flow	Present Value of Net Cash Flow
1			
2			
3			
Total			
Amount to be invested			
Net present value			

Proposal (Project) _____ :

Year	Present Value of $1 at _____%	Net Cash Flow	Present Value of Net Cash Flow
1			
2			
3			
Total			
Amount to be invested			
Net present value			

Proposal (Project) _____ :

Year	Present Value of $1 at _____%	Net Cash Flow	Present Value of Net Cash Flow
1			
2			
3			
Total			
Amount to be invested			
Net present value			

2.

3.

1.

2.

3.

Name _____

PROBLEM 24 - 5 ___

1.

_____

(blank ruled lines)

2.

Year	Present Value of $1 at _____%	Net Cash Flow		Present Value of Net Cash Flow	
		Project _____	Project _____	Project _____	Project _____
1					
2					
3					
4					
Residual value					
Total					
Amount to be invested					
Net present value					

3.

Name _____

PROBLEM 24 - 6 ___

1.
_____

_____

_____

_____

_____

_____

_____

_____

_____

_____

_____

_____

_____

_____

_____

_____

_____

_____

_____

_____

_____

_____

_____

_____

_____

_____

_____

_____

_____

_____

_____

_____

_____

_____

_____

_____

_____

_____

_____

_____

_____

475

2.

3.

Proposal	Cash Payback Period	Average Rate of Return	Accept for Further Analysis	Reject
A				
B				
C				
D				

4. Proposal ___:

Year	Present Value of $1 at _____%	Net Cash Flow	Present Value of Net Cash Flow
1			
2			
3			
4			
5			
Total			
Amount to be invested			
Net present value			

Proposal ___:

Year	Present Value of $1 at _____%	Net Cash Flow	Present Value of Net Cash Flow
1			
2			
3			
4			
5			
Total			
Amount to be invested			
Net present value			

5.

6.

7.

8.

JOURNAL

	DATE		DESCRIPTION	POST. REF.	DEBIT	CREDIT	
1							1
2							2
3							3
4							4
5							5
6							6
7							7
8							8
9							9
10							10
11							11
12							12
13							13
14							14
15							15
16							16
17							17
18							18
19							19
20							20
21							21
22							22
23							23
24							24
25							25
26							26
27							27
28							28
29							29
30							30
31							31
32							32
33							33

PROBLEM D - 1 , Concluded

	DATE	DESCRIPTION	POST. REF.	DEBIT	CREDIT	
1						1
2						2
3						3
4						4
5						5
6						6
7						7
8						8
9						9
10						10
11						11
12						12
13						13
14						14
15						15
16						16
17						17
18						18
19						19
20						20
21						21
22						22
23						23
24						24
25						25
26						26
27						27
28						28
29						29
30						30
31						31
32						32
33						33

JOURNAL

	DATE		DESCRIPTION	POST. REF.	DEBIT	CREDIT	
1							1
2							2
3							3
4							4
5							5
6							6
7							7
8							8
9							9
10							10
11							11
12							12
13							13
14							14
15							15
16							16
17							17
18							18
19							19
20							20
21							21
22							22
23							23
24							24
25							25
26							26
27							27
28							28
29							29
30							30
31							31
32							32
33							33

PROBLEM D - 2 , Concluded

JOURNAL

PAGE

	DATE		DESCRIPTION	POST. REF.	DEBIT	CREDIT	
1							1
2							2
3							3
4							4
5							5
6							6
7							7
8							8
9							9
10							10
11							11
12							12
13							13
14							14
15							15
16							16
17							17
18							18
19							19
20							20
21							21
22							22
23							23
24							24
25							25
26							26
27							27
28							28
29							29
30							30
31							31
32							32
33							33

1.

JOURNAL

	DATE		DESCRIPTION	POST. REF.	DEBIT	CREDIT	
1							1
2							2
3							3
4							4
5							5
6							6
7							7
8							8
9							9
10							10
11							11
12							12
13							13
14							14
15							15
16							16
17							17
18							18
19							19
20							20
21							21
22							22
23							23
24							24
25							25
26							26
27							27
28							28
29							29
30							30
31							31
32							32
33							33

PROBLEM D - 3 , Concluded

2.

<table>
<tr><th colspan="2">JOURNAL</th><th></th><th></th><th>PAGE</th><th></th></tr>
<tr><th colspan="2">DATE</th><th>DESCRIPTION</th><th>POST.
REF.</th><th>DEBIT</th><th>CREDIT</th></tr>
<tr><td>1</td><td></td><td></td><td></td><td></td><td></td></tr>
<tr><td>2</td><td></td><td></td><td></td><td></td><td></td></tr>
<tr><td>3</td><td></td><td></td><td></td><td></td><td></td></tr>
<tr><td>4</td><td></td><td></td><td></td><td></td><td></td></tr>
<tr><td>5</td><td></td><td></td><td></td><td></td><td></td></tr>
<tr><td>6</td><td></td><td></td><td></td><td></td><td></td></tr>
<tr><td>7</td><td></td><td></td><td></td><td></td><td></td></tr>
<tr><td>8</td><td></td><td></td><td></td><td></td><td></td></tr>
<tr><td>9</td><td></td><td></td><td></td><td></td><td></td></tr>
<tr><td>10</td><td></td><td></td><td></td><td></td><td></td></tr>
<tr><td>11</td><td></td><td></td><td></td><td></td><td></td></tr>
<tr><td>12</td><td></td><td></td><td></td><td></td><td></td></tr>
<tr><td>13</td><td></td><td></td><td></td><td></td><td></td></tr>
<tr><td>14</td><td></td><td></td><td></td><td></td><td></td></tr>
<tr><td>15</td><td></td><td></td><td></td><td></td><td></td></tr>
<tr><td>16</td><td></td><td></td><td></td><td></td><td></td></tr>
<tr><td>17</td><td></td><td></td><td></td><td></td><td></td></tr>
<tr><td>18</td><td></td><td></td><td></td><td></td><td></td></tr>
<tr><td>19</td><td></td><td></td><td></td><td></td><td></td></tr>
<tr><td>20</td><td></td><td></td><td></td><td></td><td></td></tr>
<tr><td>21</td><td></td><td></td><td></td><td></td><td></td></tr>
<tr><td>22</td><td></td><td></td><td></td><td></td><td></td></tr>
<tr><td>23</td><td></td><td></td><td></td><td></td><td></td></tr>
<tr><td>24</td><td></td><td></td><td></td><td></td><td></td></tr>
<tr><td>25</td><td></td><td></td><td></td><td></td><td></td></tr>
<tr><td>26</td><td></td><td></td><td></td><td></td><td></td></tr>
<tr><td>27</td><td></td><td></td><td></td><td></td><td></td></tr>
<tr><td>28</td><td></td><td></td><td></td><td></td><td></td></tr>
<tr><td>29</td><td></td><td></td><td></td><td></td><td></td></tr>
<tr><td>30</td><td></td><td></td><td></td><td></td><td></td></tr>
<tr><td>31</td><td></td><td></td><td></td><td></td><td></td></tr>
<tr><td>32</td><td></td><td></td><td></td><td></td><td></td></tr>
<tr><td>33</td><td></td><td></td><td></td><td></td><td></td></tr>
</table>

1. *Use the 10-column work sheets found on pages 486-491.*

PROBLEM D - 4 ___ , Continued

ACCOUNT TITLE	TRIAL BALANCE		ADJUSTMENTS	
	DEBIT	CREDIT	DEBIT	CREDIT
1				
2				
3				
4				
5				
6				
7				
8				
9				
10				
11				
12				
13				
14				
15				
16				
17				
18				
19				
20				
21				
22				
23				
24				
25				
26				
27				
28				
29				
30				
31				
32				
33				

Name _____

	ADJUSTED TRIAL BALANCE		INCOME STATEMENT		BALANCE SHEET		
	DEBIT	CREDIT	DEBIT	CREDIT	DEBIT	CREDIT	
1							1
2							2
3							3
4							4
5							5
6							6
7							7
8							8
9							9
10							10
11							11
12							12
13							13
14							14
15							15
16							16
17							17
18							18
19							19
20							20
21							21
22							22
23							23
24							24
25							25
26							26
27							27
28							28
29							29
30							30
31							31
32							32
33							33

Page not used.

Page not used.

PROBLEM D - 4 ___ , Continued

	ACCOUNT TITLE	TRIAL BALANCE		ADJUSTMENTS		
		DEBIT	CREDIT	DEBIT	CREDIT	
1						1
2						2
3						3
4						4
5						5
6						6
7						7
8						8
9						9
10						10
11						11
12						12
13						13
14						14
15						15
16						16
17						17
18						18
19						19
20						20
21						21
22						22
23						23
24						24
25						25
26						26
27						27
28						28
29						29
30						30
31						31
32						32
33						33

	ADJUSTED TRIAL BALANCE		INCOME STATEMENT		BALANCE SHEET		
	DEBIT	CREDIT	DEBIT	CREDIT	DEBIT	CREDIT	
1							1
2							2
3							3
4							4
5							5
6							6
7							7
8							8
9							9
10							10
11							11
12							12
13							13
14							14
15							15
16							16
17							17
18							18
19							19
20							20
21							21
22							22
23							23
24							24
25							25
26							26
27							27
28							28
29							29
30							30
31							31
32							32
33							33

Page not used.

2. *Omit "00" in the cents columns.*

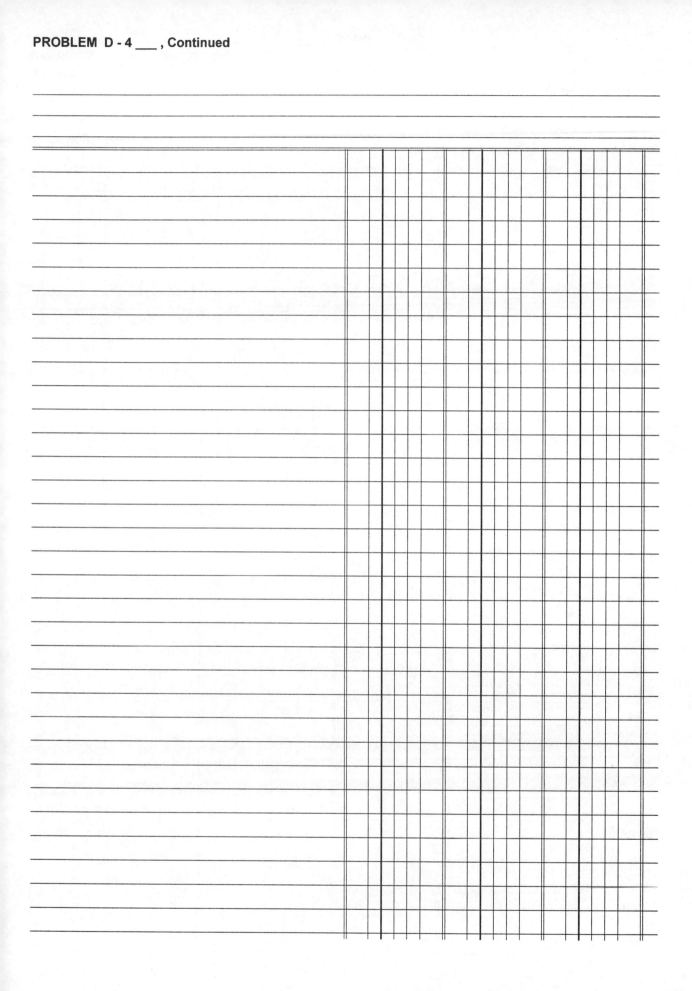

3.   *Omit "00" in the cents columns.*

4.   *Omit "00" in the cents columns.*

5.

JOURNAL

PAGE

	DATE		DESCRIPTION	POST. REF.	DEBIT	CREDIT	
1							1
2							2
3							3
4							4
5							5
6							6
7							7
8							8
9							9
10							10
11							11
12							12
13							13
14							14
15							15
16							16
17							17
18							18
19							19
20							20
21							21
22							22
23							23
24							24
25							25
26							26
27							27
28							28
29							29
30							30
31							31
32							32
33							33

PROBLEM D - 4 , Concluded

6.

JOURNAL PAGE _____

	DATE		DESCRIPTION	POST. REF.	DEBIT	CREDIT	
1							1
2							2
3							3
4							4
5							5
6							6
7							7
8							8
9							9
10							10
11							11
12							12
13							13
14							14
15							15
16							16
17							17
18							18
19							19
20							20
21							21
22							22
23							23
24							24
25							25
26							26
27							27
28							28
29							29
30							30
31							31
32							32
33							33

JOURNAL

PAGE _____

	DATE		DESCRIPTION	POST. REF.	DEBIT	CREDIT	
1							1
2							2
3							3
4							4
5							5
6							6
7							7
8							8
9							9
10							10
11							11
12							12
13							13
14							14
15							15
16							16
17							17
18							18
19							19
20							20
21							21
22							22
23							23
24							24
25							25
26							26
27							27
28							28
29							29
30							30
31							31
32							32
33							33

PROBLEM E - 1 , Concluded

JOURNAL

	DATE	DESCRIPTION	POST. REF.	DEBIT	CREDIT	
1						1
2						2
3						3
4						4
5						5
6						6
7						7
8						8
9						9
10						10
11						11
12						12
13						13
14						14
15						15
16						16
17						17
18						18
19						19
20						20
21						21
22						22
23						23
24						24
25						25
26						26
27						27
28						28
29						29
30						30
31						31
32						32
33						33

	(1)		(2)	
	Net Income $225,000		**Net Income $150,000**	
Plan	**Dunn**	**Randall**	**Dunn**	**Randall**
a.				
b.				
c.				
d.				
e.				
f.				

Supporting calculations:

PROBLEM F - 1 , Concluded

1. Omit "00" in the cents columns.

Hernandez, Collins, and Langley
Statement of Partnership Liquidation
For the Period May 10 - 30, 20--

	CASH	NONCASH ASSETS	LIABILITIES	CAPITAL		
				HERNANDEZ	COLLINS	LANGLEY

2.

JOURNAL

PAGE

	DATE		DESCRIPTION	POST. REF.	DEBIT	CREDIT	
1							1
2							2
3							3
4							4
5							5
6							6
7							7
8							8
9							9
10							10
11							11
12							12
13							13
14							14
15							15
16							16
17							17
18							18
19							19
20							20
21							21
22							22
23							23
24							24
25							25
26							26
27							27
28							28
29							29
30							30
31							31
32							32
33							33

JOURNAL

PAGE

	DATE		DESCRIPTION	POST. REF.	DEBIT	CREDIT	
1							1
2							2
3							3
4							4
5							5
6							6
7							7
8							8
9							9
10							10
11							11
12							12
13							13
14							14
15							15
16							16
17							17
18							18
19							19
20							20
21							21
22							22
23							23
24							24
25							25
26							26
27							27
28							28
29							29
30							30
31							31
32							32
33							33

JOURNAL   PAGE

	DATE		DESCRIPTION	POST. REF.	DEBIT	CREDIT	
1							1
2							2
3							3
4							4
5							5
6							6
7							7
8							8
9							9
10							10
11							11
12							12
13							13
14							14
15							15
16							16
17							17
18							18
19							19
20							20
21							21
22							22
23							23
24							24
25							25
26							26
27							27
28							28
29							29
30							30
31							31
32							32
33							33

JOURNAL

PAGE _____

	DATE		DESCRIPTION	POST. REF.	DEBIT	CREDIT	
1							1
2							2
3							3
4							4
5							5
6							6
7							7
8							8
9							9
10							10
11							11
12							12
13							13
14							14
15							15
16							16
17							17
18							18
19							19
20							20
21							21
22							22
23							23
24							24
25							25
26							26
27							27
28							28
29							29
30							30
31							31
32							32
33							33

Name _____

Extra Forms

Extra Forms

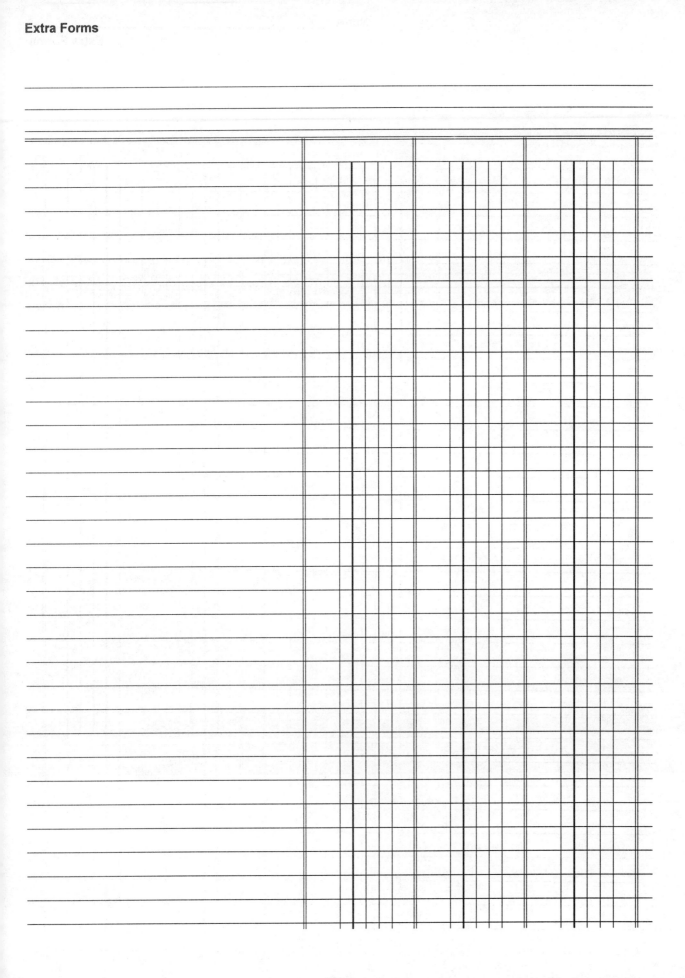

Extra Forms

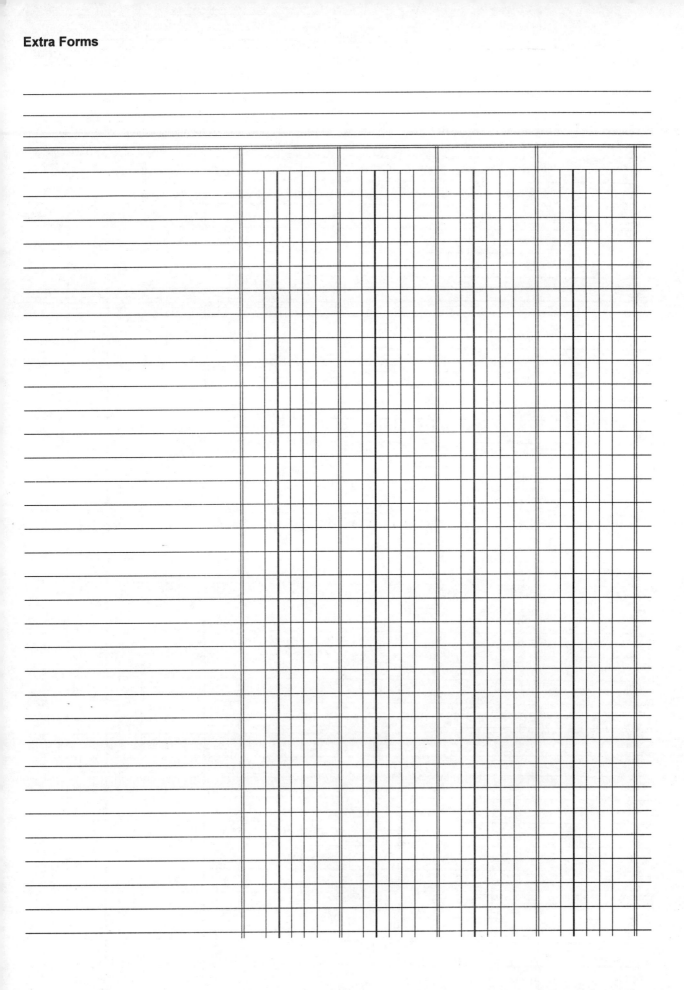